The Sh

Ambassadors of a New Age of Light

DeAnne Hampton

Cover photo:

Taken in the Shining Ones Forest, the photo is a stunning reflection of their beauty and Light. Notice the shaft of Light in the center... when I took the picture there were little orbs moving about, flashes of golden radiance all around and through the scene. The beautiful resiliency of the earth is so present, as is attunement to the rainbow bridge of a new human consciousness. I have found this image a powerful focus for meditation, to feel into and re-member within. A transformative moment extended to all.

ISBN: 978-1-300-64135-3

LULU Enterprises, Inc.

http://www.lulupresscenter.com

Cover Design by C. Stillman

Interior Design and Technical Expertise by Scott Nuce

Back Cover by Patrick Olin

Dedicated to...

The Shining Ones
whose presence, love and wisdom
serves as a constant reminder of the Mystery!

Gaia, the Earth Mother
for singing me home...

Dear Dana,

That which you dream, you are
that which you Know, is truth
Creative Vision is as you are out of mind
and in heart Consciousness!
Then all LOVE becomes a power to
reinvent the Self + Known reality.
You are on your way to that
remembrance. Beloved ~
May the light + reflection in these
pages support your journey.
With Love, DeeAnne ♡

Within me, a Light,
within me, remembrance,
within me Truth yearning to be shared
that I may know my true Self.

For it is only in living this Light,
it is only in stepping up in the name of this Light
and giving my Self to It -
that I may know the greater Truth of realities within realities~
the greater Truth of who I AM - and the peace of that surrender!

The New Human Paradigm 2013

Contents

Introduction 11

Forward 14

The Way In..17

Love Is Who You Are 21

Be Still and Know!...23

Embracing Harmony ~ Living Peace..............................25

See Imbalance ~ Feel Balance 28

Right Use Of Power and Love As A Force.......................30

Awakening...33

The Heart Of The Universe Beats Within You 35

A Time Of Endless Joy 38

The Mirror Of Your Truth 41

Give Yourself To Love..44

Fierce Heart Endless Trust...46

The Power To Choose...50

Inclusiveness As The Way of Love..................................53

Through The Looking Glass 56

The Gap To Freedom 59

The Choice Of Love 62

There Is A Place 67

The Inexplicable Nature Of Joy 71

Attachment And The Allure Of Form 74

Gratitude As the Voice On Your Path 78

Looking At The Illusion 81

Becoming Wonder 84

Trust Your Future 87

A Spirituality Of Significance 91

Walk Into It ~ A Life Unimaginable 94

The Framework Of The Heart, A New World 97

Living Love 100

What Is Old Is New Again, Inner Seeing 103

Re-membering The Light 106

Giving Rise 108

Unfold 111

Consciousness Turned Toward Light 113

Change All Encompassing 118

Bridge To The Absolute 122

The Evolution Of Love 128

The New Human Unfolding 131

The New Dispensation 133

Becoming Islands of Light 137

Beyond The Looking Glass 141

The High Side of Truth 145

Presence of Power, Center of Peace 149

Imagine 153

A World Transforming 158

Fractal World, Lucid Mind 163

Contact 167

Spiraling Dynamics 171

Chord Of Remembrance, Becoming The Song 173

The New Landscape of the Brain 177

A Day Out Of Time 180

Inspired Freedom 184

Radiant Wisdom.. 187

Vertical Trust, The Shift To Mastery 190

Peering Of The Edge 193

In The Company Of One.. 197

Reaching Out To The Improbable................................. 201

Dreaming Awake, Alchemy Of Time 206

Morphogenic Unity, The Rise Of The Feminine.................... 210

Shadow And Light, The Mystery and Legacy
Of Planet Earth 214

Interstellar Wisdom.. 218

Cooperation, Compromise And Community,
A New Season Of Being.. 222

Spaciousness, Stillness, Sacred Sound 226

Spiritual Integrity, Re-membering Love 230

Field Of Dreams 234

Hidden In Plain Sight, Giving Voice To The Mystery............. 237

Sacred Journey, Remembering Home 240

Unbound Unity, The Lightening Of A World 244

Lighting A New Star For Humanity 247

The Journey Toward Unity 251

Chrysalis Of A New World 255

A Now Before Its Time 259

Void Of Creation, The Return To Zero Point 263

The Return Path 269

The Immeasurable Now 274

Touching Center 279

High Magic Is Here 284

Bridge Across Tomorrow 290

Love Serve and Remember 294

5th World Emerging, Return of the Crystal Beings 298

Radiant Mind 302

Standing Before It, Walking Into It, Becoming the Dream 306

The Decision to Endure 311

Recognizing Center, Owning Your Light 316

Free Your Mind 321

Recapturing the Connection to our True Selves 328

A New Earth Harmonic The Shining Ones Speak 333

God Technology, Christ Light and the Birth
of a New Human Race 340

A New Earth Shambhala Entering a New Era 347

The Shining Ones, one of many groups of Advanced Light Races, are here to assist humanity through extraordinary changes in the cellular structure and DNA codex of our being. While their presence, energy and guidance has been with me since childhood, as I have grown on my own path of expansion and enlightenment, an understanding of their purpose in my life and for the many, has expanded.

The Shining Ones represent the Higher Consciousness emitting from the Galactic Core and exist along a Vibrational Continuum. I see the Shining Ones primarily as great pulses of light and energy, yet when they manifest as more concentrated Light, they are translucent magnificence in form with a breathtaking blue light at the center of their being. They radiate the Universal Principles of Love, Joy, Service, Unity Consciousness exemplified as the highest and best good of all of humanity and Earth, individual freedom and prosperity for all... and the immutable Truth of the Oneness of Creation. This Oneness is the frequency and understanding of all Advanced Civilizations and the core essence of 5th Dimensional Existence. To advance spiritually as a planet, we must assimilate, integrate and engage these energetic principles. We are known throughout the Universe according to our vibration, tone, color and Light emanations. Inclusivity, in its highest expression, is a love that transcends all.

Our inner work and expansion, the evolution of the Earth, our cellular connection to the stars and our divine origin, it is all coming into alignment to aid the awakening and healing of humanity and planet. This Intent was orchestrated by the original cause, or Prime Creative Intelligence - which has been given many names and images on Earth, yet cannot be limited to any one thing. The important point is that the energies are asking us to move with assuredness toward that which we have aligned within our heart and intentions.

In 2006, the Shining Ones revealed themselves to me visually, as magnificent high beings, intimately connected to the Elven Kingdom and the natural world. Their presence can always be found in nature and their wisdom expressed with a compassion and love that is truly palpable. It was at that time they expressed to me the desire to share their presence and insights with the many through the gift of my expression and understanding of life... the qualities that I personally embody. Thus was created a platform of ongoing messages, first in word form and then onto radio to further introduce this new human consciousness and energy as a New Paradigm for humanity. I incorporate sound through the tone of my voice, harmonics that I hear from the resonant field and lightcodes woven into the in-between spaces of their wisdom shared. Whereas I hear, communicate with and see the Shining Ones through the lens of my own unique frequency and light, they will appear to you in a way unique to your vibrational signature, as well. There is a knowingness with their Presence that you will not question, a love at once so vast and pure and yet, wholly accessible within the frequency range of human consciousness. The following discourses and tones are re-membrances you each carry in your Divine Blueprint, a timeless wisdom infused with much energetic momentum on behalf of this humanity.

In 2007, I began doing seminars and speaking engagements with the Shining Ones as the focal point. These events are always quite electric and moving, a portal for pure spiritual atomic energy. Each event is uniquely meaningful to the experience and persons at hand, as the Shining Ones work through me, creating a synthesis and synergy attuned the energy and need of the moment. The indoor engagements, along with the weekly transmissions of the New Human Consciousness on radio, have evolved to include Vortex Tours in the ancient mountains of the Carolinas, attuning more astutely with the sacred geometry and light merkabah of our beloved Gaia.

We all sit at an intersection of who we once were and who we shall become. Each individual is a living light vortex, poised to awaken and remember who and what we are. It is why you are here, an agreed upon alignment with your own Destiny. Truly, it is time to reaffirm our vows with the Light and our promise to hold the light thru all changes and challenges on Earth.

The Shining Ones are here to advance the Light on Earth and within you. They are loving Masters whose very presence serves to activate the unlimited DNA potential of individuals ready to assume full responsibility for the unique and necessary purpose of their time here on planet Earth. They are a radiant and powerful reflection of our magnificence as Universal Beings of Light. The Shining Ones are here to assist us as we step into a future that is created day by day in a hologram of Consciousness

- all that comes undone is to be repatterned and woven in a new fashion, a new human design.

May we all celebrate these extraordinary times together, becoming a living gift of empowered light for a new humanity, a new world and new Earth Star of Intergalactic Citizenry!

DeAnne Hampton

Sacred Synthesis

This book is a compilation of the Shining Ones expressions, messages and Guidance of the last several years... but it is so much more. It represents both a chronology of Light advancement on our Earth during the most profound evolutionary shift ever known to humankind, and a light-encoded transmission attuned to the highest probability at hand for our Earth and this species.

The Shining Ones are a composite of everything that is Light. As a Master Race, they embody the genetics of every possibility and expression of Life; all the Star Nations, Star Systems, all species, organisms and intelligences, the Earth herself and each individual comprising this star-seeded humanity. They are eminently skilled geneticists and are here now, present on behalf of planet Earth and in response to the Light activating in her sentient beings, to guide us through this Global Ascension.

Likewise, the Shining Ones vibrate the frequencies at the highest end of the Spectrum of Light; unconditional Love, the purest of Joy, radiant Peace, sublime Harmony, Wisdom, Truth, Creative Principle and Unity. As I write this, tuning into and feeling their presence and essence, it occurs to me that I could well be describing God. And yet, there is a distinct difference. God represents Ultimate Being... He/She/It resides in the realm of the unknowable. The Shining Ones are the bridge to that Mystery and a mirror of our own God Technology. They are accessible, knowable and here for each of us, known to each of us in the DNA Codex and heart-space of our being. They are making themselves known by calculated measure in direct proportion to the Light the Earth is now amassing, and to the numbers of those now awakening. It was never a question of just how intimately Cosmic Intelligence would participate with this evolutionary event of a planet and species... it was a matter of when.

The simplest and most direct way to attune to the Shining Ones is through nature. Gaia and these High Elves from the Galactic Center are vibrational and genetic mirrors. I know my love of nature and connection to the Earth is my love of and connection to the Shining Ones and vice versa. They are the patterns of sacred geometry, the color and tones and vibration of the Earth's Divine Blueprint, they are the properties and Lightcodes of crystal, soundwaves and harmonic nodes. With all that I know of the Shining Ones, I am aware I know very little. Yet, the information I share comes directly from their wisdom, at their prompting. They are everything relevant to this current and all important passage from one dimension into its next highest expression.

They have come to show us the way... through resonance, cellular activation and direct influence on our nervous system. They have a great love for this humanity that I am blessed to have been on the receiving end most of my life. I know, I too, am a bridge and if I can assist just one being in the re-membrance of their love, I know I have honored them across an Infinite landscape of Light.

What is equally important for me to share and you to hear as we transition into a dimensional realm we have not yet achieved as a species, is the understanding and acceptance that the return of Unity, the restoration of Oneness for this little blue planet, rests in our re-membrance. When I first began sharing the resonance and wisdom of the Shining Ones in word form, I did so in 3rd person. It did not occur to me nor did it feel natural to articulate and share this Light in my own voice. They let me get away with that for a time, but were quite clear and direct when that implied separation needed to shift. Consequently, you will find in the discourse here, that when I stepped onto the platform of radio, I began disseminating these higher mind expressions in 1st person... though still very much the wisdom and Light of these high beings. I have always hesitated to call myself a channel or be referred to as such. It feels more true to say that in regards to the Shining Ones or the New Human transmissions I share each week with thousands that I am in direct receivership with the vertical Light, connected to higher realms intelligences via the attunement of my own mind, Light body and Consciousness.

The New Human Consciousness of a New Earth is a New Paradigm of Existence for this species. Essential to the embodiment and actualization of this New Paradigm is the acceptance of our responsibility to follow Spirit first, to live the Light as our innate dispensation and to recognize ourselves as the potential leaders of a New Age of Light. This Shift is not something that is happening to us or outside of us... it is each of us waking up to the power we carry within. The New Human Templates of a New Earth and the disciplines of that remembrance are the foundational structure of a new Crystalline Grid of 5th Dimensional Light.

The Shining Ones have returned at this time because they see the gift of our inherent light - and because we have the capacity now to mature as a Collective into a New Harmonic of Being. They are everything and nothing all at once – distinct yet indefinable, which is the very essence of Oneness. Ultimately, it is we, who are everything! The Ascended Masters who have walked before us, the Extraterrestrials who observe us from afar, the Angelic, Celestial and Elemental Kingdoms, the ascended wisdom of the Cetacean Family of Light, the consciousness of the Sun and the stars of an infinite sky. No longer is it necessary to cite someone else's wisdom or authority to give voice to the Intelligence of Light. This is the Initiation of Beingness the Shining Ones are here to assist in activating, the potential of the highest consciousness ever known to this humanity. May this book, these writings and lightcodes, serve to awaken many to these Benevolent Beings of the Highest Light and Intention. Our passage to a new and sacred environment of Existence has just begun, yet with their wisdom and Love, our future as an Enlightened Race of Intergalactic Citizenry, is assured!!!

DeAnne Hampton

11/11/11

The Way In

The Shining Ones, Ambassadors of a New Age of Light is a vibrational attunement, an ongoing exercise of Consciousness turned toward Light. These pages offer light sustenance, a language that is familiar to your interior wisdom and cosmic intelligence. Yes, there is a time span of approximately five years included in this book, for the purpose of gathering as many readers as possible into the current of these very new waves of Light and movement. But within that cumulative expression is a spiraling fluidity reflecting the very real shift into a new understanding of time and relativity.

A few things are important to keep in mind as you explore, marinate in and begin integrating the vibrational light you will encounter within these passages. As we move with greater and greater velocity toward the evolutionary marker of 12/21/12 and beyond, there is a great inversion and time shift underway. As the light continues to increase on our planet and consciousness lifts toward a more unified Collective, the old linear energy influences are collapsing into a new vertical dispensation, which correlates with the movement to spiritual time: everything available, everything present, a return to balance for individual, Collective, world and planet. This is the story via consciousness and energy, of the future we are dreaming in now, a not so ordinary love story of a Consciousness that vibrates Unity.

Consequently, the content of this book vibrates the movement and continuum toward the axis shift and reset of our human potential. You may read it cover to cover, or you may jump in at any point. I greatly encourage you to hang out with it and read it more than once because, again, it represents more than words on a page. It is an invitation to Self. It vibrates wonder and the remembrance that the greatest mysteries open up to the one who ceases asking questions; to the One ready to just Be.

The Shining Ones teach wonder through the essence of being, reminding us that we have reached a point in our expansion as a species that not only must we accept responsibility for our spiritual growth but that the existence of our truest nature awakens with our participation in the Mystery.

Joy, ecstasy, genuineness and devotion, these are the emanations of the Authentic Self.

You will find many mirrors of your own devotion in this book. Your path and purpose at this time is unique to you and yet, devotion to the greater light of your potential is something all must awaken to, to grow. Your frequency and spiritual light IS who you are and must become as constant as your heartbeat. You must breathe it and walk with it and live it in each moment of each day. May these pages awaken in you the re-membrance of your own devotion and bring clarity to your perceptions of Self, humanity, the Earth and Cosmos.

With Gratitude and Much Love,
DeAnne

"Someday perhaps the inner light will shine forth from us, and then we will need no other light."

Johan Wolfgang Von Goethe

Clear the way~
and the way will be made clear.

Love Is Who You Are

May 4, 2007

There is a palpable, pulsing, pure essence of beauty that you can behold of here, yet it is but a reflection of the beauty that belongs to the 5th Dimension and the promise of the New Earth.

Each day, we invite you to turn the prism, beloveds, of the lens through which you are viewing your reality. We hear your fervent prayers for the promise of love, peace, compassion, joy and freedom to be the well-lit path of your reality. Yet, you are choosing and deciding and moving based on the constructs of the mental plane, which of course, is housed in fear. We are, in fact, observing a type of fear induced apathy from many who yearn to change and feel your truth.

So, we would ask of you, and encourage you to be still and contemplative with your answer: Do You Feel Real? Do you have a confident and centered knowing of WHO YOU ARE? And if not, where do the questions lie?

It is essential to your expansion and liberation that you get back to living a contemplative life in harmony with a wise and fertile Earth. We observe so many of you allowing your choices to be governed by perceived safety and comfort to the egoic self; and this is occurring at the sacrifice of the Self. There was a time, in the not so distance past, that your blessed ancestors knew themselves to be experiencing extensions of the Divine. They lived in harmony with the exquisitely subtle vibration of a luminous reality composed of Light and Sound. They were naturally conscious of the world of Spirit around them - a connection facilitated by creating space and time for nothingness.

Today, less and less time is spent communing with nature, with the children and with each other. We encourage you to contemplate the implications and ramifications of this fundamental construct of the way you flow your reality. Light workers are using their skills and tools and heightened mental prowess to connect with the higher dimensions, perform healings and move energy toward spiritual gain and a desired future. But there are still fragments that are blinding you to your own radiance. These fragments have to do with the essential dynamics of the heart that have yet to be integrated and re-aligned with the 3D experiences you identify yourself so strongly with, still.

You can commune with your ancestors through a reverent re-membrance and knowing of the Great Mother. She carries the essential frequencies of the heart: love, tenderness, compassion, beauty, selflessness and protection. You have the ability to heal yourself, as well as the disconnected and uncertain way of life that is your 3D experience, to restore a sense of harmony and balance and peace to your known reality and the world. This can only manifest out of a lucid scrutiny of the self and an internal inventory of the heart. You are the keepers of the Light in your soul essence but you must re-member your Self and remain true to the divine principles of honesty and right action.

The transformation of your world is hinged upon the transformation of the interior world within each of you. When the inner light shines bright through every aspect, field, body and construct of your beingness, then and only then will the Light Shine Bright upon this beautiful blue planet.

Be Still and Know!

May 11, 2007

We would like to continue on the theme of knowing your Self.

Even amongst Lightworkers and energy healers, we are observing so much busyness in your energies; activities to engage in, classes to take, new modalities to acquire for ongoing lists of credential and expertise. Do you not know that everything that you need is within your own knowing? Are your actions speaking to that Truth?

Truly, this time on planet Earth is about preparing the energetic space, heightened awareness and expanded consciousness to be able to hold center in the days and times to come. We observe what appears to be almost a compulsion to seek and do outside of the Self, to fill up the vessel with activity, input, conversation and complying to the egoic minds need to grasp onto something. If others are doing the same thing, all the better, for it further justifies the mind's agenda.

We would like to offer you a prism shift for your consideration. The act of looking, itself, implies that there is something for you to find! That you are not already absolute, whole and ready for what your wise knowing is in complete awareness is to come. That energy alone implies that there is a separation between the personality and Self. There was a time, beloveds, that the gathering and acquiring and building up of your spiritual arsenal, was timely and fitting for your journey. Now, it is time to apply. The time of practicing and experimentation is past. The time for assimilating and integrating all your knowledge for centered dissemination and action is now!

There is such a desire of the personality aspect to participate and belong and find comradeship, and we acknowledge that 3D character trait without judgment. But you are sovereign beings, each with your own soul intent and destiny, and there is a tendency to get lost in the dross of the busyness and doing and relationship as a way to feel "real" and validated and secure.

As the energies on the planet and the cadence of the concept you know as time continues to intensify, there will be a tendency to join in the spin from the mental plane of busyness; a frantic push to get everything done and be "prepared". And we would say to you, with compassion and wise seeing, that there is not enough "preparation" that you could do in your dimension to lessen the magnitude of what is to come. The primary focus of your preparation must be to re-member your Spiritual Authority and purpose through the heart's wisdom: independent of everything and everyone around you, so that when your moment comes and the Mother is depending on your piece in the complete transformation of reality as you have known it, you will be able to step into the midst of the tumult and hold center in your frequency of power.

Did we hear a Warrior Cry of yes to that edict? If not, if you felt some discomfort and squirming and uncertainty about who you are and your ability to be right now in every aspect of the changes that are to come...then it is you we are speaking to in this moment. The next time you feel the desire to take another class, to learn a new concept or teaching, to be with the many rather than to be with your Self, take that energy, that vibration of seeking and looking and turn inward. One of the greatest things you can do for your expansion at this time is to be with the Great Mother. Go to the places in your environment, wherever that may be and whatever your circumstance, where the frequency is the most pure, pristine, natural and free. And just be. She will facilitate your re-membrance and empowerment more than any knowledge gained from your plane of existence.

Those times that you are not in nature and not obligated to the social constructs that you still find yourself in, be with your Self. Sit in nothingness and commune with your ancestors and the many who are overseeing and guiding your journey. In the Light of All Eternity, there has been no other time such as the one this much respected and observed blue planet is on the precipice of. You are not alone. The entire cosmos is watching the process of this Ascension with great anticipation. Go to the depths of your most interior knowing, find the frequency and tone of your authentic essence, and allow that emerging and necessary beingness to be the one and only informer of your reality.

Embracing Harmony ~ Living Peace

May 18, 2007

If you could truly know how deeply you are loved and honored for just being here, the essence of your days would glitter. Peace and love are extended to you in each moment of your beingness from the heart of the Mother. Let go of all the expectations that you place upon yourselves and others about how life should be unfolding and allow the great adventure to manifest before you in deep joy and gratitude. Breathe~ and Love the Earth. The Presence of God awaits, to fill each day with the fullness of your divinity, Divine Love and the energy of the Light are ever with you.

Today, we would like to talk to you about harmony. Harmony, like Love, is an essence, a power, a vibration. For your world to be enlightened entirely and lifted into the pure essence of the Light, it is essential that each one of you embody the essence of harmony. This is no small task given your current state of affairs. There are, indeed, powers that be in your world and those in your personal lives that do not seek to embrace harmony. You must distance yourself from them, physically, energetically, in your minds and in your hearts.

Harmony is about Unity, Oneness, inclusion and receptivity. It is based on the principle that there is nothing and no one that is separate from anything else. There is no resistance where harmony dwells. And of course, harmony cannot be found in the circumstances of the outer world until it is secured within the secret chamber of your heart.

You must first be the Love, Peace, and Joy that you wish to see in the world and then take that essence and Light out with you to inform and guide all your experiences.

Any circumstance or person of reflection in your experiential reality that upset your flow or inner harmony is a place for you to add your loving emotions. All around you are graceful mirrors of the energies you carry in your light bodies. These mirrors come not from a place of judgment but to inform and illuminate your actions. Whatever you carry in your own luminous body will be reflected in the luminous web of the world around you. Every experience and person that comes to your reality bears a gift. The gift is from a partnership between your Higher Self and a Universal Intelligence that are collaborating on your behalf at all times. And it is all Love.

We cannot over emphasize the importance of the emptiness of space and energetic sovereignty. This must continue to be set as a priority, the allowing of nothingness, stillness and silence in your experience. You cannot engage the frequency and wisdom of your heart if you are constantly engaging the mental plane. When one looks deeply enough, one will find solutions to everything. There is an Intelligence in the heart that is directly linked to the mind of God. So many are still looking for answers rather than trusting implicitly that all the answers you seek are within.

No matter what obstacles appear before you, you must keep your eyes ever focused on the pristine path of enlightenment. Walk, drink, eat and breathe in, Life. Perform every act with focus, presence and one-pointed devotion, to honor the sacred in all human life. Do not be afraid to live in Truth. Often walking in Truth comes at what is perceived as a sacrifice to the ego. Do not be afraid to risk all. No thing can be taken from you in this dimension without being gifted back to your essence a hundred fold in the higher dimensions. Look deeply into the eyes of your loved ones, your mate, your children, your intimate relations, your neighbors, acquaintances and the strangers who briefly touch your reality. Do not be afraid to show each, who you are - the truth you carry in your heart. Now is a time of intense personal reflection that comes through inner discipline. So many are trapped in a strange sleep, imprisoned by inertia and fear, such that there is barely a glimmer of the shining light of spirit within. And yet, it is within each and every one of you to be the divine effluence that rouses another from their slumber.

We honor deeply all those devoted to the awakening and liberation of this crystal planet. The Mother is assisting you, as you assist her with your love and communion. As she is dedicated to the sustenance, protection and education of all sentient beings, so too is your power to be a light of truth and remembrance for those who have not yet found their way. You are always within the light and the light is always within you. Each and every one of you has the potential to perceive with the eyes of the heart and hear with grace, the song of harmony and freedom that belongs to the vibration of your incandescent light. We hear your questions, dear ones. We are answering through the profound and exquisitely subtle frequency of love. Love flows through every cell and transcends every boundary. Love is a force, steadfast and true; a light-stream permeating all life on your blue planet. In recognizing this sacred spiritual current within yourself, the love and harmony of the Universe will stream forth from you as luminous waves of joy, harmony, purpose and divine love!

See Imbalance ~ Feel Balance

May 25, 2007

Turn off your egoic minds and connect with your Inner God. We are sensing your restlessness and your weariness. If there is one amongst you who is not feeling restless or weary with the current energy influxes, there is need to find a deeper resonance with your heart. That endless nothingness and the intensity building toward your vast and necessary purpose in this planetary transformation is palpable. It is indeed a time of exceeding self and truly being what you know you were intended to be. This is not an ego bound prompting but an identity encoded in your heart.

The Great Mother is preparing for rebirth. As timeless as the ages, she is the wise knower, the supreme organizer and teacher of balance. All around you, the imbalance that can be seen is amplifying through weather anomalies, crimes of injustice, warring nations and the irregular behavior of the animal kingdom. Secular domination reigns over spiritual authority and as the vibrations of quantity and control are engaged over quality and sustainability, you are indeed witnessing the sacred vanishing into the profane.

The continual fall over the history of this vibrational plane is an energetic; it is about the part breaking away from the whole. There can be no resolution or redemption until the realities of imbalance are acted upon from a quantum approach to love. We have shared with you before that love is a frequency - the highest and purest vibration - that all disintegration comes from a movement away from an integrated or unified state of being and life. No longer can you look around you for footsteps of how to proceed because you that are here now, at this time, in this moment, are here to create new footsteps. You are the event you are waiting for! And you absolutely know what it is that you need to do in each moment for the sake of love.

Balance manifests from an inner state. If you close your eyes and feel in your own energy field where your vibration houses any miasm that is not of love, peace, joy, harmony and compassion, then you know where to focus your energy of intent. This is the single greatest thing you can be doing at this time; going within, seeking the imbalances within your own energy fields and expanding your heart to embrace your own misconceptions and judgments. Your world is a creation of frequency. Right now, it reflects fragmentation of the heart, with fear as the base of all miscreation. Your egoic self is also divine and an integral part of you. You must go into your heart and work with the love, compassion and forgiveness you will find there to transform your fragmentations back to original purpose. Then you will be lucid portals of light for others to find their way out of fear and disillusionment.

Continually offer your deepest gratitude to those in the higher dimensions that have volunteered to hold the energies for you to step into. Many of you are indeed hearing the wisdom and feeling the love of your own expanded consciousness calling to you now to step onto higher ground. But you must follow through. Act. Assume your place in divine partnership with the Light and release the attachments you cling to. You can virtually stand in the sameness of your current reality and step into 5th dimensional frequency all at once by the emotions and responses you choose. When you call from your own center the strength to be new in the midst of what is old and dismantling, your actions will automatically begin to shift reality as you know it. Do not be afraid of what you might lose. Trust the heart's wisdom and know that you cannot make a choice or decision in the best interest of your internal knowing without it positively effecting everything and everyone around you.

Remember who you are! Ask to be infused with the greatest insight of whatever you need to know in your now for the choices you face, and then trust the wisdom that you have to act. This is your time! Trust your God Self to bring forth to your conscious awareness all the false beliefs and attitudes that still stand in your way of mastery. Everything in your experience is a reflection of the amount of light that you carry in your lower energy centers; the emotional, mental, etheric and physical bodies. Love it all. Be grateful for everything. Walk through each day with the absolute knowingness that your creation is manifesting through your love and intentions to be only light, for yourself, for your reality and for the world. And it will be so.

When you truly tap into the unfathomable love marinating your planet at this time to penetrate every cell and layer of your being, then you cannot help but begin to embody a greater level of the beauty, light and wisdom that are your true reflections.

Right Use Of Power and Love As A Force

June 1, 2007

With so much awareness and focusing of your energies being put on vibrational shifts and ensuing Earth changes, there is a tendency to get swept up in the momentum of external action. We feel your hearts, the strong wanting and desire to realize the necessary piece of your purpose; your contribution, your return. There is an internal drive implicated in your DNA to reach for a higher order, even as all around you seems to be dismantling. And it is, indeed, of vital importance that you keep a finger on the pulse of the information and forerunners of the planetary shifts to come.

Yet, many are still estranged from the energies and implications of their own internal realities, much of which are still controlling your individual lives and keeping you from your mastery. While your service to the planet is integral to the transformations occurring, it is the transformation inside your being that is the primary purpose of your incarnation here. There is not one dynamic, creation, manifestation or reality currently in place on your planet that did not evolve out of a field of personal energy. That is the magnitude of your power as creators. Equally so, the most significant and lasting changes on the planet will be determined by the degree of personal mastery over your own individual energy fields.

You live in a reality of both shadow and light. In any given moment in your experience, there are energies of duality vibrating all around you. Dark and Light energies lobbying for your awareness, attention to, reaction, response and ultimate choice of participation. It is easy to be in peace and joy, love and compassion, forgiveness and freedom when you find yourself in the midst of these frequencies. The impetus to your mastery comes from the observation, witnessing and experience of chaos and disruption, fear and disharmony all around you, yet still holding, seeing, being and maintaining the frequency of pure light and supreme love.

We ask that you practice deep contemplation and personal reflection on this consideration. Many of you are seeing it with your intellect yet still bypassing it with your heart. Your mental plane is very much directing the energy of your decisions at the expense of your heart's knowing. The strength of the ego lies in its deception. No matter how focused and purposeful your intent in the details and decisions of your external reality, know that you are always participating in and thus being influenced by constructs that reward and praise mental execution. The unconscious gratifications and enticements to the ego are many. It is easy to get swept up and forget to listen to the counsel and essence of your heart.

Sit still and feel. We are extending to you all the love that you need to empower your hearts and lift you from the veils of doing. This pushing and striving, accomplishing and drive to inform the ignorance of others is feeding the very energy so many claim to have risen above. You, who carry the secrets of the cosmos in your intellect, can you sit still and be naked with the desires and strong wanting of your heart? Innocence and purity are the greatest threat to the deception and clutch of control on this planet. Yet, until each one can be vulnerable and in complete trust with the love and wisdom of their own hearts, love will not be able to penetrate the shadowy veils of illusion now darkening your world.

It is often easy to talk about the power of love, the virtues of compassion and the benefits of peace. Can you be it? And what does that mean? Can you let go of the persona you have so come to identify with and allow another to see you completely? Can you truly look into the windows of another's soul through the window of your own and reveal to them the purest essence of your being? With how many in your lives is this possible? We say to you the identities you wear and have come to know as who you are, are the very thing holding the illusion of this reality together. And fear is the glue. It is just no longer viable or even possible to continue your creations from this less than authentic aspect of your being.

You are everything a Master is. A Master of Light is complete, absolute, powerful, strong, perfection, harmony, peace, joy and supreme love. A Master did not come to this planet to save the world. A Master came here to love, unconditionally: to see love, be love, feel and allow love. There is no part of any creation or miscreation that cannot be quantified or dismantled by the frequency of love. But you must first allow the fullness of love in all its expression into your own life, perception, organization and allowing. Do this for your today. Do this for your tomorrow. Feel what you are experiencing and ask what love would do. Whatever you are about in this moment, whoever you think you are and wherever you believe your purpose to be, if you truly surrender to the force of love without any fear, that love will take over as the organizing principle and manifestation in all the details of everything you dare to accomplish. Trust love and the world as you know it ~ will bow to the feet of the Master that you are.

Awakening

June 8, 2007

Every moment of your experiential reality, no matter what you are experiencing, love is present with you as the greatest power and influence. Each of you is being presented with the perfect situations for you to accept and bring back to yourself those abandoned parts that you have failed to embrace with love. There is no thing that has been done to you from a place of greater power or ill influence. There are only places that you have forgotten who you were and given your power away to others. And whether or not you had the awareness to recognize it at the time, love was always there and you were always safe. Truly, to get to a point in your expansion that you know that there is no harm that can come to you and no thing of true value that can be taken from you... this is to know your salvation and freedom.

It is time to transcend your fears and learn about love, real love, which has to start with self. We observe and witness so many of you saying no to the potential of such love in your realities because it wears not the package you expect. Somewhere in your history you have been taught to deny your ability to know what is happening within and all around you. In pretending to be asleep for so long, unaware and ignorant, you have lost the remembrance of true existence. And then your journey becomes one of needing to go through the dark and fearful places of your own mental aberrations. Yet, even then, even as you wrestle with the constructs and illusions and limitations that you deem so real, there is a deep and abiding promise that everything is always in Divine order.

Each of you has a different sense of what it is to be awakened. The mind would have you believe that awakening comes from what you know, but this is not a journey of the mind. What none of you can deny is that it has to start with self-love. This love of the Infinite through you cannot come without first having a strong and personal connection with your own Beloved God. Your awareness, your wisdom, your knowing, your center of being must come from an assured and ungovernable connection to that which is indefinable, unquantifiable, inexplicable and deeply moving to your known reality: just you and your God. And you must get comfortable and adept at taking your own bright light into the places where you harbor shadow. We say to you, there is not one thing in your experience that is not a reflection of you. If you are observing others being less impeccable or loving or evolved than what you have deemed to be appropriate, they are your own shadow and fear, there to amplify where your judgments are running your experience.

Being awakened means that you see and feel everything with a crystal clear perception that carries no agenda or expectation, save to be fully present with an intense awareness that allows love to penetrate all the details of your reality. The world has not abandoned you, you have abandoned yourselves, and the way back home is through an arduous period of purification and self-revelation that must accompany the willingness to look within to find resolution. Always. All ways.

To find your true level of mastery and re-member your Self is to fall in love with each other and with life; where there is no threat to your being because you are so completely in your hearts and truly see that it is all you.

Say yes to Love. Seek the Light at the expense of all else and you will know the manifested majesty and vastness of your true being. Determine to cease once and for all projecting your illusions onto your experience and ask the presence of love pulsating in your own heart to reveal to you the greatest need of the moment. Know that the answer to your prayer is often the thing that scares you or repels you the most. Your hearts beat with the pulse of the Universe. Rise up and dare to trust that force and love to inform every experience with the highest potential. Be what you seek. Be love. Be.

The Heart Of The Universe Beats Within You

June 15, 2007

Life is never quite the way it appears but is always filled with light and color. We celebrate you and the times you are in. Each one of you is a courageous journeyer and you are being uplifted and supported by a limitless supply of love in each of your moments.

We are observing the variations on a theme of your unfoldment. So many are feeling the pulsations of change and shift and the strong wanting of your hearts to be free and in Truth. Yet, so many still feel but a faint glimmer of the brilliant light that you are. Know in your very being that you are on threshold of a new horizon far greater than you have dared perceive. This is your time to uncover the divinity within yourselves and to stop looking for it in others. It is quite simple, yet you make it difficult because you leave remnants of yourself scattered throughout all of your experiences. This is the result of attachment. Every encounter and experience you align with are a perfect fit for that moment of your reality. You come together with like energies and your only job is to be fully present and in love. No agenda, no expectation or need to know and be in control. Just join in with your joy in each experience like a child that is discovering the most splendid of new mysteries. As you are completely present and a clear vessel of receivership, those persons and experiences that are resonating with your highest potential will merge and blend into your frequency like the weaving of a most exquisite tapestry. Those that do not will quietly and effortlessly fall away. This is the dynamic and absolute of energy. The rightness, the peace and knowingness of your joy will say to you that an encounter is carrying the seed of greater potential, so stay, explore, contemplate the wonder and possibility of this resonance.

If, on the other hand, you come into an encounter or activity that does not carry flow, that bears stickiness and elicits a knotting of your solar plexus... this is your guidance saying to you that you must go quickly into the Observer and determine what past programming is running that you are currently getting entangled within. This becomes ever more tricky on your plane of demonstration because you are immersed in the density of a system of control. The more civilized the area, the denser the constructs and the more easily controlled and manipulated you are by energy that often times does not even belong to you. This is an important concept for you to grasp and embody. If you were totally present with all of your being in each experience and encounter, you would be vibrating a higher frequency of pure resonance from which to discern and interpret your current reality. In that way, the energies of influence that are of a denser vibration than your clear and present expression of being, will move right past your experience without any disturbance or effect on your reality.

Remember always, that the Universe is not outside of you ~ it is within you. The you you know yourself to be in this reality is a chosen expression of density so that your light essence could gather new levels of wisdom and power. Be not attached to the body that you wear, the idiosyncrasies of your shadow self nor the beautiful illusions that you necessarily interpret as real. You are here to lift yourselves up to the remembrance of divine wisdom and the incredible joy of your own mastery. Always and ever is the mystical realm of light glistening in your deepest knowing for you to see in your consciousness of power. The longings that you feel are not for things lost to you or out of your reach. The longings are from the essence of your dreams that need your wholeness to fulfill. Your dreams are held in their realized form in the vibration of your highest expression and mastery. This cannot be expressed in enough ways, that there is nothing for you to do here but to be present: to stand tall and embrace the Truth of who you are! Truly then, and only then, can the limitless love, support and all seeing wisdom available to you in this journey find its way to your consciousness. When you honor yourself and love the moment you are in with all of your being, people feel their own truth in your presence and gain surer footing in their own lives. That empowerment weds both the giver and receiver in a frequency of light that calls to the ages a new level of awakening. Each new moment is one to celebrate the freedom and experience gained from the previous moment. In that way, each new moment can bring to you all that your greatness allows because you have grown in your mastery beyond the walls of attachment and separation.

Know in the light of all eternity, that even as you read these words, there is a love of such magnitude in your current reality so as to lift you into the frequency of your grandest dreams of manifestation. It is right there with you wearing all sorts of guises and shapes, but love it most surely is. In the midst of your egoic mind trying so very hard to figure things out and feel its own sense of power, the vibration and resonance of your pure heart essence is emanating a call across all time and space for love to come be a co-creator in your experience. To be allowing of and in this love, is to feel as if you are living the greatest love story every known. How wondrous is that? And it belongs to you, dear entity, if you are truly present and in your heart. Do not be afraid of the power and magnitude of the heart to completely undo the world you have come to know, because we can promise you from our vantage point, that the unknown reality of your potential is more beautiful than your constructs allow you to even dare imagine. Surrender to the heart's knowing. It is speaking to each of you right now, what to do in each moment. Trust your heart. In your heart is the opening to the great heart of the Universe and the power of infinite realms of light. Celebrate who and where you are today. As the Earth Mother opens to her shift, you are opening to a most magnificent and blessed shift within yourselves. Surrender to the heart and the love that is present with you, and the door to every desire and Truth of your being will open to your mastery.

A Time Of Endless Joy

June 23, 2007

If you could sit across the porch from the God of your understanding, what would you say in that moment? What one thought or question would press itself upon your heart and mind to say to the bright sun and Beloved God of your Being? And what would your heart most desire to hear in return?

As we experience your world through you, as we are with you in your activities throughout your day, it is curious to us how we often experience a disparity between what you feel in your interior and who you express to your reality. There seems to be a divisive battle within your being that, in stillness, very much correlates with the warring nations that inhabit your world. The division and separation that occurs between what you instinctively feel and know and how you interact with your experience then becomes a mirror for the energies that pulse and vibrate out across the landscape of your creations.

In each moment of everyday across your geography, are beings that are doing the best they know how within the circumstances and constructs of their reality. They are battle scarred, broken, repaired, frightened, carrying a determined, simple, unnoticed dignity with quiet yearnings and fragile but steadfast hearts; each and every one. There is an expression by one of your beloved teachers, "there but for the grace of God, go I." What is true and deserving of your deep contemplation is that if you were born into any other circumstance, with the same conditions and opportunities and influences, you would choose and act and be exactly the way as one that you have deemed separate from you. Beings on every street corner in every city and state, country and nation, feeling the same as you, connected to your energy and beingness through a Crystalline Planetary Grid of Oneness. There is not one on your planet that is separate and independent from the totality of the Universe. As part of the whole, you are always and ever affected by the whole and you always have a choice, and thus, responsibility to engage the highest light of your humanity and the purest expression of your heart. It is within you to spontaneously feel a great, unrelenting love with all in each moment of your now. Indeed, that is your one and only true purpose; to realize your Self, as

One. This is the frequency that must now be activated and empowered.

It takes a great deal of courage to truly feel the magnitude and intensity of pure essence, to surrender to the experience of Self as Love and of the world, as God. Truly we say to you that your basic nature is goodness and light, each and every one of you. Many do not realize just how much your egoic constructs are running the show and creating your experience. You are inherently a people of Unity and Oneness Consciousness. Your natural impetus is to be the bridge between separation, the one who stands in the middle of two opposing factions and joins their hands in the middle. That is your heart's yearning and power, your innate and greatest source of joy.

No matter what geography, race, culture or religion you have come to so strongly identity yourself with, the core essence of every human being is hungering for the same thing. To embrace your experience with kindness and love is the centering Truth within all humankind and a direct link to the mind and will of God. And we say to you, all are weary of this illusion, this travesty of division and separation and hierarchy. The planet cannot bear the despair of entitlement and exclusivity any longer nor can the beings that inhabit her. It is time to remember and not be afraid of what you know in your hearts to be right and just.

Loving all that is is an attitude of loving God, of seeing and expanding the Universal Consciousness within all things. If you, just you, in your own little microcosm of the world go out and determine to, just one day, see with the eyes of holiness, speak the words of compassion, hear only the sounds of love and express the sacred to each being you encounter, the ripple of those acts would begin a movement such as you've not known before in your reality. This is the pregnant and Divine urge present, always, in every living thing, to never stop loving because there is no one or thing not to love. It is all you. It is all love.

Endless joy, utter abundance, world peace and love for love's sake are an extension of right understanding, that the love of the Creator radiates within and outward from the greatest treasure and resource given to you in this experience, your heart. You are human crystals. When we experience you, we see streams of light pouring forth from your eyes, your hearts and your solar plexus. Love as the highest frequency truly is your greatest power for all that needs healing, redeeming, transforming and balancing in your world.

Just for this day, embrace your reality with kind love. Look into the eyes of a stranger and be not afraid to share the clear heart and authenticity of your soul. Expressed love and harmony unites and awakens from the simplest moment to the grandest liberation. To consciously feel and express what truly occupies you is to experience yourself at a deeper level of beingness. The Second Coming is now, beloved beings of light and joy. Take care not to get caught up in concepts and illusion. Gentle love prevails, always, all ways. You have the total Truth inside of you in each moment to be inspired and rise up to the times you find yourself in. Be empowered by the absolute that in your wisdom, you agreed to witness and bring your mastery to this now, whatever the details. Above all else, you are here to know God and thus yourselves... your first and last intent was Love.

The Mirror Of Your Truth

June 30, 2007

Close your eyes and imagine feeling yourself at the core of your being, feeling your own love at the depth of your soul.

As your reality quickens and your timelines continue to collapse at rapid rates, there will be a necessary dismantling of your own perceptions of self and the world around you. No longer are you so entrenched in the comfort and groove of social consciousness and what has always been, because life as you have known it, is collapsing to prepare for an existence of higher consciousness, higher light, higher love. This is, at once, both liberating and desperately unsettling to the egoic mind.

There is a greater purpose and meaning to life outside the limited scope of individual understanding. Yet, you must become keenly aware of your own perceptual awareness and how much that informs all of your reality and relationships. Your brain is a hologram interpreting a holographic Universe, your bodies, living mirrors of the Universe, down to your very cells. If you view your world only through your own understanding, you will perceive only your view reflected back to you. This may sound simplistic in concept, yet we say to you, in general, that you view your experience through a small window and anything that doesn't fit into the window is either misinterpreted or discarded as conflict. Do you not know that conflict and challenge are but opportunities to deepen and evolve your relationship with self and with others? Truly conflict is love seeking a higher expression. If that is what you choose. You are being gifted the energetic spaciousness and sustenance to establish a new relationship with your thoughts and how they run the flow of your experiential reality. Each and every one of you are being asked, through the authentic energetic signature of Christ Consciousness that you carry within, to keep your mind open to new perceptions and your heart open to the highest light.

What is happening in your world is two fold in process. The old is breaking apart and falling away and the new is potentially making its way into the spaciousness created by what is no longer serving. Being in higher consciousness means stepping back from who you think you are and the world that has been your understanding to become aware and allowing; an observer of objectivity and a witness from the vantage point of wholeness versus fragmentation. This is what will provide the clarity to reach beyond your own limited sense of self and experience everything as an unfathomable mystery where the only requirement is love. This love frequency is so very strong, as pulsing emanations, for your reality at this time. It is coming to be your greatest teacher and friend, the surrender of your heart to its remembrance. You must keep your mind ever open to new perceptions and your heart open to the highest light. Only then will you be free to see what is being gifted to your process for the explicit purpose of manifesting your truth, which is the pristine frequency of this Love.

You know that you are living your own authentically empowered life of spirit when you see in the faces and experiences of your world your own brilliant and incandescent light. If your reality evokes a judgment from your being, if your attitude bears resistance to anything or anyone you encounter, know that you are not in just the present moment and your personality is clinging to an agenda other than the evolution of awareness and expansion of consciousness. Recognizing your authentic nature and your own truth is to be in a state of utter peace where nothing can disturb you because you are remembering that it is all you. Each moment. Every person. All of your experience is love knocking on the door of your perception, asking only that you recognize your Self by being true to your feelings in knowing that there is always greater love present for you to allow.

Many of you carry the attitude that faulty perception lies in another. And we say to you that this cannot be true. Because the other you experience is a mirror of what you are vibrating and attracting, from the beloved god of your being, so that you may acquire a deeper awareness of yourself. Change yourself ~ change your world. You are either flowing a thought stream of love and clear consciousness or you are stuck in the loop of a construct. There is not one in your experience that is not Christ Consciousness, offering you the mystery of being only your Christ Consciousness, so that you meet each other in the highest light. It is your power and greatest strength to meet each other and life with complete openness of heart. Taking ownership of this power is to recognize that love is an active participation in the process of life, but you have to show up first, the ALL of you.

Know that whatever your perception is, there your power lies. If your perception is one of separateness, of viewing the limitations and attitudes in another as distinctively other than your own, you are operating in illusion rather than mastery. Everything that you are contemplating is evolving out of an ineffable spirit that is ready, at last, to let the struggles go and allow the mystery to unfold. As the constructs of your reality continue to dismantle, you will have a strong desire for something that feels right, to feel the joy of your own laughter and the surrender of your own love to this life. We say to you that there is no greater joy than to live completely in the mystery ~ trusting life, trusting yourself, trusting love. As you step into each day, brand new, polish the mirror of your own reflection and determine to be in your heart of gratitude for whatever and whomever you encounter, because they come bearing the frequency of your own light and love. Accept, allow, adjust your perception and remember that through your crystalline attunement to the heart and mind of god, your awareness, knowing and trust can bring the new earth to this plane. Indeed, it is the only power that can.

Give Yourself To Love

July 7, 2007

What every being on your planet is seeking is love. Your yearning to matter, to be of service, to know a meaningful existence and feel a sense of purpose that belongs to only you... these are the seeds of love's blossom.

The struggles you encounter, the misconceptions and missed moments, the plans that go awry and the relationships that seem not to conform to the package that you expected... all love.

The resolve of your soul to not just be strong, but to feel strong, the spirit in you that lies undefeated, the knowing that there is nothing that can happen to you that you won't have the courage to face, the willingness to bend and let go and not know and allow, allow, allow... again, the holy light and vibration of love. There is only love.

Love is a shimmering circle that holds you all inside. It resides in the Earth, on all of the Earth's surfaces and is webbed throughout the galaxy. Every one of your moments is so precious, dear entities. There is no way for you to know each next moment and how completely your world can be changed because of it. That is why it is so very important to be present and lucidly conscious. To choose wisely what is there to empower you and open you up to more and more love. Every aspect of your reality is a beautiful reflection of the promise you made to yourself to remember who you are and expand beyond what you think you know and believe to be true. Every question that you ask has an answer if you are looking inside, Truth begins when you know well the voice and vibration of your heart.

There are many waking up across your globe at this time and hearing the call of their higher light and intent. Yet, it is not enough to merely wake up. You must determine to stay awake, to love fiercely and see only joy. You are needed in the world and it is time to become focused. We say to you, there is not one moment that you are experiencing that has not the offer of joy to be the foundation of whatever you are creating. All essential knowledge and growth evolve out of daring to be in an experience that is before you without any preconceived conditions on how that experience must be. Doors of opportunity such that you have never known or imagined before are opening for you now. They are opening as veils being lifted from your past experiences of fear, and presenting to you a brand new vibration for you to re-pattern your emotional reality anew. It is not possible to know even 3 months from your now what you are creating and envisioning because your reality is shifting that quickly. You must take care not to confuse your awakening and remembrance with your mind's propensity to be in control and run the show.

What we are sharing with you in this moment of your now is that who you are being right now, is all that matters for the creation of your tomorrow. Your plans and goals are a point of reference and most certainly giving the ego something to grasp onto. But everything is changing and will continue to do so. The greatest power you have to assure that you will be in the "right place" under the "right conditions" in the days and months to come, is be in a grateful heart of joy and harmony now. It is that simple. Great truth and power exist in the human heart. It is the frequencies of separation and disharmony that have created the circumstances of the world you live in today. The shifts in consciousness and earth changes to come are in response to this prevalent illusion. True spiritual inclination is freedom, unity, peace and creation. To assist the transformational process is to be in your joy and inner peace. You have come to earth at this time to remember. In that remembrance is your awakening. To awaken is to recognize that all form you perceive is but the understanding of your perceptual awareness. In your deeper mind, the level of your super consciousness, you begin to recognize the frequency of light within all form. And that it is your great joy to be present with only that light, serving and loving it as its highest potential of expression. If you deem to reside only in harmony, seeing only love in each moment of whatever you are creating, what you are creating will be your safe place and future empowerment. It is the frequency you embody and inform your every moment with that will be the foundation of your tomorrow. The heart's intelligence is a direct link to the mind of God. Be here now, in love, and you will know in each moment the next step of clear wisdom to take toward your highest light and the harmony of your world.

Fierce Heart Endless Trust

July 14, 2007

Every moment of your experiential reality is a challenge to be genuine and to seek a fearless existence. Your yearning is palpable to us and we would wish for you that our presence be equally palpable to your being. There is great compassion for the many forms that fear takes in your reality and for the very real energy that it weaves throughout your experience.

What we would impress upon you at this time is that as the shadow elements and dark forces working against the enlightening of your planet gain momentum and power for the moment, it is in response to the power and light that you have carried with such devotion and are now poised to step into with victory. In addition to the vast love and support of the non-physical realm being infused into whole of your dimension, there is a fundamental human wisdom that has existed in every culture throughout your history. Indeed, the individual soul and the soul of humanity are connected throughout the Universe through the Cosmic Heart. Your inherent wisdom and goodness, the heart of humanity, is now coalescing with a magic that is responding to the cosmic hum of the entire Galaxy. The key is to not be afraid of this great nothingness nor of who you are. The sincere and strong in wanting will awaken into their light bodies in the perfect order and divine timing of their Christ Consciousness.

Be vigilant in your self-awareness and in recovering the remembrance that there is an ungovernable basis within each of you that allows you to uplift your state of existence instantaneously. In learning to be free and live consciously, you necessarily drift in and out of remembering and forgetting. As a species you have been so imprisoned by the structures of your society that you have become conditioned to see and attract resistance. This is, indeed, a vibration that connects you into the threads of limiting constructs across the entire globe. Any endeavor to swing the pendulum to the side of limitlessness for the sake of freedom, automatically engages the energy of threat to the ego, and conscious or not, the fear of losing control over your known reality. Yet, know in the core of your being, that each time you remember who you are you bring more Light to the world.

That is why it is so important to become adept at truly knowing and seeing yourself clearly. Being able to help the world requires a personal journey to discover what you inherently have to offer to this experience that you chose. You must be unguardedly willing to open yourself up against the intense oppression that has restricted you and your ancestors before you. You are not just battling the immediate forces that seem to hold you in a state of spiritual slumber and limitation. You are stepping up in the name of all those who have come before you and will come after you as well. This can at once make you feel quite small yet serve to empower you for the sake of the many. Are you understanding this for it is very important? Be it conscious or unconscious, you are operating from and interpreting your reality through constructs that have been in place for generations. These constructs hold you in limitation and have you to believe that you are powerless and without your own unique and necessary purpose for being here now. And we say to you, you chose this moment in the earth's transformation from a window outside time and place. You knew what you could bring in wisdom and gifts and you chose the exact circumstances of your earth life so far to prepare in you and awaken this information. Now, is the time to re-member.

The rise of human dignity and the integrity that you seek flows naturally from the resolve to go after what you believe in, no matter what the costs. In order for you to be able to tap into and merge with the natural source of radiance and brilliance in the world around you, you must first trust that there is a basic law and order to the Universe and to feel that it is a very worthwhile opportunity to be a human being and alive at this time on planet earth. Second, you must step back from your experience and see every person and detail as a consenting and wise teacher; your mate, your children, your professional relations and your casual acquaintances. When you do the work to re-member and align your inner radiance with divine radiance and compassion, then you will know true joy and empowerment that knows not of the barriers this reality poses to your growth and love.

The barriers that we speak of form the veils that you cling to in your reality. The simplicity of profound change indeed occurs from the inside out. Many of you, especially those reading these words, know and love the light fiercely. Yet, we say to you that you are still carrying protection around your heart that is serving to keep from you the very thing that you truly yearn for. There is a deeper layer of being that must be discovered to truly walk in authentic presence and purpose. The single greatest obstacle between you and your authentic nature is the fear of who you are and what that remembrance might ask of you. So, you sit in the quiet and safety of your self-created world and you look outside of your being at all the things the world struggles with. You read uplifting books and perform healings on those who need your tools of expertise and then you convince yourself that you are doing all that you can from your little portion of the planet that you dwell on. And we say to you, you are limiting yourself and the entire evolutionary process with that thought stream.

Fearlessness requires selflessness, which asks for continual dissolution of the ego. What is the quality of your cosmic mirror and how often do you beseech your god to show you your true essence and vastness as well as your shadow and limitation? In working with yourselves, polishing the heart begins by telling the truth and the willingness to not know what you are doing or why you are here. In that moment of humility, you create an opening for your true Self to emerge. When you enclose yourself in the familiar with the creature comforts of what has always been, you open yourself to shadow by erecting a barrier between yourself and the rest of the world. Daring comes when you accept that in each moment you ARE the rest of the world. It is truly wonderful to be in your world at this time, but you must call upon and find a new level of bravery and commitment that first and foremost will redefine your sense of comfort and reality, as you know it.

To engage the magic of this present moment is to be in tune with the Earth. The Earth's wisdom is the new consciousness you seek. There is a cognition, tone and intelligence among the trees and all of nature that has a specific and ancient vibrational frequency. Your intuition and instinct carries this wisdom in cellular memory and provides access to a gnosis of Universality, that you can choose to engage or ignore in favor of control. You deserve the earth and the earth deserves you precisely because you have a commitment to each other to be genuine and true. On your planet, every moment is a challenge to be genuine: to look at the life you are living and be able to ask yourself if that reality is more a manifestation of your expanded truth or one of safety and known. You did not come to this now, precious beings of light, to be in control and complacent. That is the domain of the ego. You came here with your safety embedded in your heart and a fearless trusting that it is only in living in the unknown, that you will come to truly know your Self. The greatest service that you can gift to the world is to be in your joy, the joy of living an authentic existence.

To awaken your primordial self-nature is to step outside who and what you think you are and say yes to the living intelligence and natural hierarchy of the Universe. You belong not to yourselves. You belong to holiness. You are in partnership with a sacred world. Begin to allow vastness to truly touch you and inform your now. Be fierce in your desire to know yourself and unflinching in your commitment and discipline to walk in the light of your own bright sun. This is a quiet but powerful internal shift that will echo across all time and space and bring you the remembrance of your authentic nature. Meditating on these words will begin the process. When you truly recognize and accept the god radiance of who and what you are, increasing that illumination through your encoded ability to accrete more light, then you will begin vibrating the authentic essence that will awaken and send forth from you the signature of your Soul.

The Power To Choose

July 21, 2007

Life, Death, Love, Hate, Compassion, Sorrow, Joy, Separation, Wholeness, War, Peace... all experiential expressions of power, all available to the human potential, in each moment.

What do you want for yourself? What do you want for the world? Are your actions, decisions and choices everyday, indeed, reflecting what you say is your strong wanting? And do you know that it is within your power to create and allow your responses from mastery and love?

Every Master that has ever walked amongst humanity had not only a profound and abiding love for God, humanity and nature, but was accountable to his attitudes, emotions, beliefs and actions in the world. The prism shift of consideration for your contemplation on these words is not for you to see and accept that you must be accountable for your actions, but for you to understand that you now have the opportunity to bypass many steps that before were necessary for your deeper understanding. How is this possible? You must assimilate and integrate your experience from a fearless heart rather than mental prowess.

There is more guidance and energy being streamed to your reality than can be imagined. Each one of you are being uplifted and impressed with the highest frequency that your current personal vibration can attune to. What is happening at this time and being presented to your matrix is for you to be vigilantly self aware, in each moment with each experience and opportunity, of the response that would most dismantle and unfurl your constructs of self. You are being supported greatly in your reach outside of who you know yourself to be and the limitations of your current understanding to realize that, in each moment, your expansion and freedom is most dependent upon your ability to free your own mind from the limitations of its own perceptual understanding.

Every being reacts to the world in a different way, be it the immediate world around you or the greater world you reside in. Most of your reactions are unconscious and represent what your deeper self needs at the time. Reactions both repel and attract to you the people, places and situations that are necessary for your growth and remembrance as spiritual beings of power. If you are running an unconscious emotional programming in your matrix, then the lessons will appear to result in loss, lack, threat and disharmony. If, however, you can free yourself from your own conditioning, you will realize that love resides in the meaning of life that is constantly unfolding for you on your journey. It is a most unfortunate aspect of human nature that contracting the heart has become such an ingrained pattern. This is an important awareness to reflect upon. More often than not, you base your perceptions upon the very way that you have come to respond to life, based on your current level of understanding self-awareness. In that way, you are rarely responding from a moment of clarity and freedom. Your mind is then programmed again and again by your perceptions to justify and maintain your view of the world, and your identity within that known reality. It is a tough nut to crack, so to speak, a mind conditioned by a system of beliefs that have colored your reality from the moment of your birth.

Openness of heart, being completely free and fearless to respond in the moment to the love and opening present there, is greatly undermined by agenda and threat to ones sense of self. The path with heart entails being fully present without the ego and is only possible when you are acutely aware of your own perceptions. Perceptions more often than can be realized are a conditioned way of being in the world rather than the divine effluence of the heart. It takes vigilant and tireless self-awareness to consistently step outside the influence of one's own perceptions.

The purpose of life, and beautifully so, is to evolve awareness. Each experience is an opportunity to be free in the limitlessness of who you are by meeting the moment fresh and new, sensing the highest frequency available for you to respond to and take into your being. In that way, your being is constantly made new with an increasingly higher energetic of potential from which to erase personal history and be only in the present, again and again. If you would but realized how much power you are constantly surrounded with, that is constantly generated for you, of you, by you for the benefit of your own highest light and liberation. This power is, in fact, challenging you to see every experience as brilliantly orchestrated energetic configurations to evolve your perceptions, your understanding of your self, your ability to love with joyous exuberance and the current level of consciousness in your world. That is the power you have. You are that power, and available to you always, it is there to align you with the consciousness of the heart and bring energetically to you that which will enable you to map out the unknown.

Truly, there is nothing that is ultimately unknown to you or that lies outside the wisdom you possess. It is only the fear of your magnificence and the ember of awareness in your heart chamber of the true purpose of your presence here that provides the separation between the known and the unknown. Everything unlimited and brilliant and expansive is not only available to you, but is who you are in your true essence.

Do you walk through your reality each day with a knowingness of that awareness? Are your choices, your judgments, your actions and your trust reflective of the unconditional love that runs through you, by virtue of your Oneness? Real love involves a complete openness of heart that makes the evolutionary process an exciting journey filled with joy by the meaning you put into it. Whatever is before you, beloved masters of infinite potential, have that experience with openness of heart and gratitude. Let go of your fixed ideals and limited imaginings of what each next moment will bring. Engage the power of love as your highest expression by determining that in receiving your now with faith and trust, no agenda, no doubts, questions or fear, that energy of power engaged will transmute all experience into the greatest expansion of potential. In that, each moment of your participation and dance with Oneness, will not only lift your mastery to new levels of vibration, every vibration of your expansiveness will then ripple out to benefit the state of your entire planet. Such is the gift and power of love.

Inclusiveness As The Way of Love

July 27, 2007

It is within the power of the Universe and your connection to it, to change instantaneously any aspect of your experience. With that understanding and awareness comes the wisdom that any experience you are currently witnessing is not only chosen by your expanded essence for your highest good and mastery, but is love seeking your acknowledgement and conscious participation.

If you are observing your reality as having any degree of resistance or limitation, you are separating yourself from your experience, which then only creates more separation. It is only when you can embrace all of life equally without elevating or judging any aspect of it as above or below any other, that you begin to free yourself from the concepts of your conditioning.

Your mastery in each moment comes from your ability to embrace every challenge and person with just as much unconditional love as the next. It takes a great deal of self awareness, discipline, heartfelt willingness and an unwavering sense of purpose to acknowledge and accept, on going, that it is the master and love within you that brings to you experiences of pain and suffering during your journey, to awaken the mechanisms of your indwelling power! In that, each moment of your life is an opportunity to become filled with an overwhelming love for all aspects of your experience. Within that great love emanating forth from your heart, you will discover an ever-increasing desire to embrace it all, every moment and person, with the beauty and magnificence of your soul.

This is 5th dimensional living, beloved beings of light. With the current amplification and intensification of the energies on your planet, many are feeling the pressing desire and need to get on with things, so to speak, to know and BE your unique and true purpose. And we say to you that you cannot know your purpose until you are living an authentic life. Life, in Truth, is infinitely greater than what your egoic minds are capable of grasping. As you continue to expand and evolve your awareness of self and life, it will only be in retrospect that you can begin to understand and see through the vision of the inner eye just how far reaching your current impetus truly is.

Humanity in general, takes this life adventure for granted and as such, they believe and act as if they know their own true essence as well as their purpose. Life for the many is a safely regimented routine of escapisms and illusions of control in many different guises. Indeed, what you think you know, the experiences and people and materialism you have gathered around you to hold your assumed identity in tact are the very things limiting the inner vision of your Christed destiny to come forth into conscious awareness.

You are all crystals!!!!! You have the most exquisite etchings in your luminous being that are encoded with the light frequency of your mastery and ascension. This is how we see you. From every angle you reflect a color, vibration, tone and cellular resonance that is both your soul signature and cosmic sonar to awaken, remember and manifest your authentic nature. Understand that there is ultimately only One purpose and that is Inclusiveness. In order for you to connect with and manifest the Source frequency of your unique purpose, which is an aspect of the Universal purpose, you must honor the interdependence and interrelationship of ALL life and be wholly inclusive in ALL your actions. Living a life free of separation is your single greatest challenge and the call to an ever- expanding consciousness. It just cannot be underestimated just how much you separate yourselves, your experience, your actions and emotions from conscious awareness and the life around you.

Your innate and infinite nature is Joy...yet you attach your joy to circumstances and persons that you have judged to bring you joy. Nothing can bring to you that which you already are. Your joy is indwelling, emanating forth and coloring everything, as you raise your frequency to a place of being able to live in the Truth of your authenticity.

If you are complying with social constructs, tolerating a less than idyllic relationship and feeling satisfied while knowing in the secret chamber of your heart that you are not free... you are settling for the limitations you have learned within the confines of your dimensional reality. Can you hold your joy and vibrate a complete ecstasy of being when nothing in your illusive reality is stimulating your assumed sense of self? If not, then your joy is dependent upon the flow and circumstances of your reality and is thus, not an empowered and conscious state. This awareness, this knowingness within your expanded consciousness is a crucial step to the state of living that your beautiful planet is transitioning to. You must be able to hold a state of consciousness of the highest frequency to exist in the pure and luminous energies of 5th dimensional beingness.

Comfort with the unknown is a primary and necessary step. As you observe your own attitude, emotions, thoughts and actions in your interaction with nothingness, can you vibrate utter joy and unconditional love from your being regardless of your circumstances? As you align with your authentic nature and the frequency of your light body crystal, nothing can disturb your inner joy and peace because your sense of self is derived from the sacred power of your indwelling spirit. Know your Self and know your authentic mastery of 3rd dimensional existence. You are being supported greatly toward that remembrance and love as action. You are all empowered to choose now to step up in your commitment to the unknown reality of your transitioning planet. You are each here to fulfill your part in the cosmic dance of evolution. Be prepared and exuberant about getting jostled from your comfort zone. Your new day is here and you must necessarily be new within it. Begin each day, masters of a bright and evolved tomorrow, by imagining what wonderful thing is going to happen to you and then asking how you can fearlessly assist with your own necessary and unique emergence.

Through The Looking Glass

August 5, 2007

Consciousness is developing rapidly in your dimension. Everything you think is actually confirmed and you are learning daily that the power of thought, conscious or unconscious, actually creates your reality. Your mirrors are being polished through the reality you are manifesting in each moment. As the energies continue to increase and your marker of 2012 gets closer, many are feeling restless and on the edge. You are indeed, on the edge of an emergence within yourself and the planet that few, if any, are truly prepared for because there is no precedence. How wonderful is that?

The energy that accompanies transition radiates trust and prepares you for the unknown. It is a frequency that you can find the resonance of within your physical body to support and assist you as you traverse the fluid vibrational patterns of this global shift. It is essential to become more aware of frequency because it will help you to recognize your own self and to remain within your own vibration rather than conforming yourself to others. Only by recognizing and understanding that everything is frequency and is connected to everything else can you then apply the new truths to your daily life that are in need of integration. You will then be able to move forward with greater ease because you are in the center of your own frequency and not needing to extend so much energy in relation to the frequency of others.

Many light-workers address this potential by isolating and selective socializing. This is effective to an extent. But the threshold you are crossing now is all about community and inclusion and discovering your familiars, who are all being energetically fine-tuned for a coming together. Your reality is changing so fast that your greatest acceleration will come from being who you are in every arena of your reality. The teachers and the students are all merging and there will be quantum internal shifts occurring within your daily encounters. When you recognize your own truth and can be in that frequency with joy and without judgment, nothing will be able to disturb you. Truly in this now, the playing fields are being leveled so that each of you has access to just as much wisdom and vibration as the next entity. Each moment determines your next step. As you take care to let go of your judgment and separativeness, you strengthen your sense of Self, which leads to continual liberation.

Understanding the frequency of this dimension and the 3rd wave is a remembrance that you chose to be here on Earth at this time. You have a plan that was initiated from an untethered and limitless wisdom. That blueprint is deeply rooted in your cellular memory and can assist you not only in accessing your inner known and realm of remembrance, but will facilitate the necessary recognition and release of the programs you are running that no longer suit you or your purpose. Only then will you be above the density of matter such that you can attract and recognize the familiars now moving into your field with purposeful and right timing.

Yes, that is what is up for your experience at this time. Your team is coming in and those persons and experiences that cannot continue with the vibration of your intent are falling away. It is a beautiful and necessary process. You all agreed to it and you are all playing the roles of your wise knowing. There is no loss or lesser place to be at this time. It is just part of a necessary sifting, realignment and tightening up that must take place to manage the frequencies of your intent in the unknown days to come. Trust who is appearing. Trust who is leaving without resistance or the need to show another what they are not seeing. Open yourselves up, be aware what truly occupies you and be fully present. Then you will have nothing to fear because all the doors to your inner source will open to allow the new alignments and relationships to fall in effortlessly, quickly and with all the support that you need.

It is so curious to us how much resistance is viewed as a normal part of your process. It is not. Resistance is created from the mental plane and is fear based. If there is resistance, lack, limitation, doubt, discrepancy or an unclear step before you, we say to you it is about energy and a non-resonance between the program and expectation you are running and what is actually being presented to you for your discernment and expansion. There are armies, if you will, of non-physical beings with each of you right now, in each moment. If you are not sensing that or receiving the guidance you feel that you need, it is because of thought and the process of the mental plane. When you focus on your heart and your feelings and live from that awareness, surrender is an ongoing process. Surrender is necessary to let go of old patterns that prevent you from opening your heart. Surrender makes fear vanish. It takes patience and stillness to feel rather than think. Being present with passion fills you with the vibration of right timing and assures that you are always where you need to be. You are unique beings with endless capabilities. Recognize your Self, embrace all opportunities and do not be afraid of your strengths now emerging.

Every single moment of your life is a turning point. Right now, in this moment, you are not the same being you were just a few hours ago. That is how fast your reality is shifting and your perceptions in response to that acceleration. Being present in each moment with the frequency you carry allows for the newness of that opportunity to find a resonance with your cellular memory of intent, activating the codex of this current time-shift to align you with each next step in your expansion. In so doing, you are contributing to the planetary process as you endeavor to increase your own light.

Like a stone upon a glassy pool, your frequency is ever sending out ripples. Find the stillness of your true and calm center and remember that as you are looking for the clarity of the bright sun in the days to come, the reflection of power and knowingness you seek, is your very own. What you are looking for is looking for you!

The Gap To Freedom

August 13, 2007

This now of your time here on planet Earth is the most inspired and important point within which you will ever find yourself. Your world is not just randomly changing, it is irreversibly transforming. This is a time for leaps that recognize shifts in consciousness more influential and mysterious than you have yet to imagine. We will speak to you more of what it means to live in the mystery, the unknown, the eternal now of your emergence and re-membrance.

The unknown is that which has never been encountered before. Ever. This mystery is not from a lack of experiential awareness, information or knowledge. We say to you that what is just over the near horizon for your world is such that there is no reference point, no matter what intelligence or historical background is applied. It is an unknown that at best, can be described as some THING out there that is vast, daunting and truly incomprehensible from your current vantage point. We wish not to instill fear but to get your attention from a place of accountability, shared responsibility and potential rebirth into that which is only love.

The current events and state of disrepair you find yourselves in are a manifestation of the power you have given away. It is incomprehensible to us, truly, how a species of such beautiful light and divine resonance has chosen to comply and accept those things which are grossly unacceptable to the wisdom of the heart's intelligence. This unknown of Universal precedent is an opportunity that the heart's consciousness has called forth for humanity to make a new bid for power. You see, challenges ARE power. In each challenge lay the opportunity to be totally transformed, the greater the challenge the greater the gifts of power in potential. When that power comes to you in the form of challenge, how will you apply that challenge within your consciousness and respond?

Throughout a primitive and increasingly war like history, the potential of humanity has agreed to a leadership that reflects the consciousness and agenda of a few rather than the desires and wishes of the many. You have, each one of you in each moment, the choice of abiding in God Consciousness or of accepting a consciousness of control and deception. It is that simple. You have allowed yourselves to become passive and passionless in your knowledge and understanding of the Universal principles of living in peace and harmony with each other and the planet. It is not for anyone else to remedy or set aright, it is for every individual to acknowledge and accept the responsibility of power within their own being that in turn will lift the level of consciousness and imbalance of power pervading the beliefs and mind sets of your world. We ask that you become impeccable and honest observers of self and be accountable to how often you respond to creations around you, not from the highest frequency of the heart but from a consciousness of distrust and fear.

What we observe often in your internal negotiations with self is that there is much compartmentalization that occurs to justify your actions. It is easy and agreeable to your current state of consciousness to love and accept the many facets of your creations when they do not threaten in some way the sense of control and understanding of self you have managed to hold onto through these turbulent times.

Your expanded wisdom is creating many scenarios for you to engage the highest frequency possible when responding to those creations you deem unacceptable to your reality. Do you not see that there is not one manifestation of reality occurring for you in your now that is not for you to re-calibrate your own perceptual framework and choose to respond from an understanding of expansion and trust. Right now, across the globe, the consciousness of every person is poised to reach a new level of its own awareness of Self. The most potent and assured portal through which this transmutation can occur is through a repatterning of the very things that have been your own undoing in similar past scenarios. In that way, your deeper mind is offering up to your conscious awareness a defining moment, again and again, throughout your personal experiences.

Truly, we can say to you, unequivocally, that in your quiet most inner thoughts at this time, each of you feels alone in a universe of your own making. Yet, when you engage the heart in your bid for power, that sense of isolation and futility becomes ALL ONE, embracing the greater Universe of the Eternal Now. You are all connected. You come from the same Source. But you live and choose and act from a belief system and past that clearly has not served you well, one based in fear and darkness. This is not who you are. This discrepancy in who you are as a divine aspect and how you are using your power has brought you to this moment where fence sitting is no longer an option. The time is necessarily now for you to cease engaging darkness through your own response to the life around you. When you embrace ALL life without separation or judgment, you end up wanting for nothing because you are cooperating intelligently with the process of life, becoming ever more integrated with Oneness. This comes from listening to and acting upon what the heart wants, senses, desires and knows apart from mental processing, taking you from strength to strength in your challenges so that you build a true power that is whole, absolute and invincible.

The strengths you have relied upon in the past are becoming secondary if not obsolete in nature. You must take it deep into your being and heart's wisdom that to live an utterly impeccable life requires first and foremost that you be only in this now and that you then trust that the experience your own higher wisdom has drawn forth is for you to see and be with, in love. This will absolutely begin a transformation of your reality that will deliver you expeditiously to your next highest vibration of awareness and understanding, and to your familiars and support of intent. Trust what is before you, beings of unlimited potential, promise and untapped power. Listen to your heart and determine to liberate yourself from that which is no longer serving you. Even when you imagine in your mental theorizing that you do not know what to do or that you have not the courage to leap into the nothingness of an unknown reality... it is only in that leap, trusting the power of the heart to align with the intelligence of LIFE, that you will find the freedom that you seek. Your freedom from the known will reinstate the balance of power in the manifestation of your individual purpose and in your world.

The Choice Of Love

August 27, 2007

Imagine, if you will, a city of brilliant light. The sky is infinite and a blue not known to your human imaginings. The light is that of a many faceted prism reflecting pure essence illuminations as far as the human eye can see. Upon your every gaze, you observe beings that radiate gentleness, peace, joy and love. The movements you behold are movements of beingness, of trust, of allowing and of wholeness. There is a harmony that you experience here that resonates deeply with the inner knowing of your own being, a familiarity that defies the reality you have so come to identify yourself with in your dimension.

This may seem a quaint reverie amidst the many distortions you have created with your perceptions. And we say to you that the further your current awareness must stretch to visualize and feel the potential of this crystal city, is the greatest reflection of the work you have yet to master in the dominion of your mind over your heart's wisdom. For there is such a city, one of many parallel realities, vital and alive in the center of your Earth, there for the intent and devotion of assisting mankind in the evolution from 3rd dimensional orientation to 4th and 5th dimensional awareness. In a state of timelessness that knows nothing of the expectations, restrictions and requirements of fulfillment that you place upon yourselves in a reality of distrust and agenda, there are masters of 5th dimensional consciousness unwavering in their commitment to your transformation and rebirth.

The collective frequency of your planet has much lifting to embody in the days, months and years to come. The mastery of the pure frequency essence of 5th dimensional living is essential to your survival as a species. Yet, you are so easily pulled right back into that which is familiar and comfortable to your 3rd dimensional being, even if it is uncomfortable and does not bring you joy. It is a constant wonderment for us to observe so many of you feeding your minds, practicing the newest tool of enlightenment and expounding upon the virtues of a great teaching and still you go right back into your world and choose to be and vibrate density. Why is that? Go inside your own awareness right in this moment and ask yourself why, when there is only love expressing itself through the veil of your own illusion, that you choose to remain behind that veil rather than lifting it to the possibility of another reality and truth? Not incurring new karma at this stage in the evolutionary process is much easier if one remains ever aware of their commitments and interactions with those around them. Your ultimate freedom from the density of this plane is very much determined by your degree of self awareness, self understanding, attitude and the effort you put forth to achieve that which your heart knows to be true.

This is very much a lone journey for you on your planet, and we acknowledge the entanglements that occur when your orientation is so inclined to derive your beingness from outside of yourselves. Even in partnership, your experience in your reality is still about you and your unique process of expansion. Every being in your dimension has something equally essential and valuable to learn for the evolution of the planet, based on everything you have ever known in all of your many realities of incarnations and the breadth of the future unfolding. It is always available to you and always a choice. When you get your piece of remembrance, the wisdom piece, you will hear the click of your entire cellular structure as it finds and relaxes into the truest alignment of your matrix. As unique as your beautiful blue planet is, so too is your purpose in the world. As she is a crystal, you are each a facet that has incarnated to discover the unique evolutionary knowledge of your mastery, which lights up like a beacon, so that you find your place not as the identity that you think you are but as light crystal illuminations. In that, each of you is a brilliant reflection divine being, equally as necessary to magnify and express the absolute of the One.

This cannot and will not happen as long as you are determined to live in a reactionary mode of being, forgetting again and again, no matter how many times your beloved god aligns an opportunity for you to reach higher and imbibe only that which strengthens, that the vibration you engage is creating your tomorrow. Every experience that comes to you is not only a gift, but comes to you by the invitation of the vibrational patterns that you carry. There is no exception - energy is always looking for a higher implicate order to rise to. In that, your brothers and sisters are gifting you always the opportunity to shift your reality by seeing the energy dynamics from the highest light, thus taking a step from that place and opening new ley lines of creation for your own experience and for others to follow. Your mind is powerless if you dwell in vibrational and spiritual ignorance. What, after all, is spirituality to you? What does it mean to be spiritual?

Firstly, life aligned with divine will reflects greater harmony and peace, independent of the circumstances and environment you find yourselves in. Your divinity is veiled where you stray in consciousness, choosing to engage the vibrations of distrust and deception, separativeness and victim consciousness. This is a tangled web that you so weave to deceive yourselves and to keep from you the very thing that would set you free: love. What is it inside of you that has become so conditioned, to think that you do not deserve this love and harmony as your divine and true being? The fastest way for you to gain spiritual mastery and spiritual freedom is to align your thoughts, perceptions and actions with the Mind and Will of Source, the highest frequency possible for all of your experience. Truly, this is the ultimate action for all intent on healing your world once again into its rightful expression of unity and harmony.

So many of you are still operating from the lesser power of the mental plane to figure out and solve that which is not complying with your current understanding or expectation. It is working to the degree that you are still running programs from the constructs of social conditioning. Your ultimate good and necessary participation in this great evolution of consciousness requires that you step out ahead of what seems to be currently working to create a new template upon which the new earth can manifest. This template already exist in other dimensions and it is for you to align your own actions with the highest choice possible in each moment that you begin to transform what you see into what you know to be truth: for your personal reality and for the understanding of those in need of the light and wisdom you shine for them.

5th Dimensional frequency, that existing and vibrating from the beings of the inner earth right now on your behalf, is that of compassion, peace, joy, harmony, forgiveness, trust, allowing, freedom and non-doing. It is a gentle way of being in the world. Your planet is an organism and awakening to the oneness of it is a recognition that you belong to one family. She has taken on your angst and anger and ego distortions for so very long that she is weary from the density of so much illusion. In your current experience of uncertainty and breathless change, where does your allegiance lie? Every single moment of every single day is an opportunity for you to choose love. When you choose love for your self, for your experience, for those you are gifted to interact with in your becoming, you are choosing love for the entire planet, healing her with the higher frequencies you engage. And when you take a circumstance and cloak it in shadow, finding fault, casting judgment and choosing to veil it in shadow, you are impregnating that moment with more of that very same illusion for the entire planet. It is that simple and that profound. It is never about the circumstance you find yourself in dear entity but how you choose to frame and then respond in vibration; with Unity Consciousness or separativeness. Your power as a creator is to engage each moment with the highest frequency and in turn, transform that moment to its highest potential.

Rise up beings of infinite light and endless joy. You are in the gap, right now, to your freedom. Depending on how far into the void you are, how much of your being is fed by the constructs of your conditioning and how much is infused and vibrating with the frequency of your divinity, this is what determines the direction of your reach. When your reality begins to spin and things seem not in your control and your expectation is not met, do you reach back to the prison of your conditioned mind and choose to see and be and respond with the denser vibrations of your known history? Or do you allow the unparalleled frequency of love to create, transform, heal and harmonize all things, for your shifting reality and for your evolving world?

Rapid change and necessary shifts in consciousness are inspiring a renewed appreciation for meaning and purpose. It is time to be impeccably accountable for who you have been in fear and ignorance and to cut the threads of your self-created illusions. This will enable your inner truth to surface and be the power of your manifestations. It will not be a seamless shift because you are so conditioned by the known, beyond your current comprehension. Yet, it will be increasingly imperative that you are able to distinguish between that which is illusion and veiled in fear and that which is true and offering you the glistening pure essence of love. True wisdom always comes from the mind of higher perspective and higher consciousness, aligning your mind and then actions with the divine mind. Healing the world is something you get up each day and choose to do again and again with each choice and each action you engage. It is a beautiful and powerful gift for your own expansion and in transforming the density of your current existence. Even the smallest light shines in darkness. If you trust nothing else, trust the wisdom of love to transform all illusion; it is your greatest treasure.

There Is A Place

September 3, 2007

There is a place where there is no sorrow, where there is only truth and peace abounds; a place where trust lights the way of each new day and forgiveness is not a virtue that some practice, but an essence that informs the experience before there is even a need to forgive. There is a place where joy reigns supreme and all beings are a magnificent reflection of the many facets of love seeking wholeness; a place where each moment is celebrated as an opportunity to expand one's own awareness through the expression of love and the wisdom that love transforms through gentleness and grace. There is a place where you can always go and feel free to be who you are as there is only light and an answer to every question. There is a place that is the safest place you could ever be in a time of uncertainty and change. This place is within you, this place is your own heart; and the door is always open.

Beloved light beings, masters of this plane of demonstration, it is the destiny of all humankind to awaken from their spiritual amnesia and realign with the original intention of their soul. We wish to impress upon you for deep contemplation how very much you live in your mind, which is entangled with your own history and judgments. So much possibility of instant release and transformation of every imaginable circumstance is occluded by the ego's fear of not knowing what is next; of not being able to be in control of the great unknown ahead. What will you do when you know not what to do?

Challenges and circumstances such as your planet has never experienced before are upon you as a species. The outcome of all the unprecedented unknown of change, shift and reconfiguration of life on planet Earth is dependent upon where your consciousness is residing. It cannot be underestimated how much of your identity and sense of self you derive from the way you live in the world. Your surroundings, routine, relationships of familiarity, possessions, learned skills and abilities, the systems you depend on to help you flow your reality just so, all of these things you use as mirrors to reinforce your identity and belief of who you think you are. What happens when every one of those constructs suddenly disappears? What if in this moment, you found yourself sitting on a spot on the earth with no job identity, no possessions, no loving support systems of relationships, no savings account, no insurance, no reference point for your established identity and reputation? How safe and secure would your world feel to you then? Can you sit with that consideration for even a moment and find the peace and comfort you seek?

We ask these questions, as uncomfortable and improbable to you as they may seem, to open for you the awareness that you are much more attached to the illusion of who you are than the Truth of who you are. It is easy to have faith and be in peace when your world is comfortable and in the understanding that soothes your egoic mind. To the degree that your world has routine and order and a "safety net," we say to you that there is dependency on illusions and constructs that were created from fear - and not just your own personal fear, but many generations and histories of the belief in and experience of poverty, war, greed, lack, despair, abandonment, deception and grave betrayals against the truth and beauty of the human spirit. The world that you have come to know as real and have adjusted your beingness to is one built on tyranny and the power of the few at the sacrifice of the many. It is an illusion that you have become so accustomed to that you have adjusted your spirit to live within the confines of the shadow. And that world is about to topple and fall.

There is, right now in this moment of your time, a sifting and delineation of vibrational alignment occurring on your planet. It is being influenced and empowered by the ability to consciously choose, reside in and integrate a higher frequency of light, of peace, unity, abundance, truth, inclusivity, compassion and love. The highest part of you, your higher self wisdom, your oversoul, your divine mind and multidimensional beingness is shining a bright light for your personality construct to wake up and be empowered in choosing a new way of creating your reality. Every day is brand new and you are brand new in it. Yet, you live a routine and leave your passion and brave hearts for those moments when your identity has exhausted all its responsibilities. You can nurture your mind with great thoughts and have a grand vision, yet if you create that vision from the understanding and precepts of your history and known experience, you are building on a foundation that will not hold because it is connected energetically to the old world.

The new world is a world of unspeakable joy. You recognize everyone as your brothers and sisters and there is only the strong wanting for each to know the truth of their own divinity. It is a world where separation and duality have transformed into truly embracing that what you want and give to another are your own treasures secured: because there is only One. We have spoken to you as clearly as your languaging will allow the energetics we reside in to express, about the necessity of your living a new vibration before there is a comfortable or even receptive place for that new frequency to resonate. This is how the new world will manifest, by the mighty hearts and vibrational mastery of the few creating new energetic pathways for the many to follow. In that, living the way of the highest light and intent will be, for a time, the most difficult and seemingly fruitless path to be walking. But we say to you, magnified creators of magnified intent and desire to be here now, that it is the path of Truth. And it is the love inside of you extending from the greater love of Source that is binding you to that intent when much around you is denying it. It is just so very gratifying to witness the passion and awakening of the heart's remembrance and intelligence of so many beautiful and magnificent souls. So gratifying, indeed.

Be willing to be brand new in your reality for the sake of the new world soon to manifest. The ways of Heaven are coming to Earth, but your active participation is critical. And we speak not of active as in the doing of your accustomed way of being in your reality. We speak of creating your day from the greatest seat of power you possess; your vibrational core of knowingness. That is the part of you that is constant and exists throughout all time and space and within many realities simultaneously. This center is one of quiet power, allowing and non-judgement . You must be able to look right at the illusion that your mind has invested so much power in and deny its existence to create a new frequency of trust; trust in the unknown, the unseen, the unprecedented and the unimaginable. Notice everything about reality, as you know it to be, and then release it back into the shadow from which it came. This will create the spaciousness and vibrational resonance for the light to come in and perform an energetic alchemy in each moment. Surrender who you were yesterday and what you thought to be true, beautiful beings. Be right here now, in this moment, in gratitude for the present. Gratitude is the gift. You are experiencing extensions of the eternal and in this moment you are charged with the power and love of the multiverse. Use that love and power well and the new world will evolve from the brilliance of your heart's consciousness.

The Inexplicable Nature Of Joy

September 9, 2007

We will speak to you today of the tone, color, light spectrum and vibrational essence of joy. And it is our great joy to do so, for very few of you understand the vast nature and implication of this frequency.

The greatest teacher of joy, if indeed, it were something outside of you, is nature; an infinitely abundant celebration of being. Your planet, Gaia, the Primal Mother... exudes joy in just being. All of her creations, her children and her gifts to humankind are joy in infinite expression. Let us, therefore, enter humbly and reverently into a meditative contemplation of joy - the keeper of the Earth's pulsing heart center.

In contemplating the beingness of joy, you come to a remembrance of a sacred source of transcendence. The natural world of your experience is a loving, accepting, unfolding and inclusive facet of Source that binds you all together for the highest good. Joy is an expressed revelation of the beauty of the Creator. There is so much variety and stimulus for your senses to be gathered from the natural world... she is the revealer of many of the Truths that you seek and a dispenser of great knowledge. In her beingness and reflection, you will find a means of perfecting the spiritual essence that you have come to re-member, of allowing your very being to know its own dignity and immortality, of reminding your heart of its noble origin and thus, its interconnected, interdependent, multifaceted relationship with the Universe and with the Divine.

The energies being extended now to and from your planet are to liberate humanity from its attachments and delusions, into a right appreciation of its inherent divinity and the divinity of all creation. There is no identity apart from that which is your natural world and no appreciation apart from the individual finding a personal connection and relationship with the Earth. You are interdependent organisms. Your understanding of and personal relationship with your Earth, is a direct reflection of your understanding of and relationship with self. She carries graciously the vibration of your beingness and maintains that frequency through the eternal process of livingness. Divine livingness is engaging divine power, intelligence, knowledge and order - which manifests through your experience as divine love for all life. Your Earth does this instinctively and in the process attends to the wellbeing, needs and care of both the natural kingdom and all of humankind. In a singleness of purpose that defies complacency and inertia, she holds the seeds of becoming and bears the fruit of great labor, again and again, through a process that is eternally cyclical.

When joy is thought of or sensed through your imaginings it is often in the realm of emotions. As with happiness, sadness, excitement, anger, and the full spectrum of emotions that humans experience due to the thinking capacity, joy is most often associated with external stimuli, experience or the actions of others. Yet, there is a level of joy available to you that is not of the 3rd dimensional plane. It is a pristine, flawless, frequency of endurance, fearlessness and the power to vivify. The pure essence of joy is secondary only to the frequency of love. Joy is love's signature. Joy is love's finest expression, the song your Soul sings and sends to you through the vibration of your being. It may be reflected in an experience that you have in your dimension, but joy is free and independent of anything that you know as connected to your reality. Your authentic joy is radiance in form and the door into the very mind and heart of the Creator. Joy is the harmony of the spheres and the synthesis of all that is of true beauty in your world. It is possible and even natural to your being, for you to draw through your physical vehicle the frequency of joy to inform all of your experiential reality. In that way, you know only that which is joy because you use the frequency of its wisdom to transform all of your reality.

When you experience nature as an extension of your beingness, you are witnessing your own joy. The vivid colors and tones, the dance of the elements, the unfettered nature of the animal world, the symphony of sound all encompassing.... it is joy that gives voice to what would be silent. And it is all you. The ineffable Oneness that exists in the intelligent cooperation of your natural world is the single greatest impetus for the evolutionary leap from intellect to intuition. When you have truly passed the point of attachment to the distortions of material conditioning, your perceptions of your present circumstances and those of your world will shift into one that fits into the overall pattern of life, one that allows you to exercise your mind and heart toward a greater, more inclusive understanding of Oneness. There is a plan. The love of the Creator is the basic law of all manifestations and the origin of all evolutionary momentum. Indeed, an accelerated expansion of beingness occurs when the seeker recognizes that the Creator's plan for the individual is part of the Creator's plan for the world! God talks to you the clearest through nature and creation. That is where your true values and empowered knowledge lie. The gift of nature is the freedom and expressed joy to know one's eternal beingness and to leave behind the trap of identification with the temporal.

Joy is the path of return: return to love, to trust, to clear vision, to clarity of thought, to Oneness with all life, and to Self.

If you feel that joy is not always present in your reality, that joy is something you have observed yet know it not as your constant companion, then we say to you that you are not fully in touch with who you are, eternally. There must necessarily take place, a distinction between your mental life and your beingness. Your joy is always present. It is there to lift up and transform every illusion of circumstance. If you feel not the inexplicable nature of joy in all of your reality, it is the construct of thought that is inhibiting its natural flow. Joy vibrates with the essence and clarity of your heart. Thought vibrates with the density and construct of the mental plane. It is possible to align your thoughts with the intelligence of the divine mind - yet the frequency of your joy is already there.

We invite you to spend some time observing yourself in relation to your understanding and belief about joy. Find some time, as well, to be in stillness and solitude with the Great Mother. Ask her to reveal to you the true essence and vibration of your being. May you be enchanted and liberated in what you are gifted from her grace and may that joy that is timeless and eternal be the new compass on your journey.

Attachment And The Allure Of Form

September 18, 2007

We have come together with you often around the principles of Universal Love, peace, joy harmony, compassion and unity. Much aligned with the Buddhist love of the 4th plane, this cosmic love energy radiates intuition, discernment, spiritual liberation and beneficence to the whole field of creation.

More than at any other time in your history, all of humankind is experiencing a collective initiation, which will necessitate far greater voluntary responsibility. This initiation is a process of energy transmission from an expansiveness infusing your dimension with a distinctively electrical force, to jump-start the initiate into fields of increased vibrational rate. This will continue to shake up and shift individual realities beyond what is comfortable for the egoic self, which controls the human personality. The instinctive reaction to such a dismantling will be to rely on those beliefs and programs that you have always turned to when life as you know it becomes unsettling. Yet, the very gift and purpose behind this potential energy enhancement of magnetic-attractive force around the initiate, is to stimulate a higher center of energy as a new base of operation from which to integrate and assimilate the new energies that will soon be the foundation of the new Earth. In effect, you are being taught how to work with and use these creative and dynamic energies while experiencing them in a reality where truly they have no current resonance. This is, indeed, the primary causal factor of the environmental changes that are being observed and experienced across the globe. The fury of storms, the violence of earth quakes, the extreme manifestations of what use to be a natural geographical season, are all the cumulative effect of thought forms that have created an uninhabitable environment!

As a species you have lost the capacity to discriminate between consciousness and form. So attached are you to the reality of form, that you have settled into a flow of existence that is not only illusive in nature but based in an excessive identification with the material plane. This numbing of your mind with the known is gravely inhibiting your ability to be free and creative thinkers. Let us express it in relation to energy. If you are the center of a wheel that is constantly in motion, the many spokes of your wheel comprised of your house in its order and your job on its schedule and your relationships behaving just so, your Saturday routine, your comfortable balance in your savings account and the IRA that you attribute with the trust of your future, what happens to the momentum of that wheel when those personality attachments are no longer there? We say to you, you are indeed relying on that which is form for your very survival and this energy of attachment will be the undoing of many in the days to come. You do not own your house, your job is not secure and your health is certainly not in good hands if entrusted to the medical institutions currently in place. Everything that is form is subject to the little wills and minds of man, over which you ultimately have no control. Much of what you have come to believe to be true and have put your faith and trust in is but the deceptive allure of the material plane. For many centuries you have built your treasures and established your legacies based on the tangible, assured, reliable practices of the generations before you, all the while giving great momentum to the energy of entitlement and tyranny.

It is just not possible to get from where you are as a species mentally to where your transformation lies in heart-centered consciousness, until you truly begin to look at the discrepancy in your individual lives. You cannot expect to pray for peace on the other side of the world and meditate a new earth into beingness when your mind is saying, "just don't take away the comfort of my known existence!" We say to you, the greatest joy and freedom lies in the unknown, where your spirit and consciousness have the liberty to create from the beloved god of your being versus the control of your egoic mind. All the earth turbulence that is just beginning to create a momentum is the very discrepancy and duality that you walk in each day by living with division between your personality and your soul. You are acknowledged and uplifted for the creations of your intellectual wizardry on the material plane. It is the investment you have given to those creations that is the concern. Your plane of demonstration that has witnessed an ever increasing misappropriation of power and resources will continue to get spun - the times ahead on your planet are not going to get better in the foreseeable future. The gravity and devastation of potential is much greater than the days you knew as The Depression, for the very reason that there are extreme levels of what you call wealth and material dependency. The equivalent of what was known as a depression in your year of the 20's in your current state of economy will greatly upset the equilibrium and security of the human psyche with devastating impact.

The purpose and potential but certainly not the promised outcome of all this seeming upset and upheaval is to shift the assemblage points of your attachment to form and an illusive identity. The increase in energies is a gift, and offer of new life. But it comes with a decision of what master you will serve. The high frequency being extended on your behalf at this time is to enable individual minds and hearts in the mass of humanity to resist the pull of the herd instead of blindly following the dictates of form. It is imperative that you begin consciously and creatively directing the energies being made available to you. It is the responsibility of the human kingdom to bring about the 5th dimensional vibrations and Buddha energies of love, intuition, discernment, peace, harmony and compassion. No more sleep walking with one foot on either side of the fence. It is time to lift your sights and raise your expectations beyond what you can see and touch and feel a measure of control over. If you have not the courage to step out of your confinement in this moment, then begin to look for ways that you can support the light beings and disciples of the new world that are stepping out of the matrix of control. They are there, in the tens of thousands, following their heart and fearless in their pursuits. The supreme and divine love expressing Itself as conscious expansion is not concerned with single persons, just as those forging the new frontier of an enlightened world are no longer imprisoned by the restrictions and dictates of social consciousness. They are heart-centered and fully attuned to the One, their actions are manifesting toward group consciousness and sensitivity to group ideals. They are creating the templates for inclusiveness in plans, concepts and a collective, impersonal love that sees beyond apparent contradictions in their observable reality.

You know who these visionaries and pioneers are as they are observable to you and shining the light in the direction of your true purpose. If you are not yet ready to release the attachments of your own reality, be willing to support the ones who have already leaped. This is what an all-encompassing unity is truly about. It is an understanding of an interrelated connectedness to all things and the relevancy of your now to begin, however great or small, to engage the frequency of this evolutionary shift. It is the fundamental principle encoded in the hearts of all of mankind to embrace change as truth.

Imagine a divinely orchestrated dissemination of star beings around the globe committed now to the expansion of where your destiny lies. They are your star being brothers and sisters who have agreed to step out before you and reflect the light of your authentic Self. As a microcosm of the Cosmic Heart Center, they are mirroring for you the very steps of empowerment and spiritual liberation that are the promise of the new world. It matters not if you are the one living in the transformative promise of the unknown or the one acting as the bridge between them and the world of form, be inclusive in your decisions and investments and a future earth will unfold where you are all once again living as Universal love on a grand scale.

Gratitude As the Voice On Your Path

September 29, 2007

How often do you wake up with your first thought being of what powerful creators you are? And are you able to distinguish between the creations of your egoic mind and those from a centered clarity of vibrational awareness? It is much more agreeable and pleasing to the ego to attach itself to those aspects of reality that are flowing according to its plan and then delegate responsibility for all the not so pleasant details to something outside of itself. Then the emotional fires, distortions and deceptions of the ego take over in reasoning and a spin begins where there really is just no possibility for an elevated outcome.

The single greatest gift you can give to yourself everyday is to be in gratitude for all that you have created, and to find the pure frequency of light spectrum beneath the distorted illusion. There is not one moment that you are not manifesting the exact experience that your expanded Self called into being to help realize Christ Consciousness. No exceptions. You would do well to take that truth into your conscious memory and continually hold it up against your experiential reality. Especially so, those moments and circumstances where you feel anger, anxiety, hatred, resentment, discontent, jealousy and envy, because they are ego centered emotions. It matters not if you engage all or just one of these distortions over another, they represent where your current level of consciousness and energy vibrate. The ego dwells in reactive energy and strengthens itself through negativity. When these emotions are present in you they are never justified and falsely seen as caused by external factors, which is just not possible. They represent a reactive way of being in the world and most assuredly reflect a lack of emotional understanding and compassion for self. Additionally, these emotions of dis-ease have a physiological component to them that is accumulative in effect on your physical health and well-being. The moment you experience any of these low vibrating emotions of the egoic self, you are experiencing a disconnect with your Divine Self. The ego makes everything personal, which is how it establishes and maintains control.

In a world so governed by the constructs and emotional reactivity of the egoic mind, how does a being begin to move to a new and expanded understanding of the creations in their reality? It is a Universal truth and absolute that vibrating at the core of all distorted perception is the greater and finest frequency of love. To truly understand about consciousness and energy is to see clearly and sense vibrationally this love and the immediate potential for transformation and release. If you are being held captive in an experience where there exist these emotional distortions, there is a lack of self-love present. That which you perceive as separate is your reflection and is showing you the prison of your own misunderstanding. The ego just derives so much satisfaction in being right that it looks for others to make responsible for its own creations. In doing so, it creates more of the very same energy of discontent and emotional deception that allow it to remain dominant. This energy of drama is quite prevalent in your world and that gives credence to just how great the egoic power of your dimension has become. Where there is no ego, there is profound and lasting peace.

You are here to realize your Self and to stand as a sovereign being. Many take this to mean in connection to your monetary reality, yet the greater sovereignty concerns your vibrational beingness. No matter what mastery you have over the physical plane of existence, if you are not conscious with your emotional understanding and response, you are living a fragmented expression of who you are as a sovereign being. To find the love and embody the love frequency in all of your reality is not only engaging transformational potential, it is setting your Self free from ego created emotion. Begin with a consciousness of presence and awareness in those circumstances where you are engaging victim consciousness, very much a dis-ease on your planet; it is the very opposite of knowing your Self as a powerful creator. Engage a dialogue with that part of you that knows it is a magnified creator and that even the imperfections of your creations were engaged to expand your own consciousness, heart center and understanding about who you are, truly. We say to you that the contracts that you chose for this incarnation could be experienced, integrated and transformed in very short order if you were to step back from the reactive nature of the ego long enough to experience and see the love. That is when the true vibrational understanding of gratitude comes in to begin re-ordering the way you experience life! As vibrational beings you are making choices in each moment about what vibration to engage. If the energy is reactive in nature, you are in a fragmented state of being and relying upon your emotional history to determine each new moment. In becoming the observer of your vibrational choices, you see clearly who is the master of your experience. Finding and being in your joy with consciousness, no matter what the circumstance, is being the new Earth. Choosing to remain in victim consciousness, making others responsible for your emotions of reactivity and reality, is the choice to live in the ego driven known of reality.

The current vibrations of your planet, increasingly so, are folding the 3rd dimensional matter based and 4th dimensional emotion based experience up into a 5th dimensional way of living and being. The 5th dimension is that of the Light Body in which you are aware of yourself as a Master and multidimensional being. You govern your being from a high frequency of consciousness, with impeccable presence, and are completely spiritually oriented. We acknowledge that to begin to apply yourself toward this elevated intent while yet working within the dysfunction and constructs of a deconstructing reality of experience, will not come easily or without upset. Yet, the more you cling to the mechanisms of the ego to feel in control and create from its power, ultimately your creations will not survive because your planet will not sustain them. If you listen each day for the voice of gratitude in all of your experience, taking responsibility for it all in your mastery, you will begin to dissolve the old ways of creating reality.

There is only love. When you can experience that love in all your miscreations as well as those that you perceive as success, you are stepping into the vibration of an ascended being. Healing and creating the world anew, one day, one experience and one choice at a time is a beautiful and powerful gift to your expansion. Being conscious creators and sovereign beings means looking at all of your experience and seeing the master looking back. To know that presence of awareness is to know the transcendent essence of gratitude.

Looking At The Illusion

October 17, 2007

One inevitable result of the planetary evolution is that there must be more accountability in the individual process. Humanity has gotten somewhat complacent in their internal stretch, in part, because there have been so many predictions and markers for potential events for so long. Since the Harmonic Convergence of 1987, lightworkers and spiritual teachers have been preparing for change to various extents. Yet, human nature leans easily in the direction of the path of least resistance when it comes to familiarity and comfort zones. Change is not a strong suit for the personality aspects of your being, especially when you've long been dressed for a party that seems to be some unpredictable future event.

The unpredictable will continue to be a constant but the rumblings and evidence of unsettling events economically and environmentally, as well as the ensuing threats to the very life and freedom of your known reality, will continue to accelerate at alarming rates. The crises upon you at this time can no longer be stalled or held together by the false sense of power and control you have all succumbed to in varying degrees over the course of your history. You must either allow these new energies to support the need to let go of what you cling to in fear of losing your attachments, or you will be swept into the density and shadow of those forces that are bound by illusion and separation.

It can be disappointing to witness how little humans change. You must hold your focus and trust in that which is limitless and eternal with the promise of rebirth over the fear of the unknown. When you truly begin to let go, to unwind the insane rhetoric of the egoic mind, you begin to sense and feel and assimilate these loving and powerful energies that are here on your behalf. There is an excitement building energetically that, as you continue to extend your reach, carries the momentum of your creative power to fully engage and become adept at living in the unknown. There is magic in the mystery, yet you cling tenaciously to the survival of your egoic self. We have observed countless lightworkers say, "I am not willing to lose my house, be alone, not live in comfort, give up this or let go of that." That is the ego talking and in control of your reality.

First of all, those statements all revolve around loss, limitation and ultimately fear of death. Secondly, they reflect attachment energy, which keeps you in the sleep of social consciousness and imprisoned by the matrix. You are in effect saying that having these things is worth not belonging to your Self: that you trust the mechanisms of this reality more than you trust the Creator of the Multiverse. The Source of all creation wants for you infinitely more than you could dare imagine for yourselves and sacrifice is not necessary to your growth. Yet, if you insist on filling your lives with transient form over what is timeless and true, you are willingly creating lives of pain and meaningless pursuits that will never be satisfied.

This is a time for ACTION. The task before you is huge, stunning in nature and easily excused to making the responsibility for change someone else's. No longer can you compartmentalize what you view as the greatest problem you face on your planet at this time. All the traditional structures and value systems have become so manipulated by the false power and desires of the ego, nothing but a new age and shift in consciousness will turn the page to a new history. There is, indeed, a Collective Human Consciousness, a group energy that consists of the energy dynamics of every person that has ever lived on your planet over the entire course of its history. Every thought, feeling, emotion, word spoken and action taken has and continues to go into this composite energy of the Collective Human Consciousness. That is both the good news and the less than encouraging, as well. One need not look too far into the events of your history to see evidence of why in today's world you are governed by so much deception and greed and senseless killing of your brothers and sisters, so that you have the most toys when the day is done. These energies of acceleration moving through you right now are for change. They are forcing you to look at what you have suppressed, denied and ignored and at the same time, providing the frequencies of potential to rise above what has so paralyzed you in fear. The habits, attitudes and behaviors of your Collective Consciousness grew out of the very same energies you have been unwilling to look at within yourselves. That is where the action must necessarily take place today and that is what will create the repository for the new consciousness of the future Earth.

There have been many Ascended Masters and evolved beings that have walked the Earth over thousands of years. Indeed, they walk among you now. Their presence is not just to teach the principles of a more authentic and evolved way of living in the world. Each one of them opened the portal of Christ Consciousness and the potential for you to realize it within yourselves. Their mastery and power, their wisdom and their love is dancing around in the Collective of Human Consciousness, as well. Each day that you live your light, that you love as they loved, practice compassion, understanding and forgiveness as they did and walk with peace within your being, you are creating the new consciousness one act of awareness at a time.

Truly, you are living in a profound period of activation and fulfilling prophecy. You are poised on the precipice of a world that will become the new Eden. You must cease the inauthentic expression of who you are, as individuals and be willing to look at the illusions you have allowed to manipulate your daily lives. They are holding you back personally and globally. You are radiant beings of light that came to your planet in this now to be shining representatives of the new age. It is time to get serious about owning your attachments to your plane of existence. Be impeccably honest with yourself over the way you justify anger, selfishness, resentment, jealousy, gluttony, greed or even discontent. "It's not that bad" is no longer an acceptable way of deflecting energy from those illusions that you fear looking at. Christ Consciousness is. It is all around you energetically for you to continually draw upon in raising the consciousness you currently vibrate. There is so much love (the most powerful frequency of the cosmos) with you right now, extending a new Presence of power to you and on your behalf. Stop settling for the half lived version of your life and begin today to clean the shadows and cobwebs from your own closet. They may be hidden from every other person on the planet and for countless years, but they are not hidden from the unrealized potential within you, waiting to be set free. The future of the world depends on you. And when the 7 billion you's on your planet truly understand that, you will all rise together as One to a brand new day.

Becoming Wonder

November 1, 2007

There is a way of being in the world that cultivates consciousness and is available to you in each moment. So much of how your reality operates is by participating in a means to an end. The moment nearly always has an agenda such that your bodies may be present but your mind is three steps ahead or pondering your last experience. It is truly an exhausting way of being and for many it is the only reality they know. Living the expression of the mental plane becomes not just an ingrained way of being but a process that keeps you from connecting with your Soul, which is the main purpose of your lives. To connect with the highest frequency of your potential requires the ability to disconnect from all the distractions and attachments that fill up your spaciousness. This takes a great deal of trust and courage yet without doing so, before you realize it, you are reflecting upon a life that feels all too brief and filled with things that you never experienced or completed.

Life on your planet is one of the most diverse, sensually resplendent, ecologically rich existences in all the creative Universes. Your world is a wonder to behold for many other worlds and planes existing in different frequencies, yet right beside you and interwoven with your divine essence. You are not able to see or even sense these worlds and the countless beings that occupy them because you have lost the ability to be in touch with what is vital in your being and allows you to be in wonder. Humans have this compulsive need to seek and do and discover and find the answer to everything, which is an "in the box" mentality of being. Let us say to you impressionably that it this idea of "the sky is the limit" from an egoic perspective that is bringing you into a state of crises, an abyss if you will, where there is no satisfaction or fulfillment ever fully embraced or embodied.

Yet this very same species, humanity, is also the first group of beings to ever bring so much love and inherent light into the physical. It should be comforting indeed to realize that in willingly going so far into the darkness that there is even greater potential in remembering that you are Light. In so doing, you are raising the very vibration of your known reality and poised to create a world unlike any that has ever been. Imagine that right now, today, you receive a directive from the heavens that states you have accomplished everything that you came to do in this life. From this moment on, you are to just sit still, relax and be in gratitude for all you have known and been in life. Now, we are sure you will say that sounds wonderful and bring it on and let the party begin - initially. But soon that restlessness of the mind that is so utilitarian in focus will become dissatisfied and desperately seek something else outside of itself to feel useful and fulfilled.

In the midst of all this doing and seeking and accumulating of things and experience is a spark that is your Soul and is here to get to know all the levels of itself, not just what can be seen and understood and grasped and accomplished. Many believe they have a soul because you have been taught that or learned it somewhere along the way in life. Yet, you are missing so very much unless and until your physical expression of being can truly feel the unbelievable love and presence of home that is your Soul's essence; completion, fullness and the I AM of your Absolute being. Only then will your life have meaning beyond itself. You then assume a new place in the Universe because your awareness has expanded to encompass equal parts humility and wisdom. What you adore, the things that amaze you and take your breath away come effortlessly from being fully in the moment, present and at peace with the details of your life. It is the highest honor that can be given to any person or activity to receive them fully, experiencing deeply what is unique and divine in each. When you learn to observe with the movement of love from the heart's consciousness, you bring into awareness the pulsing splendor of Christ Consciousness, seeing not what is different, but the wholeness of it all. The power of presence is the magnification of the Soul, unafraid to reside only in what is at the expense of all the details. When you abide in the trust and knowingness (conscious awareness) of the moment, fully present with all of your attention, then the Christ Consciousness within becomes aware of itself, sensing deeply the unity of the world in all its mystery.

Where is your joy, your wonder, your completion? Can you answer that question without referring to anything or person in your manifested reality? It is a great gift and virtue of the heart to know the quality of appreciation, compassion, forgiveness, and love for another and one's life. But it is the state or sense of connection that only comes from the unfathomable love of the Soul for the bliss of this multifaceted expression of being that can provide a truly sustaining and fulfilled meaning and purpose. Living in a state of perpetual wonder is to have a sense of authenticity in seeing life and who you are in it through the eyes of the Soul. We invite you to continually step outside of your roles and false identities that you have grown so comfortable within. There is a grand experience of transformation awaiting those who are fearless in their trust of the empowerment and direction of the Soul over the transient creations of your known reality. Learn to observe so deeply and engage so fully and reveal so lucidly the truth of who you are, that you necessarily bring into consciousness the splendor of living in a radical state of wonder.

Trust Your Future

November 14, 2007

We would speak to you today of your future self, the new human of your potential that is calling you to a higher expression of being. Acknowledged or not, you have signed on to participate in a huge revolution of consciousness such that has never been witness before throughout the many Universes of all Creation. Many are watching the goings on and process of your planet because the implications of this transformation and lifting will have far reaching effects and consequences for your world and for many off world existences.

Your year of 2000 activated a profound shift that will take twenty years to fully realize. Think for a moment of where and who you were in the months leading up to that millennium year. The new energies streaming unto your planet carry the genetic structure of your unique and primary essence and at that time, an influx of interplanetary influence permeated your dimension, allowing the morphogenetic fields of your greater origins to be stimulated. This metamorphosis will be gradual and far reaching and will be experienced by a breaking down of old structures and false identities, dismantling the attachments and securities that have served to keep you bound to a very limited expression of who you are. You are being compelled to change. Many heard this cosmic intervention as a clarion call and leaped into an unknown of very uncertain outcome. We celebrate you because you have courageously agreed to go before where the many will soon be charged to follow.

You are magnificent creators, brilliant spheres of Light. You have no idea of the Joy you are poised to realize and awaken in the years and times to come. In the unknown that so many cringe from and keep at bay with willful tenacity, in that unknown beyond the self, you will find a more empowered and purposeful way to be creative, productive and present to the greater love and wisdom of your divine nature. As you allow these liquid light energies to pour through and heal the fear and separation of your forgotten selves, a new emotionality will emerge that will allow you to experience deeply what the higher emotions feel like; a profound experience of light, love and inflow of spiritual essence many are beginning to embrace as their own. Do you not see that there will necessarily be chaos before harmony? That for the individuals stepping into and becoming their power now, who are experiencing trauma or challenge along the way, do you not see that they are taking the earth's metamorphosis through their physical vehicles to make the passage of the many less severe? Your Earth is birthing a new consciousness that is beginning to radiate from within itself. You are destined to give birth to the same consciousness and inner light, which is so very powerful. This radiant light within the transformations, are the very soul of the Earth awakening to new life. This is all in divine order and so exquisitely overseen in detail. Many are feeling the pull of love and joy in their biology and cellular structure, knowing that to build up and transform, a complete breaking down must take place. There will be extremes in your days and times unfolding, it will take time to adjust to what is yet to come. Yet any perceived trauma and tragedies will be balanced with immeasurable expressions of love to your understanding and known experiences. It is a work of dedication and devotion and great meaning. You are being informed in each moment and your primary purpose is constantly lined up in the wings of your conscious awareness, awaiting a willingness to know your Self and align fully with your highest intent. Continue to fearlessly look to and embody the wisdom of the Earth as she shows you the way to your authentic expression and purpose.

You each have a unique task to do that will not reveal itself unless and until you have let go of the attachments and conditions you place upon your own expansion. There is a place that is only yours to stand in, it carries the vibrational signature of your inner light that glows as bright as the sun. Yet, you must be willing to be revealed. You must gather up your courage to stand in your truth, seemingly alone, until such a time that you are effortlessly standing side by side with others aligned energetically for the purpose of magnificently participating in this whole transformation. Your lesson is to love yourself enough to stay conscious and trust your greater spirit to become the primary informer of your world, as you know it. The things you cling to are as the sun's reflection in a mud puddle. They hold not a glimmer of the brilliance of the treasures that you will know when you trust life to reveal to you a new order of being, a new day. The catalyst for all of this is of course, love. Love is all there is and it provides all things to all people. As each individual steps bravely into the uncertainty of the future with ungovernable trust, they are effecting the electromagnetic field that envelopes all of your reality! They are experiencing that indescribable connection with their greater light family to such a degree that they are very much sensing the new earth now. Which is the only way for the new earth to manifest. As the old dismantles through the personal choices and acts of those who dare to be catalysts, one thing will become the timely backdrop for another.

You all have roles to play that will shapeshift and evolve continuously. No one role is less or more important than another for without each of the parts, the whole will be less than its fullest expression and potential. As you each continue to change in each moment, what is learned and embodied and shared and given out unconditionally will continue to express and support the inner expansion you each truly yearn for. We encourage you to let go of your earthbound identities enough to see and then be willing to act upon the various stages of your expansion that you agreed to. You cannot forgo any aspect of your personal journey in anticipation of the promise of things to come. Nor can you observe any one else's process in relation to your own. It is for each of you to go into the silence of Self everyday so that new light and new understanding can be born. Your fellow brothers and sisters need you. You need each other. Be not afraid of your unique role in the unknown manifesting now. Trust your heart over your mind. You are all masters with new and more expansive levels of mastery to obtain. Many are quite adept at traveling interdimensionally and connecting with a state of bliss! Yet we say to you it is about being able to sustain and ground those energies back down through the body so as to assimilate and integrate them into a more empowered and conscious walk through your reality. This has to do with your current vibrational capacity and the willingness to do the work of being the frequency of love in the midst of the nothingness of your transition.

Again, we ask you to reflect upon your experience since the year 2000, this will reveal much intuitive understanding about where you are now in your expansion and what you are stepping into in greater degrees. An initiation began that required different levels of immersion into the torsion fields of energy streaming in from the center of the galaxy. This torsion wave energy is allowing the hyperdimensional jump from your 3rd dimensional space-time awareness to a higher etheric presence where you are literally corresponding with the intelligence of your future Self and interplanetary relations. Indeed, the children of planet earth are graduating to a destined identity, responsibility and purpose that as yet, is not even known to you or prior existence. Such is the power that you carry, a power that awaits your courage and trust of the future unknown.

Somewhere within you, you know who you are! You carry the remembrance of your greater Light and primary origin. Just as when you pray for those in the shadow and are aware that they experience your light, so too when you trust and reach out to the unknown potential of your future self and your off world origins, your desire and intent is activated throughout the multiverse, opening the door of a potential only a few have yet dared to say yes to.

A Spirituality Of Significance

December 9, 2007

As you and your Earth continue the transition from lower vibrations to a higher dimensional light energy, spirituality will continue to be of major importance for the success of any endeavor. Indeed, Spirit is the light and truth of who you are. Those without this awareness will be increasingly challenged to ride the energies of awakening and activation to your highest good and primary purpose. Those with this conscious awareness will be called upon to deepen your intent and be fully awake to your experience; to take each moment and live it as Christ Consciousness, even as the dimensional shifts continue to intensify and put pressure on your experience. This is a crucial time for you as visionaries, trailblazers, pathfinders and creators of a new day, a new life and a new world. A spirituality of significance is a measure of your perception of Self; the courage and integrity with which you are able to engage each moment with conscious presence. Transformation is the reason you are here. As the whole is always dependent on the vitality and strength of its parts, your unique and individual contribution, the work of your journey in aligning your personality with your Soul, is a necessary and valued component in the Earth's renewal and rebirth.

Your greatest task in this moment is to find solutions within your own limitations and structures to create the momentum for solutions on a national and global scale. This requires that you be impeccable observers of self and accountable to the energy you are engaging in each moment. We cannot over emphasize this enough to you. Your manifesting abilities are increasing to such an extent that each breath you take, thought you engage and energy that you vibrate is as a domino, going out to affect not only your own experience of growth and potential, health and mastery, but the process of the Earth's ascension, as well. Increasingly, the unseen will be felt very strongly. Only in your hearts will you find the way through. This is a time that you chose within which to express and extend yourselves with your own gifts and talents, unique to each. Many of you are waiting versus living differently now. And we would ask you what it is that you are waiting for, as you are the gods and goddesses of the new age of enlightenment. You must go beyond the self to access the resources that will enable you to find the answers and vibrational momentum of your future self. Cosmic and galactic energies, interdimensional presence and intelligences are gathered to partner with your expansion. Personal value is dependent upon your ability to access higher levels of wisdom gained through your relationship with your Higher Self and the very stars from which you came. Energy is available to find new structures on a higher dimensional level, but you must be ready and willing to bring a presence of awareness to your own duality.

As we continue to observe and experience with you the transformation of the reality you are accustomed to, we are holding the light high for you to look fearlessly into your own resistance. Be it conscious or unconscious, you are often operating in and interpreting your reality through constructs that have been in place for generations. These constructs hold you in limitation and have you to believe that you are powerless and without your own unique and necessary purpose for being here now. This unconscious aspect, the learned and comfortable nature within your greater identity, is giving you permission to be less than impeccable with your own ascension process. There are certain ones that we are speaking to. You have called our essence and vibrational resonance in, to be of assistance to you so listen well. We speak to the many through the one, so open your heart centers and receive this guidance as if it were for you alone. This is the moment within which to gather up your past and use that tenacity and will to go forth from this day only in light. Your heart is rising and you have risen with it through many trials and tribulations. As you continue to transcend the duality of the lower dimensions in your reach for the clear seeing of the Divine Plan of Expansion and Ascendancy, you cannot take your old structures of belief and behavior with you. Every living thing is being offered the opportunity to change, receiving the vibration of its own guidance. The divine feminine of your own interior light is emerging to empower the reunion with your spiritual Self. Are you ready to be new? Are you willing to be new? Have you grown enough in the awareness of your Self to bring conscious presence to each breath, applying a higher intelligence of light and love to your experience and the world?

This is a time of being and allowing, of trusting and forgiving, of surrender and acceptance. These are all qualities of the Divine Feminine. Along with discernment and intuition, of feeling consciousness and a creative, cohesive, impersonal participation with life, it is possible to walk between two worlds with grace, ease and mastery. In this Light and awareness, the commodity of the highest value in the future, is you. Call for your highest purpose to be invoked upon the Earth now. As the dimensional shifts continue to intensify and reorder the world of form around you, drop ever deeper into your authentic selves where your inner light and wisdom will reveal to you the interconnection and collective wisdom throughout all time and space. Know that you are a direct channel for a higher intelligence of light, ready to be made manifest and applied to your personal reality and the greater circumstances that humanity faces in this day. The future Earth of unity and balance, of peace and love, of beauty and luminosity is blossoming for the potential of your entire species. As you make the transition from child of light, to teacher, keeper and lover of the Light above all else, you must bring the spirituality of your truth and essence out with you into your everyday reality and consciousness, realizing that you are a representative of a world that has yet to be realized, a world that you carry in your heart.

Walk Into It ~ A Life Unimaginable

December 26, 2007

In this, your holiday season, there is a focus on celebration; on giving and receiving and being attuned to the gratitude of your connection to holiness. Still greater than the temporal festivities of your traditions, there is a vast celebration in the higher realms for the pivotal transition you have arrived at as a species. The Divine Plan has moved to the next phase or level in your ascension process, your Earthly contracts are complete! Indeed, every person on Earth is being given an opportunity to write a new contract and script the future of your unique destiny. How beautiful is that! You have made the decision to ascend consciously and you are currently aligning with your future at a most magnificent rate. It is possible for your future to be your present now, if you are willing to be your magnificence. Your future is looking at you, curious at the ways that you limit yourself yet calling out to you to merge with it. We would say to you that the motivating force of significance working with you at this time is your future! From this moment on, the past will no longer have the same controlling influence over you. Each of you who opens more to love, will begin to glow and it is this glow that will align you with the experiences and persons of your future intent and mastery. Your familiars are lined up on the perimeter of your current reality and your only task is to respond to the frequency of their light resonance. You know each other well in radiance. Trust that and be willing to allow that gift into your current dynamic of time and space. Be aware that your visions and dreams, long held precious in your dominant desires, will become real to the degree to which you harmonize with your purpose and destiny.

Everything is in order for the light bearers to start waking up, to form a profound and meaningful relationship with all of life. This entails loving what is at all times, knowing that it is a gift from your mastery and future potential. You must receive each other and every experience as love and without the stickiness of the personality aspect. The desire to relate, to create and find the true expressions of Self through the authentic reflections in the other is paramount. There is not one who comes to you or an experience before you that is not love offering you your own potential. This perspective of understanding will empower you to discover your own spirituality, as you would most prefer to express it. Many of you long devoted to the Great Work in this evolution have been plowing through the trenches with an exclusive focus that you perceive as your personal mission and gift to humanity. May we suggest that you ease up a bit on that concept that is being driven to an extent by the ego. The transformation in progress throughout all time and space is such that what you will be ultimately doing, the service and work of your greatest potential, is not even known to your awareness at this time. This is a time that the feminine/Goddess energy is surging to an unprecedented extent, touching you more deeply than ever before. A pristine, pure love with an electrical pulse that radiates the combined effervescence of the entire star system is establishing your connections to beyond this plane stronger than ever before. You will all be endowed with a new form of spirituality and mastery where fear and unworthiness are no longer part of your matrix. You are simply becoming your truth and, in becoming, you will expand your awareness into the multiplicity of potentials far above and beyond where the egoic mind can fathom reaching.

Your opportunity to be your truth is unlimited now. You need only place your clear vision and heart on the middle path and continually return to center where you radiate vibrations of your true essence; peace, balance and harmony all around you. Rise with your hearts to the light of a new day for that new day is surely here. Observe your self, each other and each moment from a lucidity of remembrance. You have known all along from a higher light, exactly what you were doing and have stayed with the task of integrating the duality of your experience. You are honored throughout the galaxies for this courage and devotion. Ask for the best outcome always, for your highest expression and the greatest good for all. Truly, in the Light of your radiant heart, you want nothing for yourself that you do not want for every other person on the planet at this time, because you understand, at long last, that it is all you. This is a clear rendering of your higher mind perspective and that perspective is everything. Know you well that each step on the ascension ladder must be traversed and the lessons integrated to continue your expansion. Every would-be challenge is always an opportunity for growth called forth by your wisdom. When you have tapped the burning desire of your original intent, nothing and no one will be able to deter your radiant love. There is great celebration in the higher realms for you, the representatives of the future. When you have gained the knowledge and laid a firm foundation for your primary purpose, it is your passion and imagination, a faculty of the Divine Mind that will surely move you forward toward your goal. Again, we declare to you that, indeed, your work is done. The spot that is yours alone to stand on in the Great Work long commencing is there for you to but walk into. You are the divine agents of spiritual awakening. Align to the Earth's ascendancy; continue to assist her and the beings upon her in this dimensional transition. The Light of a Great Sun is upon you, see it, feel it, marinate in it and shine it upon your brothers and sisters.

Living as One is the highest expression of community. It is about seeing past all differences and separation to the unity within; receiving everyone as an invited guest to your personal reality. Recognize yourself in the other. Extend your love to all. Soul linking is the order of a new day for your experience; this act of conscious, energetic soul connection is now taking place between willing individuals to fulfill a specific portion of the Divine plan. All is in order and there is great joy. The difficulty and challenge of your known is complete. Your familiars are moving in and you will know them by their energetic signature. Let not fear or concerns of the egoic mind keep you from the sacred communion of joining together now to manifest the visions that you have long held as treasures in your heart.

The Framework Of The Heart, A New World

January 13, 2008

The powerful energies exuding from the living Cosmos on your behalf have always been and will continue to be for the sake of Love. Love is the energy that you can work with that will help you through the changes yet to come. This critical passage of the Earth is a time for all of you to realize your divine purpose and then to give birth to that which all of Creation is anticipating. Long have you been working to bring an evolution to this planet, indeed for eons, so that all the kingdoms and planetary systems could advance, many lifetimes have you spent integrating the various levels of mastery into your heart. Your vibrational path is identical to the Masters who went before you and the Light ahead, the same light shining from within you. It is now for you to trust in and utilize that light to illumine the path of your highest potential. Truly, that light, far greater than the darkness veiled upon your plane, is the only way through that which often seems insurmountable. This does not require effort or special skill. As the stars in the sky shine their brilliance effortlessly, you need only embody the incandescence of your original blueprint.

Because of the duality that you currently engage and the veils imposed upon this plane, your focus is primarily in this moment of space-time, but your consciousness reaches far into this Universe and many others. Such is the power that you possess. As you still yourself and your egoic mind, you will be increasingly able to access the higher levels of the Solar Galactic and Universal Logos that will enable you to view and feel every part of all beings that have and will exist here on Earth. The promise of the Oneness Principle is manifesting at long last and this integration of your multidimensionality will serve to rearrange the energy grid of the Earth. You have prepared the vessel well by your intent and are accessing the light codes of your galactic family, your star brothers and sisters. A magnificent re-union is in process. All are returning home from far reaching journeys where the way has been often arduous and seemingly desolate. We encourage you in this moment to place the entire etheric grid within the framework of your heart, empowering your lifeforce to be the expanding consciousness of a newly evolving species.

Right now many intergalactic species are witnessing the most advanced development and acceleration of consciousness of a planet in the history of the Cosmos. In that very observation is the precipitation of your awakening and remembrance. You in your wisdom knew the significance of this time for planet Earth and every person is endowed with the specific gifts of expression that you need to make the way clear for your unique and vital contribution. Listen well and allow the sonic resonances within these words to bypass the intellect and enter your etheric heart center. Close your eyes for a moment and connect with the exquisite lightwaves now penetrating all shadow on your behalf. Self- expression is one of humankind's most necessary requirements at this present time. This creative energy corresponds to the opening of the feminine. The surface of the planet has offered itself to assist in the cleansing of the lower bodies of mankind, to support the many Earth changes that need to occur for humanity, individually and as a Collective. What is important for you to hear and take into your heart's intelligence is that these changes need not be devastating or fearful. All chaos and confusion is superceded by the power of your individual hearts to redirect the course of prophesied events, threatening the wellbeing and future of your planet. Know that choice is a spiritual and creative force and never before have you been more empowered as a species to make a tremendous growth collectively and enter a new dimension of consciousness. As the shifts occur and the lower energies continue a pejorative spiral, align yourself with the frequency of love to walk above the vibrations of the deconstruction that must transpire. You are charged now from the creative center of the Absolute I Am, the All that is, the zero point origin of Christ Consciousness and Beingness, to bring forth your uniquely individualized Self expression to the awakening of your planet. In the center of your heart is a twelve petal lotus and this day it is glowing as bright as the sun. Each petal of your magnificence is being activated by the power of the Central Sun for the purpose of your awakening now. Surrender your hesitations and doubts about your true identity and personal luminosity for this is not a time of forgetfulness, it is a time of remembrance. Call forth your truth, call forth your right place and purpose, your courage and your full power to stand in the center of a transcendental love.

As the frequency of love continues to penetrate the shadow forces and analytical minds of those governed by fear, it is for each of you to allow that love to so fill you up that the rising heart of your future unknown becomes the only reflection you encounter in your reality. In your moments of solitude and self-inquiry, many still question who you are and what you are doing. And we say to you, cease the intellectual and ego driven need to be in control of your reality, and simply allow love to work through you toward a totality of future Earth that is almost too great for the human mind to comprehend. Don't look for complicated solutions. You have done the work of the basic levels of consciousness where your focus was need directed. Now is a time of Unity consciousness, of belonging and socializing and building relationships with others, simply open up your hearts in love and compassion, for each other, for life and most especially for Self. Put your efforts into being in your joy and grounding those energies daily onto the planet. Do every thing with love, knowing that that love is who you are. The love you express and offer to your experience is vibrating far beyond the reaches of this dimension. Let not one moment transpire in your thoughts or actions that is not embraced by your heart's wisdom. Do not be fearful and you will be able to assist others who do not yet know this love, through the transitions to come. It is time for you to truly own the power of your heart's reach to conspire with the Galactic Heart Center of pure consciousness and energy, where the birth of a new planet and species has already begun. Let your heart be the guiding principle and portal of the new Earth and trust the love streaming through you to align you with your brightest potential for the purpose of this Christed awakening.

Living Love

February 10, 2008

Welcome to life, dear ones, a life of perpetual astonishment. Welcome to a year of conversion, where everything that you want, have carried in your intent and stretched all the way to the God of your understanding has begun the rippling back to your heart center. Know that you are drawing the higher worlds to you by your intent and resonant vibration. As you continue to use intention to give more conscious direction to your life, you are placing your desire out into your exquisite world as an invocation and energized thought-form to draw to you your primary purpose. You have waited so long for this moment and your resonant vibration will continue to lift you into multidimensional levels of awareness. Do not doubt this for even a moment. This is relevant to your Now because the Earth must now evolve to fifth dimensional consciousness both for her own evolution and for the needs of the whole solar system, to itself grow and evolve.

The congruency of your personal choices aligning with your intent at this time will create the opening of your heart to connect more deeply with the heart of the Universe. This in turn will create portals and open doors for you to see clearly that which you have not been able to see before. Your new awareness of your spirituality will remind you of the original purpose of this whole Earth experiment, that of the desire to relate, to create and to find richness of Self reflected in the other. The desire to have joy, to experience and to create was, indeed, the impulse that caused the original explosion from the Source of Love. And you have never been alone in this re-membrance. Light beings from the higher realms will continue to assist you to overcome any force which may be applied against you as you flow your energy ever more with heart based perceptions, enlightening the shadows of all duality. You must continue to vigilantly work on your energy, be ever clearer and empty the vessel of all attachment and fear. You are a divine canvas and the human heart, so revered by many observing species, is that part of you that knows all things, holds all wisdom in silence and has been the center in your willingness to go through the required process of Attunement to a new Spiritual Design.

In attuning to the frequency of your heart, you are empowered to live fully in the eternal Now, with total trust in being provided for in all things, at all times. Let us speak briefly to the experience of living in higher realms, realizing that as you assimilate and integrate this wisdom, Now will be the motivating force for all that you attract as your future. For Now is your future. In the higher realms, we blend the totality of our being when we express our love for each other on all levels of our being. There is no fear of the cost to our being at what might be lost or gained, as we withhold nothing and give everything. We do nothing for a desired outcome or with personal agenda. We exist for love. We are love. We know that love denies nothing and provides everything including wisdom and the right use of power. We love absolutely at all times and allow the frequency of love to vibrate through us as the eternal heartbeat of all creation. You are now being challenged above all your other perceived challenges to be a receiver for this very same love, to change the fear based DNA that causes so many to refuse love and believe you have not yet worked hard enough to deserve such love. What many do not understand is that all that you desire, all that your high heart holds dear and that your intent vibrates, already exist! It is right there with you, always. If you are not seeing it and living it in your experience, it is fear that is veiling its truth. The greatest fear that humanity embodies is that of not being loved.

You cannot attract to you that which you are not vibrating. Every cell in your body is an antenna for the entire Universe. All that your experience and intellect has gathered as being important to you is radiated throughout the cosmos. Yet there is static in the receiver. We assure you that if any of you are in debt or lacking in any form, this is an indicator that you are denying yourself and have not yet learned to be a receiver. Your Universe is a hologram. You have your life in one small portion of it but you have access to all of it! Within every cell of your body there is all that you require physically, emotionally, etherically, mentally and spiritually to evolve into your absolute mastery. The totality of all information is available in each particle and moment of information, for each dimension is a hologram of all the dimensions. In this, it is not so much what you know, as what you understand!

You must be totally willing to release the old, to surrender fully to your experience and ever more deeply to freedom and joy! In this you will discover that your dominant desire has been with you in each moment awaiting the awareness of your heart versus your mind. Your heart knows your deepest intention but your mind manipulates what it perceives on a continual and often unconscious level. It is difficult to hold center when the mind is so accustomed to knowing and being in control of its surroundings. Your heart is always in a perpetual sense of awe about the unknown. The ability and comfort in living in the unknown is really about knowing yourselves and consulting always and only with the master within. What do you truly want for yourselves down to the last detail? Can you answer this truly without filtering it through the wants and desires of others? If you are able to admit to Self what you want and then stand in the middle of that commitment above all else, you will realize that you all want the same thing; to be and see and walk and breathe and live and give love, unconditional love and only love. Your experience is that simple and that profound. All that is available to you, all those assisting you from the vibration of your origin will merge effortlessly with your experience when you accept and reciprocate what is constantly streaming to you for your edification. It is time for humanity to join together and create one vast network of people who know they can do things with love toward a powerful transformation for your planet. Be true to your offering and you will know your own evolution and that of a planetary new world.

What Is Old Is New Again, Inner Seeing

February 24, 2008

There is a new energy giving rise on planet Earth that is available and accessible to all seekers, from the Yogis in Ashrams to ordinary people in ordinary life. All are seeking the god of their understanding and all are awakening to a hunger that can no longer be satisfied from without. More and more you will witness the many awakening to the inner light within their heart where you are all exactly the same.

Your earth is now in a cycle where the axis is facing away from the center of the galaxy so that your planet's base energy, coming from its center, is moving to a new location on its surface. The result will be a great and distinctly new change in spiritual understanding and practice that will eventually and necessarily filter down to your everyday lives. Indeed, a new way to express life is emerging. This will be welcomed news for many who have felt displaced or isolated in the way you sense the world around you and the expression you long to give voice to. The great challenge will be bypassing the conditioning of your mind, the reactive response and behavior of social constructs to finally and fiercely allow your heart to be your primary vision and guide.

It will serve you well to remember that ascension is not necessarily leaving the Earth, it is a change in consciousness. Humanity is shifting to the Unity Consciousness Grid, which will initiate a change in how each of you interprets the One reality. This movement, which coincides with the movement of the kundalini energy within the Earth, will require active, fearless, selfless participation in unraveling from the egoic self so that new chapters in your own story, as well as your Earth's history, can unfold. You must let go of what has been and what you think you know and allow the bright light in your heart to be the new compass for your journey. Know that what you are attracting in this now, the experiences, the opportunities, the persons, etc., though they may appear to be familiar, carrying similarities to that which you have interacted with before, all is new and an opportunity for you to perceive, interact with and align from your heart and light encodings. Do you see the difference? Your experience has never been so much about what is outside of you as the influence of the perception you bring to it. If you are without fear and confident in living and expressing from your heart's intelligence and light, the persons and experiences before you will shift instantaneously to that which is only light. For all is light. Trust in the pure guidance within you. It is time to pull away from the conditioning of societal constructs where the unconscious defines your reality in such a limiting way. You must begin to meet each other not as a role or sex or occupation, which serves to automatically set your union apart with division and other-ness. Receive each other as gifts, as light, and interact with the joy of this understanding. Then your relationships and experience will attract and evolve from an inner seeing that allows for a more authentic and meaningful existence with each other and with all life.

There is a higher purpose that seeks to articulate itself through the heart. What you are seeking is seeking you. What is yours to manifest and gift to the world is waiting for your partnership. Do not allow yourself to be mindlessly and emotionally manipulated by what is and has always been. Your soul is a powerful, eternal spirit that travels interdimensionally with exuberant freedom even as your Earth vessel stumbles through the internal divisions of your history. The persistent problem and great alienator to your expansion and power is thought. Your past, unique to each and a purposeful experience in your becoming, was a moment in time that served as a gift and teacher. The past is no longer, yet you remain there with your thoughts and those thoughts imprison you with a constant barrage of what ifs, doubts, fear and a relentless preoccupation with self. In this, you are never really fully present and available to receive the living guidance and energy your surroundings give you on a daily basis.

The brilliant light of the heart is the light of the world. The challenge for humanity is to shift away from the mind, from conditioned perceptions and expectations based on what was lost rather than to see each person and experience as brand new; like a coin from a land where everything shines with the purity of having never been affected by conditioning. You know in your heart's wisdom that the One Spirit moves through absolutely everything and everyone, offering the possibility of a beautiful future outside of the darkness cycle that appears to be invading your world at this time. Life eternal does not repeat itself but meets each moment with the expansiveness and love of your inner potential and light. We challenge you to look at what is in your reality now with new eyes, the mind's wisdom and your heart's inner seeing. It is, indeed, vibrationally, brand new. The outcome of your experiences and relationships from this moment forward are dependent on your understanding of the new spirituality emerging on your Earth. This moment in humanity's Earth experience is a stargate with your energetic signature upon it. The key to this interdimensional vortex is to act without thought, to see with the heart's wisdom and to allow the frequency of your mind and body to take on the higher light vibration and remembrance that will reveal the One Consciousness in the One Universe that interacts with you in each moment, with great love.

Re-membering The Light

March 30, 2008

As we observe you in your reality, we witness as yet much fragmentation. We would ask that you consider deeply this tendency within the human nature to not be fully present in your experience. There is no judgment in our observation, for you have chosen to evolve through what is acknowledged as a reality that greatly challenges your authentic nature and true sense of Self. As we peek into your experiences with your consent and awareness, we observe that you are often going with a flow that is routine and comfortable, yet not necessarily aligned with your expanding awareness.

You are in a time of great transition and by their very nature, transitions can be chaotic and unsettled in energy. The tendency is to both go into fear, even if unconscious, and to be in the understanding of the mind versus the wisdom of the heart. Just recently we were invited into an experience where a teaching was occurring. There was discussion of mystery schools and lost civilizations, Planet X and what will be transpiring in your year 2012. What was interesting and illuminating for us to observe is that there were many present who have an open connection to their own Source wisdom and a strong degree of personal awareness, yet still taking in information from outside of Self without much discernment and conscious presence.

This is what we are meaning when we speak of fragmentation and the lost art of fully inhabiting yourself. And of course, the contributing influence for this unconscious mechanism is fear. The tendency always, but especially so in these times of acceleration and uncertainty, is to remain safely cocooned in your historical tradition and beliefs. We say to you with certainty, that you must forget belief! It is time to know. Your beliefs keep you contained in a limited sphere of understanding and awareness, a fragmented version of who you are. You must continually challenge yourself to stay out of your mind and in your heart. The mind works in duality, processing concepts and limited awareness through separation and otherness. Do you see? There is not a certain way or a teaching outside of yourself that will empower you with the wisdom you seek to prepare you for the times to come on planet Earth. Your inner seeing, power and awareness has always been and is most certainly your greatest and only protection.

Mother Earth is indeed changing the world. You are witnessing this in your weather anomalies and many of you that hold her wisdom dear to heart, are taking her transformation process into states of gravity rather than unconditional trust. It is clear that she is in control and this tends to throw the egoic mind into fear. And so, you seek and grasp and give your power away and busy yourselves with activities that put your attention and center on that which is outside of you rather than within. You must determine to trust in and allow the transformative nature of the awareness process to reveal ever, deepening layers of your own wisdom and authenticity. This will necessarily re-order any aspect of your 3D reality where you are not creating through and being light in your actions and behaviors. Awareness is a great illuminator and possesses the vibrational momentum to shift you out of complacency. You simply cannot afford to be complacent with any thing and you know this in your interior. Complacency settles in when the egoic mind organizes life and experience around what has always been, what is comfortable and known, what fits into the box of belief and delegates the responsibility of self to that which informs from without versus within.

We invite you to the truth that to be fully present is to be without thought. When you are wholly inhabiting yourself, and existing in your heart, you are pure being. You will then find that each day is an invitation to expand your understanding, your awareness, your practices and your beliefs about this experience you know as life. The only thing for you to do is to be of service and stay out of fear. The inner awareness of your spiritual identity, of the light and of love must stay centered no matter what is coming into the mind from the outside. This is what the transformation process is all about. TRANSFORMING, from a limited scope and understanding of who you know yourself to be, into your mastery and accepted responsibility. Step outside of what you think you know. Expand your reality and those you are connected to. You are just beginning to experience the necessary influxes and shifts of a changing world. Know that you must change with the earth, join in her process; trust life and your future. Everything that you experience you experience within the context of an energy that potentially changes the mind and heart. Let your conditioning go and be impeccable to your highest potential in stepping out of the box of your known traditions to the light of your emerging power.

Giving Rise

April 20, 2008

There is a new level of thought and manifestation available to you now that has never before been possible. The next step in the journey has always been declared and intended by your own motions and emotions and that energetic potential is now greatly amplified. What has always been your truth is that it is implicated in your genes to reach to the next level of beingness, the next potential of self, poised for higher expression. As your earth continues her dimensional shift and expansion process, you are likewise experiencing a type of dimensional hierarchy. You are literally walking between two worlds as the collective consciousness of your reality reaches for a possibility that until now, you have only dared to dream about. As you continue to sense, feel and negotiate this dimensional overlap, you have access to the vibrational momentum to stay above what is leaving and necessarily falling apart, so as not to get ensnared and hung up in the denser vibrations. You are being given the opportunity energetically and within your own connection to Creation, to use your inner seeing and remembrance of the "other side" to experience the fifth dimensional frequencies of love, joy, peace, compassion, understanding, forgiveness, allowing, and surrender, that will soon be the foundation of the new Earth. Each day you are vibrating higher, as there is less density through which to negotiate with the reality around you. The caution and challenge here is that there will be greater potential for an overlap of what is coming in and what is leaving, causing a spin in your energy field which can draw you more easily into the drama of the lower dimension. It is wise and helpful here to realize that every dimension is a hologram of all dimensions and so, you have all the wisdom and support, clear seeing and higher guidance you need in each moment to discern, re-member who you are, and choose anew, again and again.

You are now charged, individually and collectively to re-write the rules of being human. You must never stop believing in the goodness and inherent light of people, nor in the universal justice that is always present and available to infuse your moment-to- moment reality. There is a bright future of all encompassing love awaiting the people of planet Earth, but that future depends upon humanity to move it into manifestation.

Whatever you yearn for, whatever your heart speaks to you of in the quiet moments of your as yet, unconscious momentum of daily life, you must become that. You are the living expressions of a loving God that sees the future not only of your earth existence, but of many galaxies and universes. Your participation in your own highest potential and divine partnership is essential for the continued expansion of consciousness on your planet, and throughout the cosmos. Every person, indeed, all life forms, have the inherent capacity to take whatever is and refine it into their own unique energy signature. Every word, every thought, every decision and action presented by your high self and your experience in each moment is an opportunity to fine tune what has always been, what is ensnared as false truth in the collective unconsciousness of humanity, and then breathe your breath, your signature, your color, tone, resonate harmony and divine truth into the present level of consciousness. In this way, you are continually walking into the next level of thought, creating your own manifestations and the manifestation of the new earth with a consciousness of awareness.

Every moment of your experience now is brand new. New energies are infiltrating, impregnating and marinating your now on your behalf. It is not about the war in other lands or the political and economic deceptions in your own back yard, so much as the ability and determination to look inside yourself for what you seek externally in the words, deeds and doings of others. The song of this most exquisite multiverse is dependent upon the 7 billion individual tones of those inhabiting planet Earth. There is nothing for each of you to do but to anchor your own center of being, your own inherently bright light in a place of blessed assurance and knowingness that can and will not be deterred by the shadow castings and illusions of what appears to be other. The next evolutionary shift for humanity will be invisible to your 3rd dimensional sight. It will be the result of a collective expansion of consciousness that originates always and necessarily so in the heart center and energetic signature of the individual gods you are! You each have a melody of the heart's intelligence that the entire cosmos requires to give voice to the symphony of the spheres. The time is upon you when you must truly embrace and love all of what is as a reflection and expression of a fragmented potential seeking wholeness. No matter what your level of consciousness in this moment, your experiential history or current reality reflects in detail, you have come to this duality to re-member yourselves back into your fullness and power. You agreed to this experience with the confidence and gratitude of one being given the most honored opportunity and necessary mission ever asked of a multidimensional being of light. And you said Yes because of the capacity of love that you carry in your heart.

Every day now is a greatly amplified electrical impulse activating your unlimited DNA potential. As you each go fearlessly within and step up in your own capacity to align the personality's agenda with the supernatural intelligence and reach of your heart and soul, you will transition effortlessly into a time and experience where everyone will benefit from everyone else's knowledge. You will move through your experience with ungovernable trust in your own magnificence and the over light of an intelligence and wisdom that acts through you on behalf of all. Every breath you take is an opportunity to expand into more love and in that love, is consciousness itself, seeking the inclusion of all frequencies. You are, as a human collective, dancing the edge of a future unknown. The hologram of all experience, all potential realities, past, present and future is available to you in each moment. Give rise within you to Love in action and choose to be a lucid reflection for the inexplicable nature of all your creation. Christed, chosen, empowered and charged are you to leap into the nothingness where all potential lies and live each day with fierce devotion to the Love that you have brought with you, that is with you, in the wisdom of your heart.

Unfold

June 30, 2008

Today you will find, if you so choose, a new kind of partnership emerging on planet earth. It is timely and necessary that you truly begin to allow, recognize and remember one another as a light structure; pure frequency and vibration. It is a partnership formed out of complimentary resonance, shared wisdom and higher mind principles. This very special time on your earth is for the purpose of co-creation. There are many realms and advanced beings observing this earth experiment with vested interest in the ultimate path you decide to take. It is very wise to consider that not only are you sovereign beings first and foremost, but that your earth is a sovereign planet from which you have the power and wisdom to create your own destiny.

You have been entrusted with this earth ship as representatives of a future seeded in higher mind technologies, advanced principles of spirituality and a cooperative, sharing economy of balance and peace. Indeed, there are many probable realities available to you in each moment and it is with lucid awareness and sound mind that you are encouraged to engage these future potentials. You always have control over your thought streams. It is your thoughts in each moment that are the most accurate and true barometer of your future as individuals and as a species on the verge of unprecedented evolution.

The reason for the new partnerships of intent for your species, in how you relate to one another as sovereign, transparent and radically unbound individuals is this. Receiving each other as frequency and light is a necessary prerequisite to opening up the interdimensional, interspecies communi-cations of your future potentials. The cooperation that you engage, the shared responsibility in creating new communities of sustainability and balanced infrastructure, will indeed, establish the energetic portal for the very same partnerships to be formed with advanced species, who are here to assist you.

This whole earth experiment was never to be about humanity alone. There was always in the cosmic design an agreement between races to cooperate with one another and make use of the greatest strengths and most powerful resources of each. You have had many opportunities over the course of your history to bridge the initial and purposeful division set forth by your involution into duality. In that history and over time, you have instead, gone with the path of least resistance by agreeing to not look at and so empower yourselves in the face of what your inner environment knew to be travesty, deception, untruth and without Love. This has been a most unfortunate spiral of low, density events to witness from the perspective of the higher realms.

But you are learning now to step back and engage your observer, to not only recognize where the dark forces are taking liberties with your rightful sovereignty - but to question the very fabric and structure of the game plan of illusion so insanely in place! We say to you that events in this pejorative spiral on your planet will seemingly get worse before they begin again their destined ascent. But you have the ultimate power as individuals to tip the balance back to one of peace, beginning now.

Each individual must take an inner inventory, an accountability of self, to become aware of and take responsibility for your immediate environment of creation. It is not possible to come together as radiant frequencies with lucid awareness unless and until you have prepared the vessel of your own being. The magnitude of the energies interfacing with your planet at this time, are for your benefit and acceleration. But it must be clear that they cannot be assimilated and integrated into a mind and/or body replete with density and still very much attached to the illusions and false desires of your duality.

The Soul knows the specialness of these times you are in on planet Earth. Many strange and wonderful things are on the very near horizon for your experience. You, indeed, are positioned to step into a greater expression and thus power of who you are, as individuals and as a species. It is time to unfold. Many realms, dimensions and higher beings are waiting to move forward into a future vision of cooperation and peace, leaving the conflict and division of your history behind.

Consciousness Turned Toward Light

September 21, 2008

Throughout your history as a species, humanity has been urged along by a planetary body and Consciousness that desires to impart as much knowledge as possible to its sentient beings. Through a cosmic incentive system known to you as evolution, the acquisition of this unlimited knowledge is for the purpose of developing your consciousness to the highest potential possible. As consciousness rises, so too does the development of your spirituality, which in turn, is the key to achieving a subjective understanding of the Universe. In other words, it is all about you, yet not at all about you ~ this creationary process of life you find yourselves in.

Your world, because of its current breaking down, is entering a new moment of consciousness. In drawing attention to itself by means of its symptoms, it is becoming aware of itself as a psychic phenomenon and reality. This process is occurring inside of every being on the planet as well, and directly affecting the cellular structure of the DNA Codex all inclusive.

The Universe wants very much to make itself known to those who can comprehend its language - and that language becomes more and more intelligible to you through the ongoing development of an inner moral compass and the heart. When the level of consciousness reaches a point in frequency high enough on the scale of the quality of consciousness - it then resonates with the highest levels of Creation. The energy known to you as LOVE then radiates out to pervade the whole cosmos, an all-pervading peace settles in when you truly realize that you are an immortal spirit operating on this level to gain experience.

We would very much encourage you beyond the belief that some of you know more than others and that life is a constant test of what you know or have yet to find out. More and more it is for you to imagine, believe, trust that you are at a place in the whole of the evolutionary process of getting out of our own egoic sense of superiority and separation and into the awareness that what anyone of your experiences is for the expansion and love of each other. And that you all need each other and are all responsible for each other and that there is enough of everything that you need in any given moment, but that the ability to reach out and give or the need to step back and receive, varies along the continuum of this ongoing transformation of being. Life is ever cyclical and ultimately balanced.

For what may seem like eternity in your sense of time, many of you have been carrying great responsibility for the expansion process, extending yourselves and preferences beyond your capacity at times, physically, mentally, spiritually and emotionally. And we say to you that your Soul Monad and the higher awareness of many realms and dimensions, is exalted on this behalf. The balance is now tipping back toward the foundation and support that you need to continue your efforts and true work; the grounding of your gifts into the earth's vibration in such a way that your contribution to the humanity of this time will be magnified through her power, her radiance and her own evolution. There is a significant portal of long lasting shift for every individual soul on the planet now open on your behalf. Embrace this. Allow it to penetrate deep into your heart and the core of your being. You know in your wisdom this transformation is not a black and white process such that there will be an instant change from reality as you know it, to a new and expanded one. No, each day in each moment and with each breath you are making choices and acting upon an awareness and higher wisdom that is carrying you energetically to that which you are calling in and manifesting from the future of your potential and the realization of a new world unfolding. Truly, the greatest understanding and thus intelligent action you can embody on your own behalf as well as that of your world, is to allow the support to come to you, which it cannot and will not do if you are seeking it and looking for its arrival. Know that you are walking into a future that you have already created from your impeccable intent and pure heart. The work of the ages, of many lifetimes and histories is now with you in the foundation of a new world order unfolding in alignment with an evolutionary trajectory that you have been and are a part of eternally.

We do not deny that an old world order, currently in a pejorative state, is still very much a stronghold and threat to your very life and the freedom on your planet. But you have access to the power, wisdom and right use of technologies to tip the balance toward the future you have as yet only imagined. It is being birthed and will continue to gain momentum through your respect and stewardship of the natural world and the feminine energies your earth has modeled for your edification.

You have said yes and agreed to this process eternally and in doing so have a greater capacity, breadth and wisdom of what your reality of existence is really all about and who you are in it. The only caution that we would extend on your behalf is to let go even more, of the idea that you are separate. This is a beautiful time for the humanity of planet earth; a time of coming together in unity and joy and the celebration of that which you bring through the vessel of your being to merge with, blend and create anew with one another. You must release the idea of ownership of your gifts and the unique qualities that you embody, for this truly is but another trap of the egoic mind. You are one organism re-membering itself back to Zero Point; Gnosis. There is no you and them and his gift and her strength. There is only One Love and One Truth and One Life. In healing and embracing this illusion of duality that has contributed to both the richness and unrest of your experience, you can at long last join together in harmony. Then this one's musical disposition and that one's eye for fine art, another's ability to speak the language of the stars and still another's unparalleled capacity to express and be the Love from which you all came.... all of these qualities can once again find the synergy and thus power of the infinite and inexplicable. From this, your new world will be birthed and it will be beyond your current imaginings of what it is to truly be the light and mastery of your own creations and destiny!

It is happening for each and every one of you, as well as for the planet... a call from your Soul monad, to be in and find the opening of your higher light in each moment and to be your magnificence. This is most seamlessly done through the understanding that you are here to have life!!!! It is a very fierce Soul that wants to have life and deepen the well always of your understanding and awareness of Self, through other. Nature knows this interdependence well and is selfless in what it is willing to extend for more life. No one can take anything from you and there is nothing that is not yours to have and experience, because there is no separation! It is through grace and a luminous mind that one can appreciate the exquisite way spirit invites you into your own participation with the rich complexities of this life. You all must truly see clearly now, allow the LOVE in fully and get about the work of authenticating SELF into the power and service of the magnificent transformation of your rare blue planet. If your work and individual gifts are not currently magnified around the globe, if you are not feeling the full expansion and treasures of returned expression in how your service to the planet is being received and acknowledged, open yourself up more to the world around you, to the many reflections of your own light ready to join in with the purity and joy and light-ness of your expression of being. This will be as a missing link in your current development. The right arm needs the left arm, two legs support better than one leg... the profound simplicity of what we speak of is that indeed, you are One Being expressing as many abilities and gifts. Come together. Step into your own continued evolution through the blending of all that is separate into a harmony and peace that your planet has never before witnessed or experienced.

There are radiant beings currently manifesting and fully supported on your planet with great joy in their heart and effortless daily existence. The qualifying factor for their empowered state of mastery is that not only are they living and being their gifts with felt passion, they are doing so from a free and joyful heart, just because. Not for a return and without any sense of entitlement. Thus, everything supports them and comes to them because they belong to Self and are liberated from self.

There is a rich expression of your humanity found in **The New Human** we wish to reflect back to you now. Take a moment just now to imagine yourself in this vibration of understanding and potential release:

"I was standing on the shoreline of a vast ocean where the tide had gone out, ready for a new level of spiritual power relative to my willingness to be uncomfortable, until the rhythm of my new reality began its return flow."

It is for all of you to discover the "return flow" of your authentic power and gifts of service to the world! Each of you have varying levels of personal discomfort, that which stretches the mental reasoning and story you tell yourselves. You must all continue to love one another and lift each other up in the light of your highest potential. Gather, form your light families and communities - honor this beauty and radiance in each other unassumingly and unapologetically. Be fiercely grateful for those in your current realities for you are vibrationally attracting to each other now for a profound awakening unfolding on planet Earth. Take care to not miss the portals of opportunities beyond what you have known and been. Each moment is new. Deem to be new in them. You were placed on this Earth with encodings that go beyond your comprehension. Your specific vibration and light is part of the universal puzzle that is now coming into the luminosity of all things, across all time and space. You are an important piece. Each one of you houses a highly advanced being, a structure of brilliantly vast light within your energy schematics. Do not underestimate who is in your reality today and the purposeful balance they bring to your power and light. Again, you need each other. You are each other. Embrace this. Celebrate this. Allow what is greater to be revealed. You are representatives of such a far-reaching and limitless unknown and through your love and appreciation of what appears to be other... you will find the rewards of the treasures that you seek for your own life, and a new earth transcended.

Change All Encompassing

November 16, 2008

The key to the authentic expression of your light and the unlimited potential of Creation is to live in an ongoing surrender that defies the ego and all of its distortions. Only then you will be able to develop a tremendously vast, clear seeing, empowered and unconditional relationship with all of life. Truly, this is a time for you to re-affirm your vows to the light and your promise to hold the light through all changes and challenges on your Earth.

The energy of change has recently stepped up its cadence for your world in the conviction and courage of this one individual, Barack Obama. We encourage you to reflect deeply on the spiritual implications of his acceptance into an arena that bears so much influence upon the direction your reality moves, as a body of cooperation or division. There is a quickening in the intent to bridge spirit and matter and whether or not you have a conscious awareness of this union, you have broken through a Collective unconscious that has for so long entrenched your reality in a slavery to the past. If you look at your political construct energetically, the decision of the many to shift the deceit and power of division, entitlement and exclusivity has opened a greater vortex of energy through which the higher realms of influence can assist your evolutionary progress, both individually and collectively. Whereas the election, for many, was about 2 individuals and how their person resonated with the personality construct and agendas of your 3D awareness, the energetic implications and ensuing influence is so much greater. Indeed, when viewed and embraced as a hyperdimensional election, this moment vibrates as a Shift of the Ages.

There has been, since the beginning of time for your Earth, this tension and illusion of duality; a polarity of existence that set the tone for a reality very much governed by the fear and judgments of the mental plane. So without a true sense of Self has your humanity formulated its idea of progress and advancement, that you have created, both consciously and not, a reality and life that fosters the belief that you are separate and thus vulnerable to the evil and manipulative forces that control your world. The illusion that you are not a part of everything and that everything is not a part of you is the single greatest cloak of darkness and disempowerment that the beings of your world have bought into and perpetuated through your thoughts, beliefs, actions and unconscious behaviors. You have built a history on the idea that that which is outside of yourself and your personal understanding of the world is a threat and so must be regarded as the enemy and something to be feared. Once fear takes up residence in the fragile psyche of a species in search of itself, distortion and shadow becomes the only beacon to follow. We say to you that only that which is the other gives you fully to yourself!

Right now we urge you to truly embrace and integrate the knowing that the spiritual dimensions are always mirroring what is occurring and manifesting in the material plane of existence. Because you are the empowered creators of reality as you know it and understand it to be, the spiritual plane honors that authority by becoming a mirror for what you vibrate in your choices and actions. It can only be so. The very energy and vibration of intent that you walk through your day with is interacting with all other life and energy. Everything in your world hears you. As you have felt and witnessed the division of an existence not grounded in the authority and sovereignty of Self, so too have there been warring factions of light and dark in the higher realms as well. Even as the presence of Light and conscious awareness has increased on your plane, so too have the forces of the shadow to thwart the progress of a species so destined to be a catalyst for inter-dimensional and inter-species evolution! You are, indeed, the representatives of a potential and time for inter-dimensional unity such that has never been witnessed or even possible before this current vibrational alignment, and that potential is asking you to move with assuredness toward that which you have already aligned with your heart and intentions.

In your mind's eye and heart's wisdom, can you see that the interspecies and interplanetary partnerships necessary for the future of your own species is not possible until and unless you find, see clearly and embrace the inclusive nature of your own plane of existence? Let us share a brief story with you here. On the night before the elections in your reality, there was a great gathering of Souls, those in your reality in the physical plane and those of the higher realms of influence. These beings of the heart's intelligence and of a collective mind of wisdom and insight gathered to hold the light for the highest potential outcome of this historical day. In response to the energetic capacity and quality of this gathering of higher love and intent, there was a moment within which a golden lighted net was cast from a point far beyond the conceptual understanding of the infinite reaches of the stratosphere. This radiant net was cast over your United States. Now, the love and higher mind of those within this intent was not on a particular candidate or personality driven hope for a specific outcome. The surrender and trust was toward the highest good expression for a humanity that is in critical need for new sight, new vision and new understanding of how to live together, as One. The vibrational space for a new Universe was held as a frequency of radiant expectation. As the golden net was suspended over the United States of America, small pulsating threads of light trickled down from each square unit within the net and fed light sustenance into each voting district around the country and further into the hearts and minds of the voting population. It was pure, spiritual atomic energy, a pure power source. The vision was stunning to witness from many realms of existence and still more profound in its influence.

Surely in your heart's wisdom you can acknowledge that this construct of a Presidential Election, which both leads to your year 2012 and initiates into office the 44th President respectively, was very much a spiritual election. It was not so much about you choosing with the egoic mind who you wanted to "win," but through your direct action taking a stand against that which divides; elitism, entitlement and exclusivity, toward a change which represents the release and surrender of the shadow of separation. A victory through many layers of existence has been achieved. Your conscious and unconscious statement of intent has been heard. But the victory is not the change you seek, it is your opportunity and empowered moment to be that change. This time for your humanity is a translucent example that when you are truly ready, both individually and as a collective, the things of false power and lesser importance will fall away so that Truth and the things of the utmost importance can secure a sure footing upon which to build a future: a future of equality, of true unification and of peace. We assure you that this man Barack Obama knows who he is and what he is doing. He has fearlessly accepted his appointment and has a stellar interdimensional team working with him toward a new day for planet Earth.

This moment in your Now is the expression of a revolution of consciousness. Consciousness can and has transformed energy into matter with this historical event that you have created through high minds and valiant hearts, through deep emotion and concentrated intent. This was a day of invisible upgrades and attunements within the core of individuals, of humanity and within the core of the Earth herself. Something very powerful happens to the consciousness on Earth when the humanity of the moment begins to truly awaken, stepping up in spite of fears.

Often throughout your Earth's history there has been a suspended question of the Unity of Spirit and Change All Encompassing. And yet, truly a light code activation of the 5th dimensional heart culminated in one defiant and defining moment of a species ready to embrace change at a quantum level. We strongly encourage you to now apply the power given to you. It is not enough to just access it or leave the real work of change to one individual or a few. Each member of humanity is the action that will bring change, right now, in this moment, with what is already inside of you. Do not be afraid to step into a future that is created day by day, in this permanent Now within a hologram of Unity Consciousness. All comes undone to be rewound in a new fashion. We celebrate the step up you have taken as individuals and as a collective to fearlessly be the unity and spiritual conviction that is your authentic presence in your world!

Salute! The Shining Ones

Bridge To The Absolute

January 20, 2009

All of humanity is standing at the threshold of another kind of world. These times, indeed, mark a completion of a cycle whose ramifications are felt throughout all of Creation. We have spoken to you recently about the unprecedented change rapidly descending upon you as a species, and time will continue to quicken toward your marker of 2012. As you continue this shift to a new plateau of living in your world, you must be willing to accept that everything in your reality is spiritual and begin to interact with each other and all of life through the heart and not the ego. Once you truly understand and embrace this in all of your experience, your frequency automatically shifts to one of receptivity to the influence and wisdom of the Mystery. For you see, the highest choices you can make are those that emanate from the heart, because you are then positioned to make the optimal vibrational contributions to the energetic collective of you and the energetic collective of your world.

As you enter a new year of time in your experience, it is natural and wise to reflect on what has been. This past year on your earth plane was one of great challenge and quantum change; a year of conversion and a time of transforming from one energy into another. This change took place in the unique interiors of individuals and rippled out through and into the various constructs of your world. If you remained in your heart center and were able to undergo these challenges and change from your observer, you are likely to have experienced a sense of coming to a completion, on a multitude of levels, with recurring themes that have dominated your physical experience. Indeed, to bridge the gap in consciousness between the old paradigm and a new consciousness and energy for your world, you must surrender the conditioned patterns of response that no longer serve the current momentum of your reach. This will then allow for a radical shift in perception to take place. **There is a moment of grace that comes when you truly realize that the whole of your experience has been for the understanding and integration of Oneness.**

Each day for your earth plane, the energies are brand new; offering the potential of a new future that is always your choice. We have observed the excitement and energy of promise that has lifted so many of you concerning the political landscape of your experience. Indeed, the figure stepping into position in this realm is one who has your world inspired about the future, after many, many years of discouragement and disillusionment. We encourage you to keep your point of focus on the energy of what is taking place for your species versus the details and persons who have stepped into the spotlight at this time. A new consciousness is upon you. There is much transpiring in your reality that is designed to uplift your collective recognition of the potential harmony inherent in seeming diversity. It is a time for believing in the humanity of all beings and to take great care in not closing off the totality of the many worlds that encompass your earth plane and beyond. Hold close in your awareness that in each moment, no matter the details and interactions and experiences that are perceived with the physical eye and mind - - -that you are, as a whole, ultimately finding your way back home.

This journey is crystallized in acknowledging and accepting that, indeed, you are a unified race of beings that instinctively understands the wisdom of allowing for many truths. Many circumstances and facets of your reality are surfacing to conscious awareness the travesty of living for so long as a divided species. You are realizing that the separation and division of your humanity is the result of repressing emotionally charged remnants of your personal history. More often than not, this exclusivity and emotional barrenness toward others of your fellow man is not even conscious but a pejorative and uncontested manifestation of what has come before. In this now, a ratified transparency is the new order of the day and much will be revealed in a new light as a heightened delineation of the sovereign Self emerges.

Your magnified and energetically supported power in this now is to focus your awareness on the energy that is manifesting for you as a species; that of inclusion, unity, honor and upliftment of that which is your divine nature and birthright. In that context, it is not enough for you to place undo expectations outside of your self on what changes may now occur, but to embrace with deep gratitude the energetic opening that has culminated in your now; the opportunity for you to wake up each morning and ask what you can do to be a part of that long awaited and essential change. It is not necessary for you to concern yourselves with how things will come together - simply be in a state of trusting receptivity, absorbed in the wonder of being alive. You are stepping into a time shift of accelerated expansion on your planet based on your ability to lift up with the momentum, and relinquish all tethers to the world that is leaving. Your ability to stabilize your frequency aligned with what is versus what has been is critical. How exciting to imagine that you have chosen to be part of this magnificent experiment based on your absolute knowingness that you have something of value and great importance to bring to the process. Trust in who you are, stay in your heart's wisdom rather than the mental plane and begin to harness the surge in energies that serve to drive you to peer over the edge of all you have come to know and believe.

Now is your time, to step forward in your individualism and unique presence, to create experience out of what is uniquely yours; **a sovereign energetic of heart's intelligence.** You must learn to communicate with each other beyond the nature of duality that is your reality of existence. All along you have carried deep within, the expressions of devotion born out of a remembrance of Oneness; of unity and harmony. This yearning to recreate the experience of Unity has led the courageous and strong amongst you to walk upon a path that has never been walked before. Yet, you still fall into illusion and lose your footing at times by virtue of the fact that the ego naturally assumes the role of seeing its truth as the only one. And we say to you that there is an exquisite sense of joy, a profound sense of well-being that emanates from within and waits to permeate your entire life when you can hold to your own truth with a sacred authority and profound gratitude, while equally allowing for the truth and vision of another. Are you following the implications here? **Your purpose in being present in physical form is to allow for the expression of Oneness, through the uniqueness of each.** And freedom is the ultimate goal toward which you are all striving. That ultimate freedom evolves from the wisdom of a sovereign unity.

When you are in your sovereignty, there is no threat to your being or sense of self. You know who you are and why you are here and it matters not the details, experiences and choices of another. You understand and move through your reality with an energy of allowing and love, trusting that every single person is a gift to your remembrance and extends to you a part of yourself that you have forgotten. Your personal reality consists always of circumstances that you have chosen to create, that would help you to put into perspective your inner most beliefs and certain core issues. In that understanding, all experience, no matter how seemingly separate or divisive it may appear, is actually a Soul desire for Unity. And Unity can only evolve out of separation and duality. That is the perfection and truth of all experience. You cannot know one without the other. It is in bridging the two that you will find your reality shifting toward a heart-centered consciousness of being.

Your present time frame is considered a crossroads between two worlds. This is a time for you, individually and as a species, to take great care and discernment with how you perceive and interact with each other and the world around you. This is not a time of division within any realm of your experience or your process. The energy of non-judgmental receptivity equips you to translate awareness into action. Love one another, for then you are loving Self and all of life throughout many dimensions. That is where peace can be found. Everything is different in your now and there is an exquisite sense of joy and profound sense of well being that permeates all of life and experience when you unite in Oneness with one another and with Self. Put your focus on the essence of your own experience and how you are expressing the love and honor for each other through your daily flow and choices. **A whole new energy of presence has arrived on the planet.** Be patient and allowing with the beings that are filling the landscape of your personal reality in these times. Your familiars, aligned with your heart and deep intent are present. You are each other's teachers and in your treasuring the many ways and forms through which love comes to enrich the experience of your becoming, you align more and more fully with the parallel aspects of you, patiently awaiting you in the worlds you now visit in your dreams!

The New Human Paradigm

It is a template for the new world and the original vision of this beautiful blue planet. Any plan of meaningful and lasting action requires heroic and dedicated self-effort of individuals standing side by side with an absolute faith and centered knowingness that a Collective Enlightenment is upon us as a species.

Recognizing that we all have the total Truth inside of us in each moment, this time of wonderment and Oneness Awareness becomes a joyous allowing of our inherent and sublime spiritual seeds to begin to germinate. In the germinating, the golden threads of luminous light begin weaving a morphogenetic field of right timing, right understanding, right action and righteous love to unite those of original intent with their heart's awakening.

We all have a common yearning to be of service in the mass enlightenment happening across the globe. But more than that, the purpose and role of intent we all agreed to is now being activated through the love and profound wisdom of the Earth.

All along, wherever your journey has taken you and whatever experiences you have known, each person's goal was and will always be, love. In that realization, the question always comes back to loving all that is and ever asking how we can unite with one another in a moment, a purpose, a dream and a vision of mutual compassion and cooperative offering.

The Return of Wisdom

We are the Creators of a new world...

The New Human Paradigm of a new consciousness is leading us inward toward an ever deepening connection with Divine Wisdom and understanding. As the Divine Feminine takes up a new residence in the human and planetary heart, a clear foundation set for developing the inner core essence must be our first priority. Our nervous systems are being recalibrated with frequency this humanity has never before been exposed to, all for the purpose of embodying the true authenticity and transparency of a new human design.

The Evolution Of Love

October 24, 2009

In 2001, the Shining Ones made themselves known to me. They had been a constant Presence and greater awareness within my life since childhood, but I had had no specific contact of purpose with them, nor did I know them by name. As I made my way through yet another tier of expansion within my own spiritual journey, they saw fit to not only appear to me visually in nature, but to begin expressing through me the wisdom and love of the Galactic Core. They expressed the desire and timeliness of a "greater platform" of communication and by 2003, I had both "grown into" the idea and finally acquiesced to their greater insight into my own future, by creating a website for them. For several years I have provided the space and intent of allowing for their compassionate tilling of the soil (soul) for a rapidly accelerating humanity. Working through the timelines and harmonics of a new cycle of beingness for this species, the Shining Ones have returned as part of a cosmically induced metamorphosis. These changes that are Universal throughout our Solar System entail spontaneous changes in the DNA code of our species, all life form on planet Earth.

Not coincidently at the time of the unknown of their presence making itself **known** to this one being, I was immersed fully in the training and certification of activating the DNA codex through sound, frequency and lightwaves. The Shining Ones are here to usher in a whole new cycle for this humanity through extraordinary changes in the cellular structure and DNA codex of our being.

As the crescendo continues and the center of this wondrous galaxy releases more fields of cosmic dust through the Solar System, not only is our DNA being reprogrammed at unprecedented and other worldly rates, this rejuvenation and enlivening of our Light Bodies is coinciding with an entirely new Age of Transparency for our world. The Golden Age of change is one that we get to all experience together, as One. What this means is that we are all moving into greater expressions of Authenticity, our divine roles and responsibility in an unprecedented Cosmic Event. And the qualifying factor in both this Universal Metamorphosis and our own individual rebirths as well, is that we must keep moving, stay with the momentum of change that is rewiring the minds and hearts of a humanity once lost, but at long last waking up to Itself.

So, after approximately three years of writing in the 3rd person expression for these luminous beings of such benevolence and love for this humanity, I was urged yet again to become more transparent in my own experience and co-creative partnership with life, by giving birth to The New Human Paradigm. Initially grounded through the vessel of a book, this ancient teaching and remembrance is a return to the original intent and zero point nexus of the homoluminous on planet Earth. The Shining Ones initiated this vehicle of Light Body sustenance and DNA activation as a simplified measure of returning to our Light harmonics. The New Human is a new consciousness awakening NOW within our world because it is time and because we are ready to be our true natures; we **are** the return of the Light to a multidimensional existence of rarified life.

"Keep moving, keep your lives fluid, stay in your joy and creative impulse and the future will reveal itself through love." These were the words the Shining Ones constantly expressed through my being. When the Guidance came to create a radio show around The New Human Consciousness and Energy, I knew instinctively that there were to be notes, expressions of light codes to accompany each show and that my 3rd person articulation of the Shining Ones radiance and vibrational teaching must now, necessarily shift, to my own voice. Because they are me and I am them and we are each other always, in our highest and most resounding YES to the Process of individual and collective evolution.

The Shining Ones continue to shapeshift with the whole of this transformation cycle. The Masters not only walk among us, they are we. This simple reflection of what has been a lifelong becoming for me, is to illumine the fact that the integration of Oneness is more stunning and near than we could ever imagine. For those of you touched by the Shining Ones messages over the years, their voice and love continues through the show and notes of The New Human. I invite you to join in the assimilation and integration of Light meeting Light in a unified expression of them, through me, as the new human emerging through us all. We are indeed, loved beyond measure. Guided, overseen, intricately shaped and reformed from the inside out by a limitless luminosity of being. We are multidimensional beings more precious to Gaia and the Soul of Creation than we could ever imagine. We are the expression of many galaxies and constellations condensed into form. And that form is reuniting with formlessness. As above, so below, Heaven reuniting with the Earth plane... The New Human is the consciousness and energy of a very positive spiritual unfoldment to the evolution of our highest capacity! Your mind is the Universal Mind and your love, the Love of all Existence. Ultimate Consciousness is Authentic Love, you, at long last, being You.

*****Editors note: All New Human transmissions since 2009 are available as archives.*

The New Human Unfolding

March 28, 2009

Today's "show" emphasized our sovereign identity and talked about the importance of each individual bringing their authentic nature more and more into alignment with their personality aspect and daily reality. The goal of living our spirituality 24/7 is very much the crossroads we are facing as we witness the dismantling of so much in the world around us. The process of involution that we agreed to with our incarnation continues for this dimension, but there is a simultaneous reality that exists, another probability in the evolutionary process underway. And for us to expand with this process versus being affected by it in our daily experience through loss and upset and disorientation of our being... we must increase our vibrational capacity, the quotient of light we carry, walk through our experience fully present in the moment and embodying our authentic nature.

I went to the woods after the show. A peaceful (though muddy) run in the rain, to further ground the energies present during the transmission. I will share with you that these energies directing, overseeing and guiding the intent of the show have increased exponentially just since the beginning of this newest adventure in my radio life, a few weeks ago. I have been actively and consciously working with consciousness and energy as a way of life for over 10 years now and have a good foundation in riding the lightwaves of the expansion energies. But I can say to you that these energies are much more vast and purpose driven and action oriented than I have felt before. And I am not speaking on my behalf, they are very much coming in and through me driven with the intent to assist people over the bridge that is spanning the old with the new, the known with the unknown future manifesting in potential.

So, on this joyous, muddy, slippery run high in the mountains of a nearby National Forest Preserve, I was talking with and asking the many of you (listeners and now you, readers) "are there places in your lives, any aspect of your reality, where you are not being your Self? Where you feel you have to acquiesce to certain restrictions or protocol? Are there places and persons in your life that do not know the real you?" And my response to you through the light of Spirit is that that is where your current work is. Because, can you see that we cannot expect others to respond to us with truth, with their own light and authenticity and heart consciousness, if we are not extending that to them? The only reason for not being your authentic self, not being the real you in a situation, is fear; on some level and for whatever reason, but fear none-the-less. Someone has to shift the balance from cloaking and separation and compartmentalizing, and if you are reading these words or attracted to the energy of the show, I can say to you that you are the one to "let your voice be heard!"

If we always do what we always have done we will always get what we have always gotten. There are, indeed BIG deceptions, half-truths and lines in the sands being drawn to state what is allowed and appropriate and acceptable and not, in our world. And if we listen to our wise counsel within we easily acknowledge that the BIG messes and shadows and fear of bringing the light of authenticity to the moment, have manifested from the little fears and deceptions, masks and vulnerabilities we have all held up as a shield against what might happen if we were unapologetically and fearlessly real!

I have acknowledged on the show that there is very real work to be done if we are to bridge what has been a great divide between the old world order and the new dispensation upon us. So too, many feel that to express and be love, to show our vulnerability and innocence is a form of weakness. But what I know to be true is that it is in loving first, ourselves, life and each other, that real power can move in as the prime directive and organizing principle of our lives. Our very new lives surrounded by a new family of light and a new humanity, practicing the way of a vibrational existence toward a unified expression of One life, One love. Thank you for being a part of this wondrous journey of light with me. I can promise the magic has just begun!

The New Dispensation

April 4, 2009

Shortly after today's show, I went for a run in the Shining Ones woods. I must say that all week long the building up and presence of the energies for this show have been quite amplified and yet equally peaceful. The Guidance, as it has done most of my life, is showing me through my experience how the whole of existence for us all, can be. We are at once connected to this vast system of intelligence and superior force of guidance and if we trust and surrender to it, carried along in peace, with great care to our being.

One stream of thought in today's show illumined how easily we "become" the roles of the many identities that we wear. More and more we are being asked to defy the often, unconscious conditioning of these various reflections of our being. It is not always that we have to change who we are or what we are doing so much as to LIFT the vibration of that construct with the ongoing increase of vibration on the planet.

For instance, if you are a Doctor by profession, are you abiding in and going along with the practices of a health care system that is currently reinforcing illness and in many ways dis-empowering the body's natural ability to heal, or are you bringing your LIGHT and awareness from the higher realms to your profession in ways great and small? If you are in your 40s, are you succumbing to the social expectation of what happens to the body as we begin to age, or are you practicing regenerating habits that keep the heart both healthy and connected to the wonder of your youth? Do you see? There are so many ways we unconsciously cave, give in to the unconscious expectations and tacit agreements of a life that has for so long been dictated from the outside, in. We must be vigilantly aware of what is an old construct that we no longer ascribe to or choose to buy into.

I am still running strong the same mountain trails that I did 10 years ago and I am comfortably into my 40s. There are no shoulds connected to this activity. I do it because it brings me JOY, it is so revitalizing and it is a time of amplified connection to the higher realms where all cares and seeming obstacles fall away! Whatever your practice, whatever aspect of who you are you bring to an otherwise old construct, know you are being asked to raise the vibration of that teaching and energy and bring it with you into the new energy grid that is currently activating on behalf of future Earth.

We also touched a bit on the subject of "the pink elephant" in the room that even the spiritually minded are not too keen on addressing. MONEY! I have LOTS to say about money, Spirit has been feeding me guidance and the vantage point of many perspectives for quite some time. In my life of experience today, I have an observational post that includes the middle class experience of money, the comfortable but worried perspective, the quite wealthy but with a "poor" mentality to the spiritual that have not quite connected to their dharma, to those "high on the evolutionary ladder" yet still caught in the snares of unmet expectations and feelings of lack. Exhausting gamut, yes? And all hung up on that illusive dance between a fearful clinging to the world of form for our well-being and sustenance and the world of formlessness where all things are effortlessly manifested according to our need.

I think part of the learning curve and rewiring that needs to happen here is that we are not always clear on what are the needs of spirit and which are ego driven. Just look around our world at the great imbalances within this singular construct; from billionaire sports and movie stars to the hundreds of children in your own city - their own city that go to bed hungry every night. We have ALL perpetuated that beast for a very long time. And then, when others end up with a greater share than us, we judge that and engage the energy of who deserves what and why; both from a spiritual vantage point and not. And no one is free from it and no one has it figured out no matter what their personal bank account reflects or fiscal ambition may be.

So, the higher realms are stepping in and taking matters a little more into their "hands" by assisting with this evolutionary crescendo, a shift coinciding with Gaia's growing intolerance as a living breathing life form choking from the density of greed and the incessant attachment of a species to the material plane. The higher planes of existence, are indeed, present to assist in the dismantling of the structures, institutions and planetary locations that have, over time, sustained much deception and waves of lower consciousness.

In the woods today, high up on a mountain ridge, I saw a magnificent and ancient Oak that was leaning to one side, so much so, that the roots were showing on the high end of the lean. Due to the extreme weather conditions we have been experiencing all over this beautiful globe in various ways, the root systems of many of the trees here have become exposed from drought conditions. Then we finally get days of rain that turn into deluges, saturating the ground such that these magnificent beings that have witnessed so much of our humanity are coming unearthed and falling. I have been seeing this enough in my time in the woods that it is starting to penetrate into my heart, I am feeling their sense of unsettle at being jarred from their once sure footing. Are you following me here? The energy of what nature is feeling and how that parallels many emotions and sensibilities of life for the human element as well? The foundation is coming undone, our lives as we know them are becoming upset and we feel disoriented, unsure what the next page of our story will look like, and be?

Today, I was called off the trail and over to this huge tree being, right up to its form, as if guided by a pulse and wisdom so much greater than I could possibly engage of my own accord. I stood on the high side of that tree, on its roots, and placed my hands on either side of its body, which was easily 4 times the width of me! I immediately saw a magnificent shaft of light, extending from beyond our galaxy, down through the central column of the tree, and deep into the Earth, and I immediately knew and heard that this tree would not fall. That it was anchored now in safety to the earth, through the power and light of an arresting and transcendent Universe!

As we all make our way through this transition, we must ever call upon that brilliant, reorganizing, all-powerful Light that is our power, our wisdom and our vehicle to a new paradigm on planet Earth. Look closely, with high minds and clear hearts, at those places where what you practice, what you act on, what you perceive and attach to and so, give your energy to, is old, of fear, no longer viable or sustainable in the new soil of our future. The analogy that was given to me today after my tree experience was that of a sinking ship. All the corruption and deception and greed and acts of betrayal that have become the order of the day for the humanity we have been, is the sinking ship. And we must take care to gather ourselves up into a steadfast center of who we really are, not engaging in or attaching to the illusion of what is falling in any way - lest we go down with the ship!

If you think you have trust in the unseen worlds and the unknown of existence, trust more. If you practice the frequencies of 5D Earth such as unconditional love for all life, acceptance and allowing of all seeming differences, humility in your wisdom and absolute abundance within the observation of so much lack, take a deeper breath and extend that power into the world grid as stewards of an entirely regenerated, restored and commanding species that has lifted up to the authentic light of its original intent and prime directive. This life does not exist because of us, but for us. We are so fortunate to be a part of it with the inherent capacity to disengage the old world and be in partnership with the new that is manifesting for us all. Such is the inexplicable nature of Love.

Becoming Islands of Light

April 11, 2009

Expansiveness. Grounded by Light. Like a clear pool of water, when a stone gets tossed into the center of our calm and peace, we return to stillness again and again.

Energetically, we are clear pools of water, flowing with the rhythms of a harmonically tuned Universe. In today's show, we talked about the importance of creating from stillness. The new energy is a frequency of allowing; a vibration that lifts up rather than depletes and exhausts. No longer must we go seeking information and connections and resources to make things happen. Truly, this energy will no longer be supported. With well-trained minds and heart-based consciousness, we become islands of Light in an evolving world and as such, all that we need is drawn to us by our vibrational signature. When you are on the right path, following your joy and living the Principles of a 5D World, the Universe rises up to meet you. Then everything that you experience you experience within the context of an energy that potentially changes the mind and heart, ongoing, until living the way of Oneness, of peace, harmony, compassion, joy and unconditional love, becomes an effortless creation of the new human living on planet earth.

Your Light is committed to being a part of an organically willed participation in your own process, becoming islands of Light for the many who are trying to find their way home.

A strong theme in today's show was the profound shift that happens in one's reality when we begin living our own lives from the wisdom of our heart's intelligence. So many are trapped in the creations of their egoic mind, manifesting generation after generation of what has always been and with little to no awareness of themselves as vibrational beings.

What is happening for the whole of humanity at this time is a re-organization of our cellular structure such that by our conscious awareness and lifting of our frequency and vibration, we are guiding the energy of a humanity enslaved by fear and deception and greed to one of Unity. As we do the work to lift our energy with the vibration of the Earth, expanding along with her, we will be empowered to create new technologies and structures from high minds and powerful hearts.

This is a time of stepping out ahead of what has always been, from the practices of deception and separation within our own lives to the lines of division and exclusivity within our society and world. We are not here to save the world or solve problems created by lifetimes of ignorance and fear. The greatest gift we can contribute to the world of today is to prepare the vessel of our own being with energetic integrity and impeccable intent. It is within each individual's power to become the master of energy that is your true nature thus creating lives of balance, right action and peace from that vibrational awareness and light.

I talked about how the energy of the Earth has consciousness, that she is a part of us and we a part of her. When this awareness is brought to the light of consciousness and used in your everyday decision-making and guidance, you will be continually amazed at the gifts she will share to assist you in reordering your lives to one of continual wonder and effortless sustainability. I have a story to share with you that the consciousness of the Earth gifted to me, as a validation and reminder of the very new template of living we are being lifted up to, with great love.

I was sitting on my deck late morning. I had been up early and at work on the computer, but felt the need to stop and just go be in the fresh air for a bit. I live in the woods and the back deck sits at the base of a mountain that extends about a ½-mile or so up, before it crests and meets with the blue sky. I had been out there about 5 minutes or so when some movement to the right side of my vision caught my attention. I looked more intently and saw the head of a wild turkey coming over the ridge and seemingly headed right to me.

No sooner was his whole body visible than another turkey came right behind that one, then another and another. A procession was forming and I watched in amused amazement, for it really did seem that they came over the top of that ridge knowing exactly where they were headed, and descending in a straight line right to the edge of my deck.

Wild Turkeys are not small animals! Some had their full tail feathers open, some were female, some male, and even as the first ones reached my deck and just started standing around and staring directly at me, more came. My dog was sitting right beside me, a golden retriever, yet they were undeterred. As a whole flock of turkeys communed before me, I began to count them, starting with the ones gathered nearest and then back up the single file line that would surely end soon. Seventeen, eighteen, nineteen, twenty, twenty one, and then, as if this story were not already "wild" enough, at the very end of the line, now standing on the horizon silhouetted by the blue sky, was a solid white turkey! And down it came, like the Grand Poobah of all turkeys. It made its way, without haste, regally, confidently, with purpose, down the length of the mountain, through the center of all the others, and came to stand in the middle of the gathering right before me. The other turkeys were moving around and making gobble noises and preening, but this one stood erect and proud and perfectly still. And I did the only thing I could, I stood perfectly still in unison with it, eye to eye.

After five or ten minutes max, the white turkey, the last to arrive of the twenty two, turned to the left and proceeded back up the mountain, in an exact v-shape angle from where the flock had come in. She started the procession, and one by one, the others followed, only to quietly disappear into the horizon, just as they had come.

This was a fantastical event, to say the least. But I must also share that it is not an unusual experience once you begin really fine-tuning your vibrational matrix and aligning your intent with the force of nature. These turkeys brought me a message. There was no doubt about that. And the gift of their energy is very much aligned with the energy and message of yesterday's show.

Turkey medicine in the animal kingdom is first and foremost, about shared blessings. To Native American lore they carry the energy of the give away. The turkey's very much gifted me some personal energy and guidance, the white one in particular. The master number of 22 was an additional gift. But when I went to the woods yesterday after the show, the Guidance extended the meaning and purpose of this visit to share with you, connected to yesterday's theme.

We are being asked to rise to the occasion of this NOW and ascend beyond our previous limitations, to assist in the global transformation that IS coming. When we accept the responsibility of developing our light and high mind and make that our most important job, then we are in true positions of power to create. Not from manipulating and bending and forcing our reality to fit the expectation of our egoic minds, but by building our light from within and then sending our expanded consciousness and heightened vibration out into the energy matrix of our experience here. And as you do this, you will attract and join in and unite with those of like high mind, clear hearts and pure intent to begin to share the blessings of your treasures within. We are here to Love with a love far greater than that known to the great beings of our history because it will be a Collective Love, coming together as islands of light, to form the new communities of the new day for humanity.

Twenty-two signifies mastery on all planes, the power to teach, special abilities, power of reason and diplomacy, mastery of the mental plane. These, of course, are the effortless gifts of heart based consciousness and living the new paradigm of a 5D Earth. No longer will the mind be able to guide us into the new frontiers and off world partnerships of the future for humankind. We must be fearlessly in our hearts and like the turkey medicine, find the value and simplicity of selflessly giving what is only ours to give.

Let go, surrender to the process of Life that is overseeing all of our progress with great care and a greater love. The **new human** knows and lives by the tenets of a 5D existence; that of peace, harmony, compassion, unity and a profound sense of trust in the mystery of our highest potential. Start today building your light body and vibrational signature with more commitment and passion than you have yet dared to call upon. The practices and measures are shared joyously with you in the book, **The New Human**, but they reside in your heart's wisdom, as well.

140

Beyond The Looking Glass

April 18, 2009

We live in a broken world. Driven by a story that has separated us from each other, from our Self and from life, we judge others in the name of religion, we define our success by the material comforts we have obtained and we look past what is true and of beauty in each other, lest we also see an exterior shell that fits the prototype of perfection in an appearance driven reality.

This last week we were gifted a mirror of humanity; one that at first glance, reflected what is ugly and repugnant and unworthy of our refined tastes and cultured sensibilities. Yet, upon a second glance, we witnessed the interior light and God essence found within all of humanity. And when the looking glass spoke, we were taken into the heart of our remembrance, the remembrance of our authentic nature.

"I dreamed a dream in time gone by, when hope was high and life, worth living. I dreamed that love would never die. I dreamed that God would be forgiving. Then I was young and unafraid, and dreams were made and used and wasted. There was no ransom to be paid, no song unsung, no wine, untasted."

God speaks to us from many and unusual places. In this critical time of massive global awakening, we must not only be vigilant in our awareness, but ever in our hearts for the signs, the increase in light and lucid synchronicities by which a Supreme Guidance and the God of our understanding is speaking to us every day. We are being asked to go deeper into our understanding and awareness of Self as vibrational beings and condensed light, becoming ever clear on who we are, and then acting accordingly.

We share in our mutual experience of spiritual awakening through the Luminous Web of Life, the music of the One Heart. When I laid awake in the wee hours of the morning one day last week, in a surround sound of cosmic hum, I felt the great vibration of Universal Being speaking to me through the frequency of my Soul's personal tone of being. Little did I know within that moment that that same Music of the Spheres would be sending a wake up call to so many of humanity this week, through the plain and simple vessel of one being, Susan Boyle.

So many of The New Human shows these past few weeks have redirected experiences of shadow and deception and mistrust and disillusionment back to the power we have as teachers of love and new vision for humankind. The obsidian mirror of our potential is a high magician in that, at first glance, the reflection is dark and foreboding, and yet, on the other side of our own egoic creations of greed and division and exclusivity, there is a harmonic light frequency that is tireless in its efforts and power to guide us all back home; back to the heart of the Universe.

As a species, we are a product of our disconnection from Self. No one person has gone unscathed and unscarred through this intense evolutionary initiation. The difficult task at hand is how to create a bridge of unity, acceptance and allowing within a species of beings that do not know or belong to themselves.

We are and have always been creators of choice and free will. And we are being shown, through collapse & ruin and natures unrest yet also through the simple courage of one woman's faith in her own dream, that we must employ our power to focus consciousness to the positive outcome; to raise the vibratory frequencies of our thoughts and begin to reconstruct the Universe to resonate with the emancipated hope and exalted vision of a loving world. Indeed, what we think and speak to and act upon each day will be reflected back to us across the Gossamer Web from the vantage point of our Soul and the seat of Universal Being.

In yesterday's show, I talked about a time gone by when I wore a different identity than the one I wear today. There is no judgment present, as we are all doing the best we can from the level of consciousness we house at any given moment. I spent more than half of my life thus far being a reflection of the expectations and conditionings that I was born into. We often follow the life that reinforces the character and constructs that we know, and it can be difficult at best to break free from the persona that gets reinforced as "you" every single day. Yet, it is a great disservice to Source, to the infinite being we are, to think that who we are at any given moment is the totality and end expression of our essence.

I had an experience this past week that was truly a rarified moment of God speaking directly to the heart of the seeker. I was visiting the WNC Nature Center with two little blond light beings that I have the current fortune of getting to spend time with. It was a lovely day and we were enjoying getting up close and personal with red tail hawks and black bear and river otters and couple of endearing alpacas named Bentley and B.B. King. We then came upon a beautiful peacock that was allowed to roam free within the center, and found a good spot about ten feet from its perch to wonder at its exquisite colors and fantastical distinctions.

As we made our way down the path to leave, the peacock decided it would come with us. It actually turned our way, began picking up its cadence and headed straight for us. With the one year old on my back and the three year old at my side, hand in hand, we all stood perfectly still in amazement as that peacock, loudly vocalizing some very important bird expression to us along the way, came within one foot of us and stood directly in front of me. My feet, my body and my eyes were aligned in a mirror image with said peacock. And then he reflected back to me the brilliant symbolism of a theme that the higher light and frequencies had been lifting up in illumination all week through various venues. Opening up his tail feathers in full regalia, all I can say is that it is a humbling experience to stand a foot away from one hundred eyes holding you within a plume of iridescent wonder.

Our eyes are the portals for the light we carry within. They reflect the clarity, the wisdom, the unity and vision of the Soul's vantage point, not only within this dimension but within many parallel realities and experience and Universes. When you truly look into and connect, unafraid, with another through the eyes, you go beyond the details and circumstances of that person and yourself as creations of the egoic mind, to the light and beauty and love that is infinite; to the place we are all One.

The new human more than anything, is fully present to all experience and thus, sees everything through the heart, through the eyes of the Soul. The New Human has learned to bypass the constant chatter and dictates of the egoic mind and tune into the higher realm frequencies of 5D world. As responsible creators of conscious awareness & intelligent action, the new human is centered in the knowingness that the very energy and vibration of intent we walk through our day with is, interacting with all life and energy. Stillness, Sound, Light, no thought, Higher Mind Principles and Love, these are the vehicles of manifestation for future earth when aligned with the Cosmic Source Motion that creates and shapes all life.

One Love, Love of the One...

The High Side of Truth

April 25, 2009

After the show yesterday my immediate experience was one of utter stillness. I felt like I was in a vacuum that was totally devoid of this sensate reality. I had no thought, my mind was completely silent and I felt a low whir, a vibrational hum that enveloped me in a cocoon of peace.

It took a while to ground back into my physical aspect and I looked forward to getting out into nature to fully integrate and be with the energies of the show. I always get a lot of feedback from the higher realms on how my energy was running during the show and a clear stream of insight to enable me to continue to ground down the mystery and unknown of this commitment. I am very aware that the Guidance is constantly attending to the different configuration of energy present as the listening audience expands and more people are called to the intent and work of The New Human.

I went to one of my favorite spots on the river and as I walked with Samadhi Blue toward a nice deep spot for her to swim in, I heard, "water is a magnificent conductor of energy." Of course, I "know" this from my work with DNA and a comfortable understanding of quantum physics. But, it was as if I was being guided to engage this principle with the gift and opportunity of the river, right then.

As each moment is always perfect with everything that we need, Blue and I emerged from the woods right at a place that had a vibrant, dancing rapid cascading over some large river rock. I took off my shoes and waded out to the center of the rapids fierce kinetics. The water was about thigh deep, but just as I turned to face the flow, my foot found a large rock beneath the water's surface to stand on, lifting me to a poised position. I closed my eyes and let go fully to the moment, completely surrounded by the clear, cool, ever flowing waters of life. I saw a swirl of light lift from the water and spin a vortex around me, at once clearing, lifting, adjusting and exchanging light waves with an interdimensional presence of support and acknowledgement. And I knew the non-physical realm was working with the intelligence of the water, in that moment, on my behalf.

About this time I felt something warm on the back of my leg and opened my eyes to the gentle nudging of Blue, reminding me that I had promised her some stick fetching time on this beautiful afternoon.

One of the themes in yesterday's show, directly impressed upon me by the Light to share with the many, is that now, more than ever, we must suspend disbelief. We are indeed, entering another profound stage of our evolution. We have always known, with spiritual understanding, that our connection with the earth is invaluable. Yet, there is something changing within our core, right now, to align us further with Gaia. We must ever look to her, abide in her and move with her to assure safe passage in these next few years to 2012. These new and powerful energies arriving in our current experience, that are affecting our sleep and making us less tolerant of dense, stagnant energies, creating a sense of urgency that there is something that needs to be done, yet we aren't quite sure what!!!! These energies are to provide the necessary push and momentum that we need to fully align with our divine purpose, our positions of power and necessary action. Attuning to the earth, to begin considering her as the loving, breathing intelligent organism that she is, is to begin to grasp that not only is her metamorphosis our metamorphosis, but that her dimensional shift is felt throughout the Universe and as such, we are all part of an immense moment in all time for the entire Cosmos.

So, what does this mean for the individual still very much attached to the 3D reality of an existence supported by social consciousness and man-made structures? It means that everyday each of us would do well to look at what aspects of our life are supporting persons and institutions and societal practices that are hurting the earth; choking her, dishonoring her, taking her for granted and thus diminishing all of life. We have gotten so far out of balance with over population and the creation of poisonous food sources and endless streams of artificial stimulation and synthetic substance, humanity has forgotten that we are here to re-member, to wake up and return back home wiser and more loving than when we entered in.

Whether conscious of it or not, whether we put our high minds and heart to it each day or not, our emanations, the vibration and light of our etheric bodies permeate not only the immediate space around us, but serves ripple out into the greater sea of consciousness. As such, every thought, action,

146

belief and emotion joins with the group voice of our planet and then journeys out to untold civilizations, penetrating many layers of existence. Gaia is the communication center of our Solar Dieties chakric grid and many realms of existence are listening, observing and counting on this upward moving humanity to remember that they came from the stars.

Let me share something with you, a DeAnne moment within a life that keeps me constantly attuned to a consciousness and energy beyond reason or my mind's ability to comprehend. I was reading some material from a scientific journal and was reminded of a basic science lesson reflecting that it takes approximately eight minutes for the light of the sun to reach the earth. Based on that fact, we can likewise infer that when we look at the sun, we are actually experiencing a time delay and in effect, looking at the sun as it was eight minutes ago. Bear with me here. Now, following the same premise, the brightest stars in our night sky are so many millions of miles from Earth that it conceivably takes years for their light to reach us. And so, when you are sitting out on your porch one evening after a long day at work within the delineation of a life very much defined by the perimeters of a societal driven ideal, the stars that you observe in that moment, may no longer even exists! And what so impressed me with this chain of inferred wonder is that this is the kind of phenomena that is occurring ongoing while the majority of humankind have their minds and concerns on things of transient importance.

"Tell them to suspend disbelief," the Shining Ones whisper in my ears. "Talk to them of the things that speak of wonder such as the animal kingdom seeing your frequency and light beyond your humanness; impress upon them that guidance is everywhere all the time reminding each individual of the promise they made to bring their Light and power to the compulsory transformation of your planet, and compel them to trust their cosmic identity more than they trust the fear that is constantly knocking on the fragile psyche of their finite experience of self. Tell them that the mystery, the unknown and high magic is real. And most of all, tell them how much they are loved."

As we move up the great serpent of light, the cosmic spiral where time folds in upon itself to stand still at zero point, we begin to interface with higher dimensions and duality begins to lessen because our understanding becomes such that we see the whole. The whole then envelopes us within a spaciousness where all is peace, all is abundance, all is Love.

Everything is different. The New Human understands this, sees this and welcomes it as the new day on planet Earth. We are restructuring at a cellular level, recalibrating and balancing ourselves out as individuals to prepare the ground for what is the new Earth vision and potential for our species, Communities of Light. Yet, those communities of light are dependent upon the light within; a light that has endured much density and shadow and must be lifted and embodied as the greatest import in the way we run our day and organize our life in this unprecedented now.

An enlightened state of consciousness, a mind free from thought and fearless in its surrender to the Soul's reach, perceives the reciprocity in all things. To elucidate the new paradigm of 5D world and the feminine emancipation of Gaia, all must experience mutual relationship in every moment, knowing all exists within everything else. I exist in you, you exist in me, the rivers in nature flow through our body and the stars in the night skies are the vantage point of our inner sight. To know these truths, is freedom. To live these truths, is love.

Presence of Power, Center of Peace

May 2, 2009

I had a dream this last week that remains with me still. Seems that many of my experiences of late linger in the contemplative stillness of my awareness, inviting me to turn them like a multifaceted prism, so that I might capture the wisdom one may find beyond casual consideration. In the dream, I had been traveling for some time with quite the cache of belongings. The journey, though long and at times rough and treacherous, was completely out of doors across an endless landscape of lush and verdant green. I was happy to be making the journey and quite sure of my destination.

After some time, nearing the end of my sojourn, I came to the edge of the landscape, which stopped abruptly, only to be presented a dilemma. Though I could clearly see my destination and was so close to arriving, there was a fairly large chasm between the land I stood on and where I needed to be. It was a canal of sorts, about twelve to fifteen feet across with an equal drop to the water's surface below. There was no hesitation from me. I knew only that I needed to get to the other side and though what I carried with me would be much worse for the experience, I jumped with fearless determination.

When I hit the water's surface, I quickly discovered that the weight of what I was carrying prevented me from swimming to the other side, as had been my "plan." I was pulled, as if by an anchor, down down down into the water, all the while watching the surface of the water fading from my site. All these events were happening in rapid succession. In the next instance, a huge tunnel, opening (yes, it was like a worm hole) appeared to the left of me with a centrifugal force that sucked me right into a dark, fathomless womb!

I had a moment of panic at being taken away from the direction of air, lifeforce, my breath, and woke myself up. I got up out of the bed and got some water and then went back to sleep. And I was taken right back to the very spot in the dream that I was when I had panicked. Only this time, a very bright light appeared. Coming from the direction of the vacuum that had, moments before, been utter darkness. A bright light shone though the water and in that instant, I knew I was safe. I relaxed and followed the light up to the surface, right to the place I had been headed all along. The only difference being, I carried nothing with me. I had been set free from the weight of my journey.

Each day I ask the Light, how do I share this love that I know? How can I teach the faith that comes with being given so much inner sight and fullness of heart? What might I say or do that impresses that with profound trust, we are given access to a world within a world where peace sustains you, joy inspires you and love beckons you to an experience of tenderness and beauty and immeasurable treasure? In our finest hour, humanity knows that problems are but evolutionary drivers for something of greater meaning and purpose trying to emerge. My evolutionary drivers, the presence and force and i-magi-nation that get me out of bed each day are these questions from the ancient grace and wisdom of my Soul.

Immediately after the show yesterday, my whole body was buzzing. It was as if I had an oscillator beneath the surface of my skin, and I felt the urge to just lie down and drop into that for a brief time. As I relaxed across the foot of my bed, I could hear a low hum to accompany the sensations I felt, and then my awareness shifted to an unusual smell. Now, I have been noticing this smell off and on at odd times for the past few weeks, especially so. But, as it was not something I readily recognized or could put my finder on. I would just observe it, acknowledge it and then let it go.

In this moment however, with all senses already so heightened and with a LOT of Presence still hanging around with me after the show, I knew I was being invited to lift my awareness to the clarity of this energy. I "looked around" intuitively with my mind's eye and engaged the moment with my High Self. The smell was very "clean," fresh, almost like the sensation you get when you stand real close to a large waterfall and the water's mists dance in the air. And then, as clear as a bell and with the same impact it came to me. I was smelling the Light! I could smell the luminous, radiant energy of Light. The Light. Sigh. And I did the only thing that I could do in that moment. I opened my heart in gratitude.

We had a few themes running through yesterday's show, but I could tell that the Presence and intent within this new human consciousness was more than anything, endeavoring to pull people into their center. It just cannot be underestimated how, as a species, we just don't know what it means to be only in this moment, in the now of your experience. Our power and potential for co-creative vision and ultimate peace lies in our ability to be fully present to all experience. I can't help but ponder sometimes if our tendency to divide our attention to many points of focus at once is a symptom of the duality that has shaped our current world.

Keeping with the theme of building our light bodies to align with the Gaian vibration rising on our planet, we talked of the need to cooperate with the reorganization of our DNA that is the transmutation into light body. The cosmic energies currently radiating through the atmosphere and into the body of Gaia, are here to assist us in clearing the emotional body and attuning to the heart and frequency of Love. There is a 3rd strand of DNA being recoded, which plugs into our 3rd chakra, our power center. And with this 3rd strand activation, we will experience the co-creative passion of the yin and yang, the masculine and feminine and of electricity and magnetism as they connect at the subatomic level. This is the rebirth into the higher dimensions and dependent upon our ability to clear emotional debris, surrender the ego and transcend the cultural imprints of masculine and feminine energy, from without and within.

The lower chakra energies still dominate our planet. Our experience of love as a species is emotion centered and we suffer because of that. What we term love is a manifestation of the lower chakras energy of desire and sensuality and reflects this instability of the emotional body. The Guidance present in the show yesterday especially addressed the male light-workers who have so much wisdom and gifts and ancient civilizations of knowledge to share. Yet, spirituality cannot be aggressively pursued at the expense of emotional wholeness. The healing of our individual lives spirals out into the healing of our greater world. We must bring light into all elements of matter and allow the tender lucidity of the feminine energies to come in and take the helm of the important work we are here to ground into this existence, lest the ego throw an evolutionary cog into our expanding reach toward greater light.

When we lift our light body through the conscious, tireless practice of increasing our vibrational capacity, we are capable of pulling the strength of Gaia through our bodies and into our Soul. This perfect balance of feminine and masculine energy is our personal evolutionary process in this NOW moment and it is in conjunction with the Earth Mother. I love her so much. My experience of the natural world is such that, if no other thing happened in my life than my time with her, I would be wholly complete. And thus, I am wholly complete because of her wisdom and love for me.

Nature has always evolved in a direction and progression that is good. If we take in the details of our world today through the limited scope of our egoic mind, we will not be able to see past the details to what is true. What is true is the vision that lies in the mystery. We have only just begun to peek through the veils to a world of joyous and limitless Light; a world sustained by the mother's profound love for all sentient beings. A vision that includes effortless manifestation of all that we need, shared gifts in a co-creative existence and communication and travel via clear and high minds that have re-membered their star origins.

My vision of the future is of a world where we experience and interact with each other as light, seeing through all differences and illusions to the ONE LOVE within us all and all life. We are all part of a quantum change and we are each being invited to participate more fully and necessarily so, toward evolving a new vision of the world. There is only this moment. And it is perfect and whole and complete and wholly Love. I encourage you, The New Humans of a new world emerging, to identify your JOY - where it is guiding you to express your creativity. We are a Universal humanity and it is that creative urge within that will reunite us once more with our hearts, with this profound existence and with the Heart of a very great Love.

Imagine

May 9, 2009

The day before the show I woke up early. It looked like it was going to be a very wet, rainy day and though I usually reserve that space on Friday morning to prepare and be present with the energies of the next day's show, I was strongly guided to just go to the woods. Don't think about it, no breakfast, just throw on some shorts (I did grab a cup of hot tea) and get to the Shining Ones woods before the rains come.

We have had a lot of rain lately and so, when I got to the trailhead, the river was so full I had to take off my shoes to cross rather than just hopping on rocks as I usually do. I ended up having to take off and put my shoes back on four times in this early morning and chilly adventure. But I was on a mission.

I was guided to go up the center trail of the forest, which offers a nice high loop to the right and left, as well. Each trail is mystically unique with its own special nuance of energies. I always tune in and ask which trail I "need" to take on any given day to support the exchange underway between my 3D process and the impressions that the higher realms are extending on my behalf. And the answer is always clear. This early morning under a very pregnant and overcast sky, I was pulled magnetically to the top of the Shining One's Central Column trail.

On the way up, having already waded through two streams thus enabling the waters to clear and prepare my energy field to an even greater level of receptivity, the bird kingdom was just lit up with activity and such joy. It was as if I was in a surround sound of birdsong and every voice was amplified, their energy very palpable. It felt as if all eyes were on me! Even as I write this reflection, I feel the pure emotion of one being seen and loved so clearly and wholly and unconditionally. I felt celebrated.

When I reached the top, I followed my customary practice of turning to face the sweeping landscape that I had just climbed, taking in all of that expanse and then with a personal mudra that I use to ground my being with the natural world, I acknowledged that all of the rich, endless, breathtaking scenery that I was beholding, was indeed, a reflection of my own personal wealth and abundance.

As I stood there in utter stillness, eyes closed, deeply engaging my breath, I still had the sense that "everyone" was watching me, from all sides, I could feel the presence of hundreds, if not thousands. Then, a great white luminous being appeared at my left and right side, simultaneously. And no sooner did I acknowledge that, then there were two more, on either side, then two more until there was a hastened quickening that resulted in a row of Ascended Masters to my left and right as far as my physical site could see - that continued still with my inner site to form a grand sphere of Ascended Masters, my body being the electric arc of this vortex.

Initially, the circle encompassed the entire Shining Ones Woods, which is easily hundreds of acres. Then it expanded still to orbit the entire world. And I just stood there, an extraordinary moment within an ordinary life, hand in hand with all these beloved Masters, suspended in a timeless realm of unity and love. Within that circle, all was Light. Light radiated from their heart center to mine, which radiated to the heart of our solar deity, which then magnified all inclusive, the purest of frequencies, radiant, scintillating Light back to the Earth, deep into her core and settling as a soft blanket upon all her sentient beings.

When I felt complete with the moment, I opened my eyes, and every tree was a being standing before me with the honor and presence of a royal court waiting to serve their beloved leader. I did not see trees I saw life. I felt their energy, their heart and the story within their purpose for our species. We acknowledged each other in a reciprocal moment of recognition. I turned to the left to run the semicircle trail back down to the trailhead. Blue was dancing with excitement, clearly having witnessed and felt the energies of the last fifteen minutes or so of no time.

As I "glided" back down the mountain, all my thoughts and strong wanting were focused on the show the next day, on you, and all who would be listening. I asked the Higher Realms how I could begin to impress upon the many, still so connected to routine and expectation and obligation to the sensate world, "how do I impress upon them that this experience I just had is running parallel to the mundane in their everyday lives?" That an existence that allows them to follow guidance and intuition and impulse in each moment IS theirs, if that is the reality they are ready to embrace and stand in the middle of with their power and light.

Everyday, we make choices and with each choice, we are either creating more of the same or, with a little daring and imagination, creating a new world for ourselves and the future of our Earth. At one time, our species thrived in an experience of life that was sustained and nurtured and informed by the natural stimuli of the Earth; the wind, sea, rain, animal kingdom and movement of the stars. Yet, today we are increasingly dependent on artificial stimuli that is robbing us of the ability to imagine, to dream and be inspired and reside fully in the purpose and gift of each moment. Graver still, our obsession with and entrainment to the many wonders of technology is serving to plug us ever deeper into the artificial, superficial, soulless circuitry we know as life in the twenty first century.

In this advanced society of brilliant minds and intelligent reason, there are billions of people just living out their lives; uninspired and feeling powerless to break free from the mundane of an existence that has been passed down through generations by those oblivious to their internal workings. We have become so conditioned, for so long, to the unconscious, stealth manner in which we are programmed by external drivers, that we have lost touch with our predisposition to create and envision and dream new worlds out of nothingness.

It is a profoundly exquisite time to come into awareness for our species. There is a phenomenon occurring - a process underway supported by evolutionary drivers connecting the entire cosmos, whereby we can now detach from this simulated world of illusion and need and the ego's imbalance, to re-attach in Unity. But we must gain a command of our mind; breathe new life and intent into the art of mindfulness and the ability to be present to our experience; to life. Don't believe anything you see, but act as if it were real. Become indifferent to externals and then every problem becomes a challenge to test ingenuity and mental acuity. When we realize that we are nothing, then we become everything.

Consciousness can be focused and rewritten in anyway the imagination desires. The New Human is a new consciousness; one that understands and sees energy and then engages that energy as an interactive dance based on the advanced technology of intelligent mind and high magic. So far, in this human experience, we have been pawns within a giant chess game where all our moves have already been anticipated by egoic minds and indifferent hearts. The love we have accepted as holy and true is actually a love of conditions; of rules to follow, criteria to meet and needs to fulfill. We must stop this madness. To be free and authentic and belong to Self, which is to belong to God, is to turn your eyes inward: to the mystery of the unknown and the nothingness of nonexistence. From there we have the vibrational capacity and mettle to act with imaginative response, with inspired spontaneity and without prior thought or motive.

Our lifeline is our Will, our unbending intent and sense of impeccability in being accountable to something greater than the false sense of self and security we invest so much of our time and energy in today. Much of our world is constructed as a distraction from the greater Truth of our inherent power and light. We are distracted by fear of death, religious tenets, dependent relationships, sexual shame, mindless jobs, political deception, drugs, pain, and ongoing tragedies within a repetitive mental time loop. Every adversity we ever face is just love endeavoring to get us to let go, think outside of the box, bend the rules, free the mind. More than anything, we are prisoners of our thoughts; our thoughts create our reality.

We have the opportunity now, in this moment of our humanity, to disengage; unplug from the world of form, conditioned thought and externally controlled lives: to suspend disbelief and dare to live lives abundant with purpose and inspired everyday with meaning and value. The only way to be free is to be heart centered and internally driven. What is happening everyday in every part of the world, to all people and within all cultures, is happening to us all. There is only One of us and there is only this moment. Be fearless in your determination to live your Light and only that. Dare each day to make choices and decisions that unplug you from transient existence and leave you with only your imagination and a profound trust in life to create your next moment. Every consequence that results from decisions made with a free mind empowers you with greater light and wisdom than before that decision was made.

We are fighting for a new start as a species, a new way of being in a new world inspired by the power of the present moment and the imagination of those daring to live free. The New Human knows that our greatest currency is energy. Build your light from within and move without thought through the holistic spacetime continuum where all interconnects seamlessly with everything else. Then and only then will the ordinary moments of our journey back home become the extraordinary existence of One who has remembered their destiny.

A World Transforming

May 16, 2009

I am sitting in a chair, sharing. It is a simple act and though my words are soft and gentle, within me they feel impregnated with import and intangible grace. To the casual observer, I appear to be sitting all alone in that chair. In Truth, there are many luminous beings gathered round me, filling my mind with their wisdom, my words with their expression and my heart with their love. And in my stillness, in my trust, in my remembrance of my Self and the greater family of Light present within all uncertainty and unknown, a high magic transforms the moment into one in which a few gather to listen to my words. Then the few become a dozen, the dozen becomes thirty and then seventy five and ever so purposefully, within my allowing and TRUST, suddenly I am expressing the consciousness and energy of the Inner Light, to listeners expanding around the globe. Such is the transformative invitation extended to each of us, calling us out of the predictable cocoon of all we have known, to the now visible horizon of future Earth.

Coming into your Authentic Self is a dimensional shift. It is the undaunted stepping up into an experience that offers no assurance, no safety net and no predictable outcome for a species that thrives on control and the comfort of the known. And the easy question would be, "why would a person choose to be the One who follows the inner voice into an experience and life beyond reason, when the gift of Free Will also allows for the choice to remain in the comfort and safety of predictable outcome?"

I think all would agree that something of significance is happening to our world, to life, as we have known it for many lifetimes. And that something is more than a repetitive history of failing infrastructures, time specific wars, governmental anarchy and the presence of pandemic disease. It is the awareness and Presence of a new language to detect and vision to recognize a world of frequency and color within the finite existence of the world of form. It is the supreme gesture of those Beings of High Intelligence and Greater Wisdom willingly stepping in, to engage our limitation toward a new possibility for our species. A partnership is being extended. And the greater question is, will we take the red pill of our considerable potential, or remain closed and static and unbelieving of just how great and wondrous the love of Source truly is?

There is a non-local conscious awareness that we can tap into, visually, audibly, the whole of the sensate self, that enables us to enter a time zone where there is no time. It is the activation of and access to the quantum brain versus the neutronium brain, by which we can talk directly with the Higher Self, the Divine, God. This is our scientifically validated and documented capacity to see other dimensions, irrefutably impressing our rigid mentality to doubt, with the knowingness that we are, indeed, all connected within a luminous, intelligent, timeless organism of life.

The show is gathering momentum every week. It is illumining through simple exercise, through stimulated thought and tangible experience what is available for those ready to accept responsibility for their power as creationary beings. Within our current manifestation as a species, we are highly monitored, anticipated, regulated and fed continual streams of ignorance through a pervasive level of deception and unenlightened power. And the great majority of mass consciousness goes along with the triviality of existence out of fear; fear of the unknown, fear of death and fear of the unprecedented destiny we are charged to step into.

The work of The New Human is to prepare the frequency of our light body to SEE with new eyes and be able to negotiate the vibrational shift of a New Earth breaking through the structures of the old one. To take part in the awakening process of ascension is to fine tune our physical aspect, which directly coincides with conscious awareness. Our consciousness and our energy body are intimately connected; you cannot think or pray your way to conscious awareness and an open mind while remaining in a safe, orderly, routine existence of predictability. If you always do what you have always done, you will end up with more of the same. We must determine now to be fluid in the way we map our days and remain flexible, without attachment.

The ego can only exist in isolation. It soothes you with routine and order and known comforts, luring you into illusion with the promise of safety, security and predictable futures. I can honestly say to you that I imagine my ego dies a little bit each day. Each time my heart catches in my throat by yet another leap into nothingness, each time my egoic mind heckles me with how alone I am on the path I have chosen, each time a holiday comes round and I witness generations of families get together to engage in their time worn traditions of "what you do," year in and year out within lifetimes of cultural, racial, and socioeconomic histories. Yes, the spiritual journey is one that sets apart and is relentless in the impetus to a greater experience of life, of existence, and of love.

We can look at the state of our world today and reflect, from a safe distance, that the division and exclusion, the imbalance and inhumane atrocities of our conditioning will somehow work themselves out and so, the best thing any one person can do is to keep as much flow of order and comfort as you can within the perceived safety of your finite reality of existence. Or, you can, in the stillness and luminosity of your interior world, within the planetary activation of Gaia's DNA simultaneously activating within you, you can determine to step into the evolutionary consciousness within which you are called to the awakening and applied knowledge of your necessary gifts.

We talked yesterday of a great reboot underway, in preparation for the return to zero point, within the year 2012. The love and wisdom of infinite realms are here with us to guide us safely through the recalibration and lift to a 5D World of existence. The humanity of this time, in its infinite potential and radiant light of possibility, is witnessing the fall of an old structure and the rise of a New Earth now manifesting. As a species of free will and choice, we can imagine two elevators side by side; one that is dense and heavy- laden with transient debris and egoic desires and thus, descending, going down. The other is fresh, new and comprised of only Light, the very Light and color of the Spiritual Self, and thus going up, up up to the unknown realms and worlds of future Earth. And in this moment, the most important moment in our history, we are called to the future of our choosing. But we must make a choice.

There will be more dismantling in the years to come, both in the structures we have created and in the breaking away and rebirth of much of our natural environment; the body of the earth. It is a time of cleansing and renewal and revival for us all. Every act, every choice, every decision you make to no longer support and be a part of the deception and broken infrastructure of an unsustainable and soulless world, you are contributing a frequency of light to the upward spiral of transformation for our species. To endure, settle, acquiesce and justify a homogeneous existence of what has been at the expense of what could be, is to become the lesser forms of intentionality and hopelessness of those still in shadow.

By now, if you have been following the show and the accompanying notes of The New Human, you are on to me that I go to the woods, out into nature each week soon after the show. I go into the mystery for a recapitulation and synthesis of all the energies present and the mystery fills me with the fullness of all that transpired. And what I want to impress here is that the Guidance set it up that way; the freedom to go into nature after each broadcast, as well as the portal of 11:11 that happens every show, providing a doorway within which all who are ready, will be transported to their next highest expression in this partnership.

Yesterday, true to the usual flow, I went to the river with Samadhi Blue. I sat on a huge rock beside the eternal flow of life within the river and in the peace and stillness of that moment a small gathering of cerulean blue butterflies came and alit beside me. I reached my hand gently into their center and delighted in their willingness to walk onto it, lightly touching their sinuous legs along my fingers and palm. And then, a moth came to join the energies of the moment. A small brown moth, about half the size of the butterflies, just flew into the mix as if it too, belonged. And what I saw and felt within the wonder of this experience was a reflection of the dance underway for our species at this time.

The butterflies embody the energy of transmutation and joy. They are the beautiful mutation of our fullness, encompassing many frequencies of color and light. The moth is a creature of metamorphosis, reminding us that in each phase of transition, each new adaptation to shifting surroundings, we must determine what stage of our expansion we are ready to embody and become: egg, larva, chrysalis or flight? With their willingness to come and merge their nature so freely with my physical aspect, the higher realms offered the insight into the full scale transformation underway right now, for all of humanity.

When we truly embrace our Divinity, the inherent Unity and creationary power we have to create worlds out of nothingness and to do so for the One purpose of Love, a sense of Supreme Joy overtakes our human condition. We then see ourselves in both the chaos and the confluence, the separation and the unity, in the one who has forgotten their way and in the one who has remembered their destiny. Then, the most important thing becomes our full love and participation in the determination and intent to bring the whole spiral with us to a new creation of existence.

Fractal World, Lucid Mind

May 23, 2009

Going into yesterday's show, I felt strongly the possibility of doing the whole hour in silence. And though the energy of the show flowed with much clarity and powerful presence, again, when I began creating the space for the notes to come through, nothingness. There is a dance going on between a continual stream of very new information coming in and my mind's ability to articulate it. I typically do one of two things when the way is not clear, when movement between 3D reality and the timeless worlds isn't fluid: I meditate or go to the woods. In this case, I did both.

After lying in stillness for almost an hour, I began receiving the movement of the language the Guidance wanted me to express. It was not until I went to the Shining One's woods afterward, that all the images, my experiences of this last week and the energies of the show yesterday began to coalesce in such a way that I could express them to you meaningfully.

Now, I am surely one of the most non- mathematically oriented persons you could imagine, but what was given to me today, the information streamed to me, is that I am seeing fractals. The mathematical, geometrical imagery that I see clearly in nature but that is slowly taking over my entire interpretation system, are the patterns of a world constructed of fractal curves and angles, waves of light and color spectrums that form the nucleus of an entirely different story of life than we perceive with the naked eye. I even sense that the voice of the Shining Ones is fractal in nature. To see this way is to see Unity and to move through reality this way allows the physical body to become liquid light, capable of accessing any point on the holistic time/space continuum; retrieving any information that you need or that the higher realms deem to communicate to you. As my reasoning mind continues to stretch, it occurs to me that new information is on its way before I am even aware that it is coming or consciously seek it out.

Several years back, there was a craze of popular culture called stereograms. I was given this as an example to share with you as I endeavor to put to words what is second nature to me now. Stereograms are pictures that look like just a bunch of color, lines, angles and circles but when focused upon, you can find a picture within a picture. Seeing these fractal patterns is similar in nature but perhaps reverse in concept. Our brain is divided into left and right hemispheres that interpret our visual reality through a combination of reason and logic, creativity and imagination.

What I shared in yesterday's show is that nature, because of these fractal patterns, is a huge key in lifting the divisions between our left and right brain, enabling us to see and know other aspects of Life and Self. Much of this information is not new, but what is important here is that I retrieved the same language and data that the studies of science and quantum physics has documented, but I did so through wonder, innocence and joy. I allowed the Mother, Gaia, to teach me her world of existence vibrationally and it resulted in the same intelligence and conclusion as the mind's training through scientific research. Further, because I have learned to drop the sensor on my reasoning mind, to move without thought, I have discovered that with each move into the unknown, it is possible to discover ever, new realities and they are all Self discovery, Self Actualizing; pun intended.

I absolutely acknowledge this as a manifestation of the thinning veils, of time folding in upon itself and of the hyperdimensional shifts that are occurring in anticipation of an entirely new vibrational reality unfolding. But that is only part of the equation. The qualifying piece within this awareness is that of partnership. We are part of a unifying whole and at a point in the evolutionary process where the gift and necessity of partnership emerges as the nucleus of all that is unfolding. The marriage of science and spirituality as mutually respected parties of world transformation, the principle of yin/yang union in grounding the higher realms to the earth and lifting the earth to the higher dimensions, the reciprocity of exchange in what we take from the earth and what we give back to her and the cooperation we mutually work toward in creating a sphere of life on our planet where we see every person and all of life as essential to the level of balance within our individual lives and a sustainable future.

Gaia is changing in her cellular structure. She has always been a merkabah of beauty and perfection, sacred geometry and architectural gnosis; alive with patterns of energy that repeat in endless cycles. Doesn't really sound like the same body of mass that humanity has ravaged and decimated, suffocating with concrete and senseless refuge through lifetimes of disregard and irreverent abuse. She has suffered long enough and her energy is lifting to a new spin of lucidity and light, to the principles of 5D world. We have the choice to lift with her by attuning to our heart and feeling nature. Life not only wants to survive but to enjoy survival, through our willingness to return to innocence and live from our joy.

The destiny of the world is written not with words but with consciousness and energy, frequency and light, geometry and color. Human nature is preparing for a huge leap. What does that mean? It means cellular change has been initiated and we must change our habits, actions and the focus of our attention to a new level of consciousness. We have the awareness now to acknowledge the senselessness of supermarkets the size of a football field crammed full of environmentally detrimental substances that hold food sources as toxic as their containers. We have created a culture of consumerism by consent and demand and that is the only way we can reverse the spin from negative to positive; from form to formless and from shadow into light. We have to rise above the fear of letting go to a higher level of instinct and intuition that says this is a beautiful world that is aware and intelligent and knows what she is doing. It is time to get to know her better and learn the language of her wisdom.

Last week I shared a story with you about butterflies. As they walked up and down my fingers and hand, I observed them really close, merging as best I could, becoming the butterfly in my imagination. And what spoke to me interiorly is that these delicate creatures of the One Love and One Life, accepted me and trusted me via their feeling nature. They move through life without thought or attachment, willingly venturing into unknown territory, interacting with creatures very different from their own species, not by logic or reasoning... but through instinct and energy. They are guided by the interconnected web of life that finds harmony and unity in the language of light that informs through a Universal Consciousness. This is our doorway, as well, to roundtable creation forums including the high minds of many sciences and worlds toward the vision of emerging Communities of Light.

Every day we are making a statement of intent that echoes throughout the cosmos via a vibrational signature that is intimately linked to the fields of the earth. When we are aligned with Life, with the beauty of this world, contributing our gifts of creativity and practicing ecological responsibility, our heart actually beats an entirely different rhythm. And the consciousness and energy of that rhythm empowers us individually and collectively toward a new way of life for the humanity of planet earth.

Contact

May 30, 2009

In preparing for the energies of this week's show, I was sitting by one of my favorite places on the river. Everything is just so lush and tropical right now in Western Carolina, after a rather zealous rainy period. Samadhi Blue was almost fully hidden in the tall grasses beside me and I sat peacefully gazing into the fullness and rapids of the river; suspended in a space of no thought.

It was not long before that reverie was abruptly shifted, by the piercing calls of a family of geese who had just rounded the bend of the river. Of course, this made Blue stand up to see what all the commotion was about, which really got the dander up of the male goose, fiercely guarding its family. Understanding whose territory it actually was, I told Blue to sit back down and we both just allowed for this nature moment to remain in the flow of its natural rhythm.

Because I am at this particular spot on the river often and have never seen geese here, I attuned to the synchronicity of them appearing within my intent and open receivership to the theme and messages for the show. And when the whole family of five came back round within the hour, almost like a deja-vu time loop in experience, I knew there was wisdom of significance to be found within their energies.

Geese provide an invitation to the netherworlds, calling the questor into dimensions and enchanted realms where they can enhance their spiritual journeys. The attention evoking call of goose is a harbinger of movement toward the fulfilled promises that only great spiritual undertakings can bring to Light.

My heart is quite full for the great initiation of so many within this full-scale spiritual awakening that is encompassing our globe and humanity at this time. I don't pretend to have the instruction manual and do not subscribe to the tenets of any one sure way to bridge the great divide between 3D reality and the freedom of an interconnected, multidimensional existence. I only know that each day I am guided by what I can only express as Supreme Consciousness, an all-inclusive Love that through an ever spiraling, dynamic reflection of experience, is asking me to share the possibility of sovereign existence found within the language of Light.

This NOW is a huge portal within the whole grand scheme of evolution, one in which we've got to shift our perceptions. It just cannot be underestimated how much change is occurring at a subatomic level and to the degree we actively engage the energy of change, we are hooking into a force that we may not fully understand, but can feel in the compelling urge to do something different. This unexplainable impulse that drives you beyond the reasoning of the egoic mind is the Creative Force of the Universe; we are unifying our field of awareness with the quantum field of non-local reality. If you are not feeling this and acting upon it, you are not paying attention.

A magnified portal of shift was grounded into this dimension with the election of President Obama. But the essential piece of awareness that many are missing is that this historical moment of forward movement set into place a fresh new energetic within which every person has an unprecedented opportunity to break free from much entrenched belief, unconscious thought and patterns that are no longer serving them. If you are not doing something different in your reality since the inauguration, some visible, tangible reflection of change within the understanding and life structures of what has always been, you are missing an extraordinary opportunity to realize a new freedom from the known, static, perimeters of a shadowed, unconscious history; individually and collectively. Our spirituality is important to this planet. Learning to harness and work with energy enables us to gain insights and heightened awareness that ultimately liberates our creative vision toward a joyful and empowered humanity.

What I so love about the show is that it is my own portal of illumination, as well. I get to learn what I teach and be what I know through a continual spiral of light dancing with the consciousness and energy of all who are drawn to this medium. I am then guided into experience with them, enabling the frequencies of Ultimate Consciousness to perform intricate twists, turns and inverted maneuvers lifting Light to more Light. What I know as absolute is that this collapsing of duality into fluidity happens through the heart and beyond the control of the ego. It is a whole new level of insight and understanding into the mechanics of consciousness for me, to guide people energetically by watching and attuning to their energy through the language of Light.

My ever-deepening relationship with nature has taught me to see through illusion and awaken a truer vision than the one governed by thought and visible reality. Life is rarely what it appears to be yet many still make their decisions and follow guidance based on what is known or been experienced before. I know few that engage the fearless power of allowing the mystery to inform each next moment, which means to disarm the ego and trust in the nothingness, the pure essence of this moment, where utter peace resides. In nature, I experience no time, the ability to reflect and refract light and color. The language of nature, which is the language of light, enables me to come into and move around situations from a myriad of angles with perception that far surpasses the limitations of form, thus challenging rigid awareness and prompting the energy of change, ongoing. The Earth is a relentless expert at what she does, teaching balance, beauty, cooperation and the eternal rhythm of life sustaining itself, with love.

Yesterday, in the Shining Ones woods, I contemplated this awareness and continual illumination that renders me a greater level of freedom each day. And I asked, "am I now a teacher of nature?" I am talking so much to students, the listening audience of The New Human and friends about this pivotal piece. I do know nature, am confident and have a calm center of Self in that regard. But, I certainly did not set out to gain wisdom therein, that I could then articulate to the many. Then I got an "aha" moment of revelation that I strongly encourage you to take to heart. The extraterrestrial realms are entering through Gaia's field, because it is the one place within all that humanity has manifested and created, that remains pure in essence, without influence of an adulterated ego. This partnership is destined in our lifting to a peaceful planet. I have Shaman friends that don't really like be-ing in nature? This mystifies me. I imagine there are many hidden clauses within the ego's realm of influences that set us up in so many ways, caught in the snares of discrepancy within our own lives.

What we must truly begin to understand and grasp about energy is that one decision, one simple act connects us into a whole web of conscious and unconscious thought. So, if you are a light worker, i.e., you work with Light, and have your intent set on 5D Earth, you cannot justifiably maintain a cushion of safety and security, for instance, because you are then making the energetic statement that your fail safe is invested in the 3D foundation. That is not trust. That is not walking the talk. Now, I realize that this is hard core in principle but I wish to illumine here that we are preparing for a whole new world of existence, and the portal of ultimate shift closes in. There must, by necessity, be greater and greater numbers that are willing to cross the bridge to nothingness, impeccable with their actions and words, for the new grid-work and foundation of 5D existence to be laid for the many. We speak of Unity and the desire for peace but our actions speak duality and lack of imagination. We cannot keep playing by the old rules while simultaneously voicing the tenets of a new way of life. This is not teaching and way showing, this is an example of trust that is still very much governed by fear.

I am reminded of childhood when we are so often asked what we want to be when we grow up. The question feels huge and daunting from a perspective of life that is still so limited in experience and understanding. How in the world do you choose? We are entering a whole new level of awareness about who we are, why we are here and where our responsibility lies from the level of the Soul. We are lifting up, supported by a mystical illumination that shines a new light into all that was once perceived as valuable. To experience the world as energy and ourselves in partnership with that Divine Light, that Nirvana, that Christ Consciousness and Oneness, is to know that where It goes, what It experiences and sees and transcends into, that we are going with It. Then a whole new level of yes emerges, realizing that you already possess the greatest treasure of all, a life free from all that binds; only to reveal a joyfully authentic and new expression of what it means to be human.

Spiraling Dynamics

June 6, 2009

It stands to reason that when you have a species on the verge of Self-discovery, there will necessarily be a confluence of energy seeking a higher order. The photon energy currently radiating from the world of Spirit to the world of form is to provide for quantum change within all levels of being.

There is a binary process underway whereby the human aspect is being infused with the electromagnetic rays of its own potential, causing an assemblage point inversion of body, mind and spirit, of instinct, intellect and love. The necessary collapse of the infrastructure of our sensate reality is synonymous with the integral synergy of the egoic mind and heart consciousness.

As we do the work of world transformation, the historical power and perspective of the ego must not be underestimated, lest we lose sight of the Ultimate Vision we carry in our interior light. The ego wants what it wants when it wants it, and will stop at nothing to achieve its goals. Yet, Unity is a manifestation of love, all inclusive, uncompromising love.

When I look into the sacred symbiosis modeled so exquisitely for us by the Earth, I observe synchronous mutualism, a seamless cooperation and inherent trust of many diverse organisms living together in harmony. Nature has perfected the art of transparency. The life expressing there is authentic, a gnosis of perpetual creation and spiritual integrity that evolves not by agenda or mental objectives, but with selflessness and a consciousness of love. The purest and most powerful way to access Universal energies is to link with the power of the Earth.

As we make this great transition, each ultimately in the exact level of awareness and understanding aligned with their individual process, we ever have the opportunity to attain and maintain a greater lucidity of consciousness and heart-centered awareness. As long as we are still incarnate and influenced by the circuitry of egoic influence, we must vigilantly attend to the work of spiritual transformation, ongoing. It takes diligent responsibility to fulfill the Soul's purpose, to know your Self as an actualized Spiritual being. Our greatest work here is ultimately energetic: emotionally, physically and spiritually. To follow the golden strand that leads to the center of the Universe, is to practice Cosmic Consciousness, everyday. The foundation of our mastery within this plane... is love.

This last week, amidst the ever-present drama of 3D theatrics, I came across a blog entry by a fairly well known author and spiritual teacher. She was commenting on, responding to the "brutal assassination" of an abortion doctor, recently in the news. Her post went on to illuminate this event as an act of terror against women, in general. And where the Guidance took me in perspective is that though her arguments and logic may have had truth in them, the whole exercise was still engaging the old thought paradigm. She was, in effect, using her light and energy to draw attention to what is wrong. And when fragile psyches of varying degrees of awareness connect with negativity in any form, that negativity and shadow is then compounded within the collective unconscious. We cannot begin to fully appreciate how the force of photon energy is impacting the mental plane, but we can ever empower the evolutionary process by focusing our energy on what is right; trusting the higher frequencies to restore balance through Universal justice and the eyes of Truth.

As energy continues to amplify and quicken, our thoughts, emotions and feelings, conscious or not, will manifest into the spiral of what is both lifting and dismantling. Our consciousness and energy, as it has always done, will ultimately determine not only our personal future but the future of our planet within the whole evolutionary schemata. The New Spirituality being transmuted through the synergy of the planet's DNA and ours simultaneously is the fierce embodiment of 5D Earth even as we witness so much that denies it.

The New Human is the Light of a New Consciousness. Authentic spirituality requires a commitment to all life, all that is, and that includes the interior life of our reunification with Self. By anchoring peace within, on an individual level, peace will then be disseminated to all: as above, so below, as within, so without. Our totality, the highest potential of our mastery lies within, but we must be true to our Light and greatest point of power, the frequency and Oneness of Love.

Chord Of Remembrance, Becoming The Song

June 13, 2009

One of the many gifts of The New Human radio broadcast is the Unity gathering there. It is such a beautiful example of how simple and effortless life can be when we allow love to create the experience. The family of Light within The New Human audience is an eclectic gathering of political, Christian, metaphysical and scientifically persuaded beings of differing age, race, sex and sexual preferences. And it fills my heart. Through the influence and energy of Ultimate Consciousness, I am observing a small world forming, a microcosm of the greater world manifesting by the power and intelligence of Love. It is the new human being birthed, subtly yet ever so purposefully and with center, from the Unity of Cosmic Mind. And it is all so perfect.

The Light is calling us into a resonate field that expands us beyond seeming separation and differences, to an understanding and life chosen from the openness of scared space, the emptiness and totality of the mystery that is the Light. The void of the unknown beckons us to our joy, to beauty, to passion and our authentic nature. We have a great responsibility to be ourselves. We must learn the language of Light and do the work of extracting ourselves from all previous scripts. Everything is brand new, I feel this every day, and the new is being empowered by energies that are activating change in the way we connect with each other and life; the way we are supported within a continuous opening of the higher mind to all of Creation.

Each show, by necessity, becomes a deepening into the understanding and inevitability of the homo-luminous, our ability and capacity to transcend the perimeters set in place by an extremely polarized existence. We are here to define ourselves spiritually, within a duality that constantly reinforces our humanness. We so long for a sense of belonging and unity but we have come at that emptiness and void from a consciousness of separation. As we become more and more a part of the Greater Consciousness that is as committed to the process of integration as we are in our interior, we are lifted into new levels of awareness, stepping into a synchronistic flow of life. From that perspective we can begin to lovingly detach from the mind, allowing all the meaningful, interconnected Guidance of Higher Mind to wholly shift the perimeters of what we have come to trust as true.

The energy within the meditation for yesterday's show provided a powerful unification and alignment with the I AM dimension, Oneness. But, it also illumined the hyperdimensional stargate of the pineal gland, drawing more awareness to our ability to access many worlds and realities through an alignment of our breath with the Central Column of Light. In receiving this meditation, I kept seeing spirals and orbs and concentric rings of light, all interacting in this fluid wave of cooperative intelligence. As I went deeper into the stillness and nothingness of my Ajna, I had a panoramic view of the Cosmos... impressing upon me the extreme capability of this vast portal to transmit and receive lightwaves from the center of the galaxy. All within the computer that is our brain.

It mystifies me ongoing that a human can have such experiences (and I know I am not the only one) and yet, still cling so much to the things that have brought us pain, that have divided us and engendered greed and deception and an obsessive addiction to materialism. And what is emphasized here is that we have a choice of what kind of human we want to be, in each moment. The energies of celestial beings and heavenly bodies are within the cells of our bodies, within the intelligence of our hearts. We have the opportunity now to fully awaken to that and embrace ALL life, by willingly relinquishing the structures of indoctrinated belief, unconscious habit and fear based thought. Transformation means leaving the old behind. By learning to work with the new energies being offered to us, integrating and assimilating their essence, we are empowered to a place of fierce non-attachment.

A prominent theme being extended through the teaching of The New Human and highlighted yesterday through story, metaphor and guided experience is the critical objective of changing our bodies; working with the Luminous Self, to accommodate the changes of the Earth. Her form is changing and ours must change, too. We are being shaken up and synchronized by our own process for the purpose of taking us to a new place, awakening to a world of many realities, which is not possible within the confines and determination to cling to what is falling away. We are just beginning to energetically grasp the depth and awareness available to us now, and the potential of this apex of transformation to catapult us to an utterly unfathomable existence. But we must first surrender the egoic mind and the many false identities that for so long have been the glue of conditioned culture. The ego cannot go with us in our return back home.

I can say to you empirically that it is possible to embody and become one with the Earth, to feel a love and responsibility for all of humanity as a Mother feels for her children, along with the knowingness of what is best for them. Her desire and the ascent of her energy is that of harmony and peace. And she is singing us home. There is an entirely new energy field enveloping the planet, a gossamer web of power and balance comprised of the feminine principle and Light. And powerful it is, a star tetrahedron of shimmering light frequencies that carry a vibrational hum. It is the heartbeat of the Goddess activating a new center of being capable of balancing the chaos and disharmony of our fearful ignorance. We must move in unison with her, willingly and cooperatively stepping up vibrationally into her merkabah of 5D Earth.

We are in preparation for a new vibration of Light in 2012. This now of our individual and global expansion is to prepare us energetically for what is to come. As vibrationally aware and empowered beings, we will no longer need the structures of support we have long depended on for false security. By attuning to nature and the Goddess, you hear a new language of Life, becoming invisible to all that is in shadow and thus, guided by a song, harmony and vibration that is in the rocks and trees and animals and stars; the Symphony of the Spheres; the frequency of Love.

The New Human is a consciousness of Mastery. It is a return to the innocence, wonder, intelligence and freedom of Love. To live life from a center of stillness, calm, no thought and non-attachment is to live free, with no boundaries. Then all of reality shifts. This is the path of becoming an authentic human, leading to the birth of the new human, the homo-luminous, in 2012. Who will you be in just two and half short years? Blessed and empowered are we to choose.

The New Landscape of the Brain

June 20, 2009

"Listen. Can you hear it? The music. I can hear it everywhere, in the wind, in the air, in the Light. It's all around us. All you have to do is open yourself up, all you have to do is listen."

The above quote is from the movie August Rush. Imagine my gratitude, within so many dimensions, when a friend gifted me the experience of this movie last night, right in the midst of the theme and emphasis of sound, frequency and Light that we have been discussing on the show for the last few weeks. It is as if the world is at long last, waking up to itself with a harmonious connection between all living things, the song that all of life knows. The synchronicities are amplifying such that we barely register a conscious thought before we're soon presented with a series of parallel phenomena, magnifying our every desire into a synergy of harmonious flow with the world around us.

Within the consciousness of mastery that is the new human, there is a growing realization of just how connected we truly are; that out there, a series of higher tones and scalar harmonics, governed by the laws of physics and mysterious worlds beyond, are lifting us to a new spiral of creation, an overtone, energy wavelength that we are capable of attuning to through the heart and an increasingly transformational frequency of love. Life is righting itself. The old world no longer exists energetically because the cellular structure of all life form on our planet has been altered, such that, the conditioned, exclusive, regimented world that we have come to understand as life, no longer exists! Our work now, is energetic, lifting ourselves up to the new world of light on the horizon.

The reason we are positioned to lift to a mass enlightenment in 2012 is that there will be a considerable shift in yin/yang polarity, favoring the front side of the brain. The Mayan Calendar tells us that the cosmic polarity that has, through our history, dominated the human mind will be increasingly conducive to a shift. As we draw ever nearer to the enigma that is 2012, more and more light is falling onto the frontal lobe, humanity is pivoting out of the shadow of unconscious creation to a time when the 7th chakra opens to the full capacity of a translucent mind.

I find this so fascinating and magical because this is all being lovingly mirrored for us within the Earth's process, her metamorphosis, and willingness to "turn up the volume" for our edification. Human beings have gone through different magnetic orientations of consciousness that are, level by level, coming into play in the evolution of consciousness. We are shifting to a higher octave of being, spontaneously changing within our genetics by our ability to attune to the Earth and let go of our attachment to the hollow shell that is the world of form.

I shared a meditation in today's show (6/20/09) that came to me in nature. It is a gateway meditation meant to take you deep into the void of the pineal gland vortex. The journey of this exercise is a way to bring what I experience in nature, what I see and feel and hear in the elements, into everyday consciousness and practice. The energies are talking to us, telling us how to change the course we are on, how to heal our bodies, free our mind, align with Oneness and understand the new rules of ancient wisdom that will guide us back to peace and harmony for our world. I can say to you that the Earth Song is especially sweet right now. When you learn to attune to her you are transported back to innocence, a child-like receptivity and fluid connection to all existence, able to connect with your personal sound frequency, the song of your birth.

Last week I took two little girls to the local Nature Center. The peahen had just hatched 5 chicks and was freely exploring the open grounds within the complex, delighting all the onlookers with her brood. And as we watched the babies shadowing the mama up and down the banks, behind trees, over the sidewalks and into the tall grasses, the three year old asked me why the babies were following the peahen around like that. And I told her that the mama peahen was showing her babies how to be in the world, how to find food and take care of themselves, what to trust and how to be safe so that they could grow strong and have a beautiful life.

And as I heard that simple reflection to a child, I could easily step back from the moment and apply that same simplicity to the intended relationship between the Earth Mother and the human race. Vibrationally, within the folds of harmony, peace, heart -centered consciousness and joy, the Earth is here for us. Everything that we need to know and understand and learn and surrender to can be found within the layers of her eternal wisdom. When I gaze out my window to the resilient, timeless beauty that is her world within so much that is superficial and soulless within ours, I feel the full impact of grace, that we ever have the choice of what life and existence we want to attune to as a species.

What I know to be true, because of the inexplicable nature of our planet to adjust the frequencies within our mind and heart, is that she holds the key to the New Crystalline Grid of 5D Earth and connectivity. The resonate vibration of all living things is being augmented for the attunement of all consciousness to heightened levels of existence. We are in an upward spiral within which a luminous, radiant energy is shining light on a new part of our brain where we have always been authentic, free, living in abundance, without disease or physical decline, co-creating in Communities of Light: loving the Earth, loving each other.

In order to realize the potential of our journey, we must be willing to LET GO through the tumultuous, unknown of change, knowing that the insight, wisdom and fortitude needed in all possible scenarios, is within us, as it is within the Mother. She is our Soul Compass. Our song is within her song. Our new life within her new life and the sound, color and Light of her heart is showing us the way back to our own and the heart of all Creation. The whole of the Cosmos is cooperating with her contraction as she determines to give birth to higher levels of Oneness and love.

Each of us has an intended transformation within this incarnation, a predetermined course that is our spiritual destiny. We will arrive right on time, right where we are meant to be. That is Truth. The only variable is what we give ourselves to along the way, how we choose to love and the level of exquisite JOY we allow into our experience and heart. The birth of the new human, the homoluminous, has always been about the interior and our relationship with the mystery. The light, color and Intelligence of many worlds hums in the stillness of our inner-being. When we have fully surrendered to that, beyond mind, beyond thought, beyond the ego and fear, then the resonate harmony of this rare blue planet will once again, be love. One Love. One planet. One people. One Life, Complete and Free.

A Day Out Of Time

June 27, 2009

I was sitting by a bubbling brook, in the cool shade of some majestic trees. There were huge boulders placed randomly around me in this particular section of woods. I had come to nature to sit and be still and listen intentfully to the energies, the tones of silence and the crystal light essence that so easily penetrates the auric field in nature; allowing the mystery to re-order the mind with timeless truths.

Every Friday before the show, I give the day totally to the spiritual realm in preparation for The New Human energies. I surrender my 3D reality to the mystery and allow the Guidance to foresee the audience, oversee the whole of who will be present, and prepare the space for mental, physical and spiritual receiving. It is a sacred time within which there is no need, no directing, only willingness, openness and deep gratitude for all that is.

And as I sat there in the gentleness of peace, a ray of sunshine broke through the lush canopy of nature and streamed light onto the dancing waters below, forming a fluid, shimmering heart, a foot and half in diameter. Now, just "how" the Light was able to manipulate the branches and leaves of the trees above, such that, they could assist in orchestrating this outline of the Creator's love, is beyond reason. But the fullness of its meaning and purpose within the frequency of this teaching I have stepped in to steward, spiraled into my heart. It was Ultimate Consciousness at its finest, shapeshifting reality to illumine my own.

As the veils continue to thin and the light crescendos alongside the dismantling of form and what is known, it is for each of us to present our own unique versions of Self, the authentic expression and heart resonance of who we incarnated within this time to be; a genuine reflection within so much that has been taken on and experienced and made to come undone by the Laws of Sacred Remembrance. When I view humanity through my own clear seeing, I see a landscape of crystals just now waking up to the internal structure that has carried them through so much density. Greater still, I feel the Earth's Crystal Grid as it pivots into its rightful place within the Cosmos, generously and unwaveringly infusing our new minds and new bodies with the frequencies of our future.

Since the fortuitous opening on the Solstice last week, there is much awe and celebration within the coinciding chaos of the 3D reality. We are realizing the fruits of our spiritual labors with meaningful manifestations and astounding accelerations within everyday experience. And what I want to interject within the upsweep of what we are seeing and experiencing within linear expressions, is that the new and heightened manifestation energies are being reflected in the more nebulous realms of seeing, awareness, insights and inner knowing, as well. Our manifesting abilities are lifting both horizontally and vertically; the art of discernment being greatly amplified. So, it is not just about what we literally see in our everyday reality that reflects these new energies. It is about the unseen connectors of our future Self, peering through the veil at us, such that, a new peace and vision completely unrelated to this now, is taking up residence in the heart.

I am finding a whole new level of serenity and allowing settle in as I witness the metamorphosis of those who are experiencing the New Human energies. And as I have expressed on the show, it is more than the words that the listening audience hears or that the readers take in intellectually, it is about the energy and light and supreme love that this ancient teaching exudes. Like a seed of the finest frequency safely planted within the heart, the haunting melody of a mystical world of color, sound, light and higher intelligence is shifting the focus of the mind to a new seat of power.

It is so very important in this Now to hold the vision and awareness of what is ultimately true and destined for this species. We have a responsibility as varying reflections of Ultimate Consciousness, to steer what is deviating energetically from perfection, back to center and the power of love. It is that simple. It is one thing if we are seeing and calculating the potential of a bleak outcome for this unprecedented ascent, but it is a disservice to the Collective of what remains unsettled, to predict and voice into the unformed realm, more separation and duality. Now is not the time to stray from love's power.

We have energetically sidestepped so many prophecies of ungovernable finality and we did so, as a Collective, by attuning our minds and hearts to the mystery; learning to trust what we feel and intuit with the heart. We must be mindful and respectful of the fact that what we personally hold as belief, we are ever perceiving in reality as a way to validate our own awareness. This is spiritual integrity and a fluid, ever mutating invitation, even as we use our high minds to tap into the future, to go back into the heart's intelligence and embrace our own power to return ALL to love, once again.

We have so many mirrors reflecting within today's pivoting world, where and who we have been. The untimely, unnecessary death of Michael Jackson, and the egregiously perpetual deception of our health care system to assist the unaware toward decline versus regeneration, just begin to touch the surface of how we have all participated with varying degrees in the separation of body and consciousness. We are pressed, in the Now of our future, to redefine the way we interact with the world and each other. We are only prisoners of our own thoughts. Everything else is a realm of magic. And we have the power and vibrational assistance, within this current portal of evolutionary ascent, to engage intelligent action every day, removing ourselves from the illusion, the downward spiral and the things that steal our luminosity. It is essential in continuing to assimilate what is coming in, to simultaneously release the density that will keep you from functioning fully at each new level. No matter where you are in the process, you can engage the energy of cooperative partnership by breaking routines in your reality, spending more time in stillness, creativity, and nature and determining to stop participating in anything that diminishes your joy. Densities held at a cellular level cannot be carried forth to the levels of reality we are spiraling to as a species.

I shared an experience on the show that is just SO telling of where we are as a humanity; what we have come through and how admired and loved we are for our impeccable intent. The higher realms are very much present, participating and engaging the process we're opening up to at this time. If you were not able to catch the show live yesterday, I encourage you to do so, but basically, I was transported to a place of no time. Even as I stood, very grounded in the midst of this experience and reality, I was lifted to an in-between dimension that was not a day, or month or year within a certain location or place, it was an energetic reality wherein hundreds of thousands of masters gathered around me to acknowledge what is being done on this plane to activate the energies of peace.

We must continue to allow the process to direct us toward this peace, toward Unity Consciousness, compassionate love and fierce surrender to our hearts. As we get out of the way and cease trying to direct the process, where it is going and what the end result will be, we can begin to savor the experience of transformation and the beautiful energies that are spiraling within and without and through it ALL. The motion of ascension is a perpetual motion that will manifest very naturally in its own time. We just need to let go, get out of the way and begin practicing and being the wisdom of the new human, grounding those perceptions ad understandings and steps into our everyday reality.

There was a stillness behind the show yesterday that exemplified the prism shift of these new energies. Those who have been with the show for months and/or read the book expressed that the love behind this template has gifted them a huge change in thinking, that they feel more open and free and have developed an essential trust in the Universe. I imagine that is the truest barometer of peace; a consciousness and energy that allows us to be utterly still within all that is fleeting, transient and bound. This new human paradigm is a timelessness of genuine existence wherein we trust the magnitude of the Light within us, and Love above all else.

Inspired Freedom

July 4, 2009

I was posed the question earlier this week, who some of my heroes are. And to my surprise, without thought, I listed myself among those who have inspired me to reach beyond. Undoubtedly, this is a time of developing unwavering trust in ourselves, confidence in who we are and the Light we came to bring to the world. It is a time of holding ourselves, and Life, to a higher standard; one that embraces the responsibility we all have to steward future generations toward peace, harmony and love. We are being cellularly formed and reformed, ongoing, by our willingness to change historically ingrained mindsets, awakening to the awareness that this whole wondrous hologram we know as reality is simply a magnificent reflection of self. As the planet returns to her rightful place of spiritual balance, we are being offered the opportunity to re-mind our limited, mistaken identification with form and be in the joy of one born anew into a realm of heart-centered consciousness and clear seeing love.

Yesterday was a special, holiday broadcast of *The New Human*. All week, leading up to the fourth of July, I gave myself and focus, my observer and intent over to the higher realms in consideration of what it means to be free. And through story of everyday existence and expanding awareness, the show, more than anything, reflected how much freedom there is between the higher realms and those of us incarnate; that even as a higher intelligence guides and informs us, serving as our conscious compass, so too does it allow for an intense descent into various levels of awareness, with linear time as our transport into a world of merging polarities.

The first thing that I was compelled to do right after the show was to lie down for about thirty minutes. There was a sense of just wanting to savor the energies that were present, allowing them the space to fully ground into this dimension of awareness and understanding. I then went to the Shining Ones woods and was richly aligned with some out of the ordinary animal encounters, including eye-to-eye contact with both bear and owl. It was not lost on me how these two animals appeared to reinforce the teaching and new thought paradigm we touched upon in this day of honoring freedom. It is clear that we are emerging at a place where many worlds intersect. As the veils continue to thin and the magnetic fields to weaken, more mysteries and phenomena will be revealed to those with open minds and the heart of a child. It is time, as a species, to shift our awareness to the greater mystery of a duality that is an infinite multiplicity of quantum elements, of geometry and color and light and sound right alongside the human conditioning of emotion, behavior, action and thought. Light is the geometry of existence and within its infinitely expanding and interconnected web, an entirely new frequency and consciousness of LOVE is forming a new stratum of planet Earth.

At this time of transformational liberties, the new human template serves as the beginning of a world where all will find fulfillment of their dreams and desires and longing for Unity. We are deepening in the understanding each day, that life is a shared experience founded on trust. And as we mature as a species, we see this time of metamorphosis as our opportunity to become co-creators in a reality of experience that is meshed together in vibrating fields of infinitely expanding, interconnected points of Oneness. The nature of being at this dimensional level of conscious awareness is love and those awakening to new minds are decidedly heart centered and determined to stand up for lives of meaningful purpose.

So what does love and consciousness have to do with freedom? In earlier times on our planet, humanity, like the animal kingdom and nature, was strongly connected to the luminous web, the song of One Life. We made decisions through our attunement to hypercommunication abilities such as intuition, inspiration, imagination, remote healing and sensing, and telepathic exchange. These powers and gifts are awakening once again as we ascend through the lightwaves of dimensional initiation, to a new octave of being. I shared stories of the dreamtime collapsing into real-time and interspecies, mind to mind communication, of an everyday flow of experience where we can actually reach through dimensions and sing energy to us by attuning to the sounds and tones within the overall vibration of Creation. When time and distance is understood as holographic in nature, Creation and our place within it, is unlimited. Somehow, by grace or love, harmonic adaptation or a fierce determination to re-member ourselves back into our rightful kinship with the stars, the resistance to hearing and seeing has lessened and we are attuning to the constant stream of messages from the realm of Light.

This is a time of decision-making. Making decisions that are about love and genuine relationship, inspired living and the creation of joy over the insistence of egoic reaction and thought controlled existence, are essential in ascending to a future where we care less and less about things and false power and more and more about spiritual freedom and each other. The 5D World of our potential and destiny is not subject to the temporal perimeters of density and polarity and neither is the new human that will be residing there. A mind free from emotional debris and fearful imaginings is one that knows only this moment. Our wholeness and peace is not about what we achieve, the "ideal" of our mental constructs and imaginings or the destination upon which we long, at last, to arrive.

Life, this experience, is about this moment and how freely you can be in it - in your joy and with loving detachment. It is the essence of our lives here, how we love and forgive and practice compassion, the awareness and understanding we bring to all experience and relationship that determines our mastery and true level of freedom. We will never be able to extinguish the corruption and evils within this duality, but our alliance and trust in the vitality and beauty of the Light assures its exalted contrast against any and all shadow.

We must be able to attune vibrationally to anything that comes into our reality, or shift away from it with quickened lucidity. Each successive level of our expansion is dependent upon our ability to mirror the Creator's mind and love. As the Earth continues her pivot to her rightful position in the multiverse, we have the opening and opportunity to shift as well from a bound, outer directed people to an internally driven knowingness of who we are and why we are here. There is no reason why we cannot understand who we truly are. Every individual on the planet is equally empowered. With awakened minds and open hearts, with intuition and breath and a courageous awareness of Self, we are awakening codes of light to assist the whole of humanity in advancing to higher mind technologies and the power of love. That is evolution and the true measure of freedom.

Radiant Wisdom

July 11, 2009

There is such joy and meaningful understanding when you can wake up each day, not only knowing, but feeling that who you were the day before, your actions and thoughts and love, made the current day brand new. That each day, you are no longer the same person as you were even moments before, because you are no longer participating in the world of form but in partnership with the world of Light.

Yesterday's show had many magical elements. It is so curious and wondrous for me to witness and experience what occurs each week, because what transpires within the hour is as fresh and new for me as it is the listening audience. I am fully aware, especially when I go to the Shining One's Woods after the show and am then shown the connective threads, that whatever comes up or is addressed in the show is being energetically and intentionally influenced through the quantum field, independent of time and space. In this case, the little Indigo I spoke of in the show, has now shifted vibrationally, the trauma that she has been undergoing physically, she is now free from. All the energies of everyone present, within all dimensions, contributed to that.

When I was in the woods after the show, there was a lot of stillness. The Presence and peace was palpable. What is being impressed upon me, is that as greater numbers continue to move up to the 4th dimension and learn to reside there full time, that they will need to get more and more of their sustenance from the Zero Point Field. I am aware of (and have been aligning my daily reality with this principle increasingly so over the course of this year) that we can indeed draw any missing nutrients within our physical structures from this ultimate source. This occurs naturally and effortlessly in alignment with our own vibrational attunements. As we continue to lighten up our energy bodies, it will be increasingly challenging to get comparable, sustainable sustenance from the 3rd dimension.

I had a conversation this morning with a listener that illuminated what is happening within the overall template of The New Human Paradigm. So much is dependent upon our ability to create from and interact with the current shift as vibrationally sovereign. Much of the changes that are taking place within our cellular structure are such that there will increasingly be no reliable frame of reference for what we are experiencing and stepping into. We are in the process of integrating the momentum of change as a population, all the while learning to trust in and rely upon our own interior process. The only way to expand and grow within these rarified energies is to find your way through the interior - observing the energy of all things - and then continually taking a strategic step based on that. It is naive to imagine or assume that you can do things the way you always have and take uniformed liberties with your personal energy field and how that is influenced by the energy of persons and things in your environment. We must be meticulous and very wise in how we are using, spending and nurturing our energy in each moment and in so doing, the energy (Source, pure Guidance, Gnosis, the Zero Point Field) becomes the sustenance and "map" of our destiny.

Today in the woods I felt the presence of Lord Sananda so strongly, he might as well have been walking beside me - (and perhaps was!!!) Did he not say to us, "I am always with you, never absent to anyone in any situation?" And the wisdom and insight that he shared with my consciousness is that all the really great Masters knew that it is in innocence (which means without thought) stillness and pure energy that our true power lays! These beings who mastered the lower realms of consciousness existed only in the moment and from an impeccable and confident center. There was no need to question or second-guess what another was doing. They were not concerned with how their teachings and wisdom would spread because they had surrendered to a higher understanding of how consciousness and energy works. They lived lives that many would deem unstable by today's standard, without concern for themselves, who would follow them or revere them, love them or remember them. They just were. They RADIATED truth and didn't really need to say a WORD - you just wanted to be around them. And that was because their consciousness and energy was heart centered.

Their lives and what they gave, the faith they had in humanity, was for the purpose of creating an energetic template more powerful than the illusion and disillusionment created by the egoic mind. The example the great ones set for us was how to live free from thought, in only the present moment, knowing and trusting energy and following the Creator's impulse vs the mental plane of reasoning. Their lives and energy today serves as a Pilot Wave, a vibrational scout that they sent into the future generations of planet Earth for us to draw upon and embody in our yearning and intent to get back home.

In truth, they have never gone from us - they reside in parallel existences that are very much available to us if we choose the way of love over fear, of heart's intelligence over mental constructs and compassionate objectivity for a world that has long existed in the pain of its own creation. Within the current spiral of our collective evolution, we are ideally positioned to choose which version of the world we want to live in and then do everything in our power, (and everything is within our power), to continually lift our vibration to the highest potential within ourselves, each other and the world. It is not about who is left with the gold after the great Mother completes her metamorphosis, it is about how many can be empowered to join in the Golden Cities of future Earth.

The spirituality of the new Earth is one in which each day is an amalgam of intelligent action and high minded principle where we participate with each other and all form as a fragile, endangered resource. It is not some idealistic fantasy of practice that is available and fulfilling to some but secondary to what has been a consensus reality of separation and isolation. If we are to be Unity, we must behave as Unity. What we do, what laws we are governed by and beliefs we uphold, affects the whole of Creation in ways great and small, for the better or for worse. That is the power that was entrusted to us, the new humans of future earth. Anything in your world that is static, of diminished joy or a finite replica for what could be imagined and creatively unleashed, allow it to move on with the remnants of 3D Earth, so that you can line up with and receive the new that is coming into view. We will know what is true by the light it emits. Just as you will be known throughout the Universe, by the Light you dared to step into.

Vertical Trust, The Shift To Mastery

July 18, 2009

There was great movement within the momentum of the show yesterday and the impact it is having on personal awareness. I received several correspondences in the hours immediately after the broadcast and each person, from so many different walks of life and beliefs and understandings of spiritual phenomena, all communicated the same basic response; a supreme desire to feel and be the experience that is truly theirs. There was such joy expressed over the possibility, which the new human energies so generously allow for, that we can be unique, uninhibited beings with the complete freedom to experience this life in totality rather than through the filter of conditioned, uniformed response. Many are feeling and acting upon a renewed vitality with the return of wonder, brilliance in everyday experience and the essential balance of body, mind and spirit.

As a species, we are in a perpetual spiral that is serving to lift us up, moving us from a shadowed existence into a fierce determination to KNOW SELF and align that knowing with a supreme trust in Life, in all of Creation, and in Love above and beyond all else. The return back home that is often illumined within spiritual wisdom is really about a return to innocence, with the understanding that the ultimate creation for this humanity is and has always been, the spiritualization of Life on Earth. The living organism that is this rare blue planet and all her sentient beings began this whole existence as spiritual essence, pure, sovereign and seeded with the intelligence and heart centered consciousness to transform a plane of duality back to its original form. Within the momentum of this evolutionary spiral is the realization that there is no separation, no time or distance that would indicate other, only this ongoing moment that affords us the unconditional invitation to be brand new.

Yesterday, shortly after the show I went to the Shining Ones Woods to just marinate in the love and forward motion of the rarified existence we know today. The week leading up to the show was replete with encounters and experiences that are occurring around the globe to awaken spiritual transformations in all who will let go and be still enough to receive the impetus.

When I shared some of the ongoing phenomena that I experience in these woods, I emphasized the wisdom in the Guidance consistently guiding me into the mystery via a directional pull to the left. The message being that when we are in a state of absolute receptivity, independent of our mental censorship, the Divine Feminine within is able to align with Its mirror in the higher realms, turning the mundane into a reflection of the many realities and worlds we have access to. I encourage you to relax into the possibility that my shared experiences of entering deep space through an Earth Portal, of ancient civilizations appearing within this dimension and the high magic of entire realities appearing and disappearing from awareness, are but beckoning glimpses into the true essence of Oneness.

I was completely charmed by the persistent and playful deja-vu moments when I found myself on a certain section of trail, with no awareness of having covered the trail that got me to that point. And then in the next instance having the distinct feeling that the section of trail I was walking on, I had just covered several minutes before. There is just sheer joy and a constant sense of "okay-ness" when you step into the vibration of reciprocity that accompanies the "I AM" center of awareness. There must necessarily be balance between our understanding of and participation with the higher planes of existence, even as we dance with the allure of the material plane. Ever cognizant of the truth that in the Mystery lies our greatest potential as Life waking up to Itself.

The New Human is about an assemblage point shift that redirects our focus and priorities from a linear perspective that simply recycles thought and experience into different versions of the same occurrence, to a vertical alignment that allows for a completely new possibility and experience within the very well worn groove of human behavior and thought. The brain is capable of extraordinary things when it is clear. We are endowed with so many gifts that we've surrendered to the ordinary, to sameness and inertia within a consensus reality that has lost touch with the magic of imagination! Ultimately, what delivers us from a dualistic paradigm of unconscious, conditioned response is a determined shift from the identity of seeker, one always looking outside of self for validation and assurance... to knower. This is the beginning of a perfect equipoise between the power of the Divine Masculine and the sublime love of the Divine Feminine. We must stop moving through this existence autocratically and embrace the uncertain fluidity of one in tune with all of Life.

Our Soul's initiative and greatest desire is to fulfill our own unique purpose here, which in turn, births Heaven into the everyday existence of all beings. We have to believe that. In wholeness, in our joy and finally, in unity, we can create something very beautiful and lasting and positive for the future of this planet, something that reflects the highest light and potential of our authentic nature, which is fearless in its trust in love. I ask my Soul everyday how I am doing, if I am mirroring the Love and Trust IT has in me to radiate my Light out into the world. Surely that question alone opens up the attainment of its desire. I am equally humbled and comforted each day in the knowingness that to the degree we have been broken, is the potential for ultimate wholeness, that in the depths of our greatest sorrow is an equal measure of bliss and that each time my mind questions my fearless reach into the unknown of existence, that my heart reaches a new level of freedom.

We are not there yet beloveds... we still have much work to do, and the greater portion of that is within the thoughts and beliefs we still hold about our true essence. We are being lovingly empowered right now, in this moment within all Eternity, to free our minds from the tyranny of disbelief. We are stepping into a new frequency of our own divine nature where manifesting dreams and ideas, comes effortlessly by focusing our intentions UP! We have a new found strength, forged in the collective misunderstanding of our lives here, to finally and forever let go of the myth that we were ever separate. Everything you do matters. We are poised, as a species, on the edge of a whole new experience of life and who we are in it. There is an unconditional invitation to step into the Isness of Christ Consciousness and allow, allow, allow, the transformations and transmutations taking place. The outcome will likely be different than anything we expected or could imagine, but within the Light of Love, it will be the realization of Peace.

Peering Of The Edge

July 25, 2009

I can hear their voice long before I see them... the hauntingly piercing call of the hawk. Shortly after the show I headed to the woods and was guided to a section of forest where I rarely go. I had to cross over two mountains to get there, each time, descending deeper and deeper into the mystery; virgin nature, unspoiled energetics. Eventually I came to a giant tree that had fallen down, too heavy for the mountainside soil that had receded at its roots. And though much nature in the form of tall weeds and looping vines had grown up all around it, I knew I was to somehow climb up on that tree. The position of elevation and panorama that the aspired lookout afforded me made the entire trek to this magical spot worthwhile.

The Shining Ones are moving in so much closer to the human element, I am feeling this all the time now. Not closer to me, as I have always felt them intimately, but more into the front line of the current spiral of humanity's evolution and attunement, which they have come to assist with. Just as human beings are implements of a divine plan, the Shining Ones are instrumental in preparing humanity for that inevitable fulfillment. They are positioning themselves with great strategy and care and the first awareness I had when I was finally perched about 6 feet off the ground on this fallen tree, was of them. I was also keenly aware of many from the animal kingdom watching me from hidden places. So I began to tone, sing, loudly, because I know that the sound of my voice is vibrationally attuned to the harmonics of the natural world, and this would lift the experience to one of assurance and peace for both the animal kingdom and me, in the middle of such wilderness. I toned and radiated my heart energy and gratitude to ALL that was present with me and set an intention for these words I am sharing with you now. Then I stood perfectly still.

Within moments, I heard the cry of a hawk coming directly from my left. I had the thought, "could it be responding to the tones and frequencies of 'my' call?" And no sooner did I register that thought, than another hawk, exactly to my right, responded to the one on my left. And there I stood, in this precarious position of center that I had been guided so surreptitiously to, with these two regal messengers and visionaries of the air singing my heart and intent back to me. And we were all One.

This entire week of the Solar Eclipse has been a stunning reflection of how these new energies are transforming the way we experience life. Synchronistic opportunities reaching across infinite distances connecting otherwise strangers in spiritually dynamic, co-creative endeavors, relationships constantly shifting toward authentic alignments, doors simultaneously opening and closing. It is the energy of pure magic and it is a realm the Light beckons us to with fervor, if we would but listen. I know, trust, believe, in my heart that there are so many more people attuned to spiritual life than those who dare to give voice to and actualize it in their experience; in how they interact with their reality and who they are to the world. On four separate occasions just this last week I have had four different people comment to me how fearless I am, how brave to speak about the mystery so unapologetically. In response, I might borrow a line from *The Little Prince*: "Here is my secret, it is very simple. I see with my heart, everything that is essential." And I follow that unwaveringly.

One of the things I talked to the Light about today as I climbed over those two mountain passes, was how to describe the mystery to those who have never felt it, experienced it and even fear it? How can we move people more and more into the energy of life, the innocence of pure essence, and out of so much that is predictable and conditioned? How can we get back to the natural flow of existence that is in harmony with all things and all beings, when so many are dependent upon and cling to the very things that have led to such an egregious state of imbalance for this planet? With so much progress toward unity and compassion evidenced within so many facets of 21st century humanity, we still very much dwell in the energy of separation, compartmentalizing our lives into safe and orderly constructs, projecting into the future that it will more than likely be but a different version of the same. It just occurs to me so strongly that if more could feel the Mystery, the freedom and authentic sovereignty of beingness that envelopes you there, that much more actualized spirituality would come to pass. The Mystery is in the hawk's cry to creation, it dances in the Northern Lights and rises with the Sun over the Eastern horizon. It explains why some of us were born with fair skin and some dark, why some can defy life and live many decades while other beings never make it out of the womb. The wonder of our world today is that we are positioned now to not just fathom the mysteries of the world, but to become them. Yet we must let go of our mental proclivity. Surely the majority would agree that we don't live in a reasonable world! Why would we continue to rely on logic and "sound reasoning" and the promises and actions of a paradigm that has continually led us astray, to decide the fate of our future?

Within my work and understanding of the world of energy, I am constantly observing the predilection of humanity to remain in their thoughts, to be guided by and fed by, reinvented by and deceived by thought; again and again and again. Just to test the waters of how we are doing with the whole unity and oneness and loving one another thing, I periodically post statements about being supportive of our President, of seeing his victory within the many trials he has inherited from his fellow species. And there is always a noticeable dearth of those willing to chime in and agree that our belief in his efforts matter. And what I want to expound upon here is that I am not making a personal statement about my party or politics or who I did or did not vote for, I am lifting the view to the greater possibility that God is a God of all things; and that this man, who is now in the greatest position of power in our nation, is there by the grace of One God. A God endeavoring to get all Its children on board with change and that to allow that change, we must be it. In ALL that we do and are, we must acknowledge, give voice to and model a new level of existence our everyday choices within life. As the smallest and wisest among us would say, "don't love me with your words and promises, love me by your actions."

We also talked a lot about innocence in yesterday's broadcast of *The New Human*. Innocence, far from being naiveté or ignorance, is a quality of pure essence, and interior alignment with the Divine. It is an undiluted receivership to the natural phenomena and wonder of the world that sees everything and everyone not as they have been conditioned to be, but as they are. I challenged the listener to consider that the vibration of innocence is a true source of power because it allows us to move free from thought, without judgment and expectation based on preconditioned agenda, able to embrace each moment with wonder and a full and fearless heart. We came from a realm of no boundaries, a world of interdependent, interconnected Unity with the awareness that everything we do matters in the light of all Eternity. We came empowered with the remembrance and confidence that we could, indeed, recreate that Unity within a plane of extreme polarization. I am up for that, are you?

This journey to awakened consciousness that we are all on together, is for the purpose of ascending together, lifting ourselves up to higher levels of existence in unison and cooperation with the Earth Mother. There is so much Presence, beings of High Light and experiential wisdom co-creating with us, side by side, toward a new day for planet Earth. Be fierce in your determination to know your Self beyond this here and now, to acknowledge that everything is different for the species we are today and that in our love, in the innocence of our heart's lucidity, we can realize an even greater humanity for the species of future Earths, unfolding.

In The Company Of One

August 1, 2009

There is a sonic hum that I am increasingly transfixed by, each day it grows louder and louder to my conscious awareness. I hear the harmony of it at the center of all my activities, in the midst of nature, in the cacophony of traffic on a busy afternoon, in the flight of the hummingbirds as they zoom outside my window and in the silence of my interior when I make time for stillness in my world. When I tune into this vibrational sweetness, every thought, every question, every uncertainty and all unknown transforms into a measure of undisturbed peace. I know unequivocally that it is the song of the Great Mother and that she, along with the entire Cosmos, is singing of a new life, for you and for me and our planet.

Yesterday's show just felt like a love song to me. And it wasn't about what I said or how I expressed the information that I was sharing. (Well, maybe just a little.) But more importantly, it was about the vibration of Unity that laced its way through every moment, lifting our conscious thoughts to the awareness of attunement with the rhythm of Creation. This show, that focused on the necessary changes occurring in our bodies and minds, perceptions and understanding of who we are, was elevated to a place where the forces of nature joined into the dance and expression of just how interconnected in consciousness and energy life on this planet truly is. Not only did the animal kingdom participate in the show yesterday with glorious exuberance, but the energies of the wren and squirrel were in perfect alignment with what the Guidance was expressing through me in each moment. It is time to be bold and unapologetic in who we are, get real with ourselves about the current focus of our reality and then get busy with the steps and mastery of those things that will allow us to step out of the mind and into the heart, where all of life is brand new. Indeed, all memory and judgment of the past can give way now to gratitude and humility by a species that has begun the journey home.

All this past week, there has just been a constant ripple of new, the energy and momentum of change pouring into a seemingly unmoving reality! I can feel this consciousness and energy of pure Life, pure Love, a strength and clarity and beauty within all things just fill my whole being and every cell of my body, with radiance. And I know that this ever-growing audience of listeners and participators felt this peace, as well. What is beginning to happen is that we are connecting through our cellular memory, recognizing each other by the personal tone of authenticity within. Anytime you can partake in an experience where nothing else seems to matter to the moment than to be fully in that moment, an experience where your body relaxes and you feel the joy of just being and the pull of your own desire to know Oneness, rest assured that Ultimate Consciousness is present, allowing Love to seal everyone and everything up in an essence that just plain inspires.

It did not surprise me in the least as I drove to the woods shortly after the show, that I saw not one, not two, but three different families with loaded up vehicles, in the process of moving. Now, the naysayer and mental deliberator amongst us might say, "it was Saturday afternoon DeAnne, people move on Saturday, what is so divine about that?" But what I know and recognized is that on any given day, I go to many different woods and can drive several different routes to get there. But on this day and on the path that I chose, the Light reflected back to me what my personal reality of late and the message of the show is impressing about the dynamic enveloping the whole of humanity and our planet at this time. We are moving! All of us, individually and collectively, to a new experience of life, a new understanding of who we are in that life, and the very new abilities that have been set free from the limitation of thought and belief and fear. And with that move in consciousness and energy to a greater possibility for the humanity of this time, we are granted a new freedom to live as the highest expression of our potential, liberated by the great Light of the Creator's love for us all.

Everything is changing. Reality is expanding and the foundation we have been granted to now build upon is brand new. This now is all about learning to be with these new energies, to work with them, talk with them and communicate with them as Presence, because they are. I've always seen the possibility of more than one reality existing side by side, a hologram of infinite possibility that reflects not only our humanity and the complacency of settling for what is, but the reflection of One Soul that has let go enough to leap into the nothingness with the trust and innocence of a child. I imagine that this constitutes Christ's greatest joy, to witness a creation of beings that embrace the fullness of life and live with the passion of one who dares to know Self; independent of the many identities and boundaries of control imposed by the mechanism of imprisoned consciousness. Our society is set up for isolation. To recognize this and how our technologies of cell phones and televisions and the speed of conveniences keep us from truly seeing and interacting with and participating in LIFE, we are that much closer to an awareness that goes out from our field of consciousness seeking a new level of beingness, a new mind and fierce heart that not only brings us continuous joy, but reminds us that we are here to share that joy with a world that is sorely lacking in this essence.

Everyday last week, without exception, I was visited by a snake, small ones and large ones, blatantly lying across my path within the many directions of my reality. I was even gifted the rare wonder of seeing snake eggs playfully strewn across a trail as if to make certain that I "got it" that this energy carried a message of attunement with this now. Not only do snakes symbolize life, they represent healing on a cellular level. Their bodies are "light"weight and flexible, with the speed and agility to allow swift changes to enter into their world. And the changes that snake so beautifully models for us in their connection to life, is the death of what is old and a birth into something new; untapped power, creativity and wisdom. It is the guardian of sacred places and the keeper of hidden knowledge.

Within all the uncertainty and unknown, the as yet, seeming division between those sitting on the fence of this current global ascension and those willing to jump off the edge of what might ultimately become of this rare and beloved species, there is a promise that is Eternal. Christ Consciousness prevails for the humanity of planet earth. Each day as we grapple with our childish concerns of what is right and who has more than they should and where our sustenance and comfort will come from as we toil our lives away in an existence isolated from true community... there is a consciousness and energy that permeates within all that is lower nature, lifting the Christ within each high into a harmonic that attunes the world to Oneness. When connected as One Soul, One Voice and One Humanity, we begin to comprehend what it feels like to know each other across the luminous web of Life and the Earth as a vital part of Self. Then a new world and understanding opens up to you and dawns like a brand new day such that the totality of who you have been and what you've experienced comprises a new level of gloriousness about your true identity.

The **new human** of future earth emerges as one whose evolution as a human dares to honor the evolution of their spiritual essence. No longer content with just reading of heroic realizations of Self and the awareness of angels, superior intelligences and high beings of Mastery, the Authentic Self of embodied Christ Consciousness recognizes this momentous now as a time to be the Greater Light that is One. One Life, One Joy, One Truth, One Power, One Being, One Love.

Reaching Out To The Improbable

August 8, 2009

"Not that which the eye sees, but that whereby the eye can see, know that alone to be Eternal and not what people here adore. Not that which the ear hears but that whereby the ear can hear, know that alone to be Eternal and not what people here adore. Not that which the mind thinks but that whereby the mind can think, know that alone to be Eternal, and not what people here adore."

The above passage is paraphrased from the Upanishads, ancient scriptures of India. They are beautiful lines that illustrate for the discerning mind the level of freedom that comes when our conscious awareness becomes independent from the physical world. "Not that which we adore," idolize, lift up and revere as separate and outside of Self, but the essence of that divine impulse through us as living light receptacles for the Eternal. Our existence here is not about the form and content of our creations, that which we can define and cling to and use to separate us from our fellow species, it is about Love and the infinite ways we can reign the ego in by embracing and exemplifying a Love that is all inclusive.

I am so grateful to know an experience of life that can read sacred scriptures such as the Upanishads and feel the love and passion of the Vedic faith and devotion to the God of their understanding, without judgment or opinion or the need to separate my awareness and beingness from theirs. The concept of Oneness as a Collective humanity cannot begin to be realized without a thorough analysis of the hearts of all who comprise it. Perhaps we are not here to learn anything new so much as to awaken to a dimension of pure essence, truth and utter stillness that is the Creator's love through us, all of Its children, all inclusive.

The show yesterday permeated the theme of its focus, stillness. The search for the true Self begins with stillness. In stillness there is no need, only the present moment. Only in the moment can we experience the spaciousness that carries a depth and fullness that is not available in our active mind. In the present moment we can just be, without thought and free from the investment we have in the egoic identity. In stillness, there is no conflict, no other, only an organically willed determination to know life through our feeling nature and heart rather than the conditioning of an outer directed understanding of this existence and who we are in it. To know the totality of your Self in each moment is to fill every cell of your body with the aliveness of being, without the need to think and hold others accountable for our experience, but to just see beauty in the world around us, and within.

Brain researchers have documented that our sense organs, such as our eyesight and hearing, only determine ten percent of what we interpret as our world. That leaves ninety percent of what we experience as life as being determined by our perception, our prejudices and beliefs, our attitudes and habits. The astute observer of life recognizes that beliefs are self-affirming, that our social identity and the secular tribe we gravitate toward often constitute a means of limiting one's true essence from becoming part of the greater family of life. The brain is attributed with the ability to create its own reality at any given moment. Consequently, it takes ninety percent of the information we need to understand the world around us from its own reservoir, making what we believe to be true, a mere construct of our mind. I imagine this incessant busyness of the mind, always interpreting and planning and judging what does or does not fit into the world of the ego, is a very clever and ingrained ruse to avoid the clarity of all that stillness engenders.

Being only in the moment with lucid awareness is terribly threatening to the egoic mind, because to be in the moment without thought, is to exist in pure consciousness. It demands the deeper probe of who we are as essence, if we are not the many things we give our attention to. Can we be utterly still without the need to fix things or improve them or remake ourselves or change others? Can we just allow and love the moment simply because it is? That reveals an entirely new level of faith, trust in who we essentially are and the True Source of Power behind this beautiful creation we know as life. It is a radically new emergence of what it means to truly KNOW God.

The New Human template and understanding is about shifting our awareness out of the mind, to energy. Seeing and witnessing, experiencing and embracing reality as a fluid, unlimited field of pure potential out of which we can know each other as Light. We cannot truly know each other with the mind. It is way too analytical and interpretative for that. We can only know one another with the heart's intelligence, wherein there exists a love free from demands, without even the demand to know each other, just to allow each other to be. Learning to keep our energy neutral in response to all the various stimuli and scenarios of our holographic world, we are then empowered to move forward as architects of a new design, co-creators of a world that vibrates in alignment with a future of harmony and peace for all.

For those who have become faithful listeners to the show each week, you have become accustomed to the use of personal story in redirecting world situations (which are no more than a magnified reflection of collective consciousness) back to the moment, which is continually brand new. We always have the choice to separate ourselves out from such absurdities as the CEO of Cigna making roughly one hundred thousand dollars an hour in income, or we can step back from the emotional distortion of a reality gone awry and see how our own actions and beliefs have contributed to every construct and facet of the existence we know today. We have "bought into" the belief that our health needs to be insured and somehow guaranteed by an institution that diminishes our innate capacities to self heal and correct any imbalances of dis-ease before reaching a crisis state. We have fed the mechanism of this monopoly by our own fear of death and the use of synthetic means to maintain the misunderstandings of self we so cling to! Those who can courageously embrace all the world's imbalances as a mirror for the work that must be engaged within are the most probable candidates for liberation from the pain of a imprisoned consciousness.

This new earth we deem to steward in for the sake of future generations, is one that has surrendered the manifestations of our own confused impressions of what it means to be human. It is fairly universal, across continents of great division within our world, that all beings believe they carry a spark of divinity, a descendant of their Brahman, Allah, Christ, Shang Ti, Kami or Krishna, to name a few. How then can we collectively conclude that our inherent divinity is somehow separate from who we are in this reality? We cannot be divine in nature while simultaneously existing in a microcosm of self serving belief that what we do in each moment, what we believe, the choices we make and the actions we do or do not engage in, somehow don't matter in relation to ALL life and ALL beings in the ONE world we each live in. Everything that constitutes a lower vibration on this planet, from injustices to ignorance to beliefs that extol unconditional love but practice separatism and exclusivity, all illusion of division is a product of our fears. No God exists in fear. The new earth of our clarity and acceptance of who we are as a unified expression of One Life and One People, One Truth and One Love, is a self actualizing organism of the higher vibration that is comprised of compassionate action and fierce determination to see ALL with the eyes of the I AM Presence.

The good news for the species of planet earth today is that we have a rare and precious opportunity NOW to stop creating with our minds, conditioning and thoughts, and to begin creating with our JOY - the frequency of our Light and the true vibration of a free love that is unconditional. These vibrant, electrical, molecular new frequencies of our bright potential as new humans with the power to transform what it is no longer serving us, are comprised of the compassionate love and harmonics of attunement that can set our species free. The fullness of who we are is within. It is in each moment and breath of sovereign beingness. When we can embrace life with that awareness, surrendering all need and questions to the unknown potential of a brand new day for our planet, there is a decided air of peace and joyous gratitude that settles into the core of who you know yourself to be.

Upanishad means "sitting down near." You will find the symbolism of this expression within the heart of all religions across the landscape of a potentially renewed existence for the family of humanity; all long to be held near to the Infinite and Eternal of existence. When we go within and get to know our Self, independent from the many roles and identities we think we are in our thoughts, we will not only come to understand this life and all beings in a new way, we will be able to embrace the whole of our species as One Soul, and adjust our individual lives and prejudices accordingly.

I encourage you to get to know yourself as the resplendent, multidimensional, talented and wholly loving being that you are and these new energies of shift and change marinating our planet at this time, as Presence. There is a new frequency of love and high intelligence here to teach us a new way of being. Our bodies our transforming to their crystal essence and we are charged to bring that new vibration out into every facet of our realities and aspect of who we are. To start moving forward in this radical transfiguration of beingness, ask yourself everyday how you can understand what is happening to you in a new way and make use of these new energies in transforming your own life, for the evolution of Self and the highest good of all. These are the questions of your Authentic Nature, the actualization of the new human of future earth.

Dreaming Awake, Alchemy Of Time

August 15, 2009

As I ran through the woods today, my feet drumming a trance rhythm into the earth's soil, I felt a wash of wisdom envelop me with a compelling force of loving observation. My inner sight filled with the images and emotions that the earth has for so long embodied on our behalf. And I am just humbled by and with deep reverence for the mirror of dis-ease she has agreed to be for our unrest.

I was with a friend this last week that needed to run an errand in a large supermarket chain that I do not normally shop in. It has been my practice, as one of the many small things we can all do to counter the destruction of simplicity on our planet, to shop locally, support our local economy and farmers, and minimize my use of packaging by buying nearly all my consumables in bulk. So, when we made this perfunctory stop on a hot, sunny day, I went and sat in the breezeway of the store's entrance as my friend disappeared into the belly of the beast.

I sat there in reverie, watching people move around in little bubbles of mostly unconscious thought, and my awareness was drawn to one woman in particular, who was driving around on a mobile shopping cart. She easily weighed 300 pounds and had a breathing tube inserted in her nose. She and the gentleman she was with were looking at watches at the jewelry counter, and I could see that she was adorned with many flashy rings and shiny things, randomly accessorizing her misshapen physical form. And what I noticed was that there was no radiance in her energy body, her light was all but extinguished. In that moment, the question that found its way to my contemplative deliberation was, is our material world, the false measures of security that we enslave our lives to, making us truly content? The answer was not far behind.

The voice that spoke to me from deep within, the same voice and energy I felt on the trail earlier today, reflected that there is no reason for the species of planet Earth to be so pitiful. To look at our humanity today, the isolated, dispassionate, dis-ease ridden and materially hypnotized beings we have become, it is almost as if there has been a collective agreement to resign ourselves to indifference; even if that indifference is to our own divine essence. Did we turn on the Earth because we have turned on ourselves? Can we so easily abuse and disregard her care because we are so numb to our own inner needs? Can we decry the wars and wonder at a government that can't be trusted when there are wars that rage within and little trust in the true nature of our own inherent light? One giant hologram, billions of points of light all reflecting where the mind has focused its belief, and fear.

One of the most pressing reasons for taking *The New Human* live on radio was to share the energy that is present within this ancient to future teaching. The world I know and have experienced most of my life is the world that our species is finally waking up to. The inner plane of our dreams and the spaciousness of our imagination is a fertile landscape, where the mind is informed not by dictatorship and conformity, but by the compassionate wisdom of a benevolent influence here to steer us away from our own destruction. Beyond the gifted sight, sound healing and intuitive knowledge of a few awakened to our future potential as a species, is the empowered partnership with very evolved, spiritually and technologically advanced beings with the goal of Universal Peace. They are here to help us create a new reflection for the world we currently know as home.

These new ascension energies continue to come in on waves of stunning magnitude and impeccable cosmic intent. I felt a lump catch in my throat during the show yesterday and I feel it now, as I tap into and allow for the strong wanting and compassion of the higher realms present with us here. The Shining Ones, along with full participation of the Star Nations, have gathered in council for this inexplicable metamorphosis of a species long disconnected from its Source. We must be open to their presence and help as we unplug ourselves from those industries of world power that have been deftly running everything, and acknowledge that it is part of our evolution to move past the controllers, reclaiming our freedom and divine destiny.

The only way to change the fabric of our reality is to change the fabric of our minds. Our physical bodies are receiving upgrades to our DNA structures so that our light bodies can endure these new, higher frequencies currently enveloping this luminous blue sphere. As the higher realms work with the grid of our planet to change its frequency, we must be ever mindful of who and how we are being in response to these changes. I shared a dream that I had recently of the "new soil" being prepared for the new consciousness and energies of an awakened humanity. Surrounded by the peaceful flow of living waters and the abundant grace of dancing waterfalls, the new soil of our mind's potential is dependent upon our active participation in our own loving detachment from the known.

This now is brand new for all of humanity. It is part of an organically willed determination to transcend our own learned and conditioned ineptitudes. We have a clean slate vibrationally from which to realize a new earth. By opening our minds to the greater possibility of what it means to be human, we allow the conscious shift that has to happen. We cannot be controlled by the fear tactics and agendas of an assumed world domination - if we have mastery of our minds. Our greatest threat is perhaps emotional and psychological warfare. Knowing this compounds the necessity of each of us detaching our minds from the inevitable collapse of all we have become so dependent upon and shifting our trust and intent to the new dream being birthed from within.

Nothing happens in ordinary life until it happens in dreams. This is the experience of our world. The challenge of this NOW is learning to be still in response to pure energy, the new voice of the interior redirecting the chatter of an errant mind back to the present moment, wherein every potential and coveted peace resides. We are receiving more vibrational sustenance than our awareness can currently hold, but as we learn to assimilate and integrate these higher frequencies into our daily reality, we will be able to translate this new energetic data into action. We are being downloaded with information to form a new reality and the steps of learning to manage energy within the new human template will assist in this process of freeing the mind and becoming the language of your dreams.

When I woke up from my dream of the new landscape being prepared for our awakening humanity, the message the Guidance had freshly planted in my mind was this: *if you travel to legendary places in your dreams, then the legendary places will become you and you them. For you see, the dreamer and the dream are one.*

We are, indeed, dreaming the dream awake. Planet Earth and all of humanity, is being fortuitously guided through a cosmically endowed thrust into a new position in the Omniverse.

Pull your energies and focus, your awareness and efforts away from the mundane in greater and greater degrees. This will create the spaciousness and opening for these new energies to continue to come in and work with the interior of your cellular structure. To empower your light and strengthen your mind beyond this now, you must surrender the known completely. The force and freedom of Presence teaches directly through the moment, the NOW of our unlimited future. The signs of new, of promise and a great and infinite love are everywhere, all the time, inviting you into the mystery.

As I came down the last stretch of trail today, so full and grateful for life and the beauty of this world, a Peregrine Falcon swooped down in front of me. It flew deliberately ahead of me as if inviting me to follow. Eventually, it perched in a tree I had yet to catch up to, waiting patiently for me to arrive. We stood for a time, eye to eye. Peregrine Falcon is a messenger of opportune action. They exude grace, timing, precision and acute mental perception. They hold the medicine of how to use ones capabilities to the fullest by attuning the mind to the harmony of life.

All life is extending an invitation to the humanity of this NOW- a species inherently beautiful in essence. Harmony and balance is being restored to the earth. All that is not harmonious and in balance with Universal Law will continue in a downward spiral and cease to exist. Where you focus your mind and energy is the intent you will connect with and thus create your future from. The new human lives free from the mind while attuning to the heart and harmony of a Mystery that is just beginning to make itself known to our species. I celebrate that gift everyday!

Morphogenic Unity, The Rise Of The Feminine

August 22, 2009

It is happening. We are connecting across the planetary grid of consciousness and energy, forming new alignments of empowered service and loving kinship with our Light family. It is an incredible reflection within so much that still remains in shadow, of how strong the frequency of Light truly is on our planet. And it grows every day. Within a Cosmic Process that often leaves our conscious awareness feeling disoriented and questioning of our sanity, it is so comforting and reassuring to have our gifts and light reflected back to us from many and far, unseen places by those aligned with our Soul. We must continue to expand who we are, our minds and vital essence, our understanding of existence and each other and our ability to embrace a seemingly non-ordinary reality, infusing our everyday life with magic and greater purpose.

There are many things occurring in the 3rd Dimensional Reality of this NOW to evoke fear to our perceptions. Our government calling for mandatory inoculations and the proposed regulation of National I.D. cards for travel are just more of the same control mechanisms and attempts to imprison the mind and emotions in powerlessness. But I can say to you that the vibrational now emerging, hidden in plain site and existing side by side with the illusions so many cling to, is exquisitely beautiful, with a frequency of even higher love and more brilliant light than we've known before as a species. We can anticipate even more love, greater peace, abundant happiness, joy and prosperity - but we must first let go of the lower vibrating energies that are still creating imbalances in our lives. Many are being "tested" through the constructs of job, finances, relationships, sicknesses and untimely deaths. When things intensify in such a way, it can be seen as defeat or as a time to truly stand in the center of who you are, and reclaim your power as a divine being. Ultimately our evolution is intricately interwoven with the mind and our ability to gain mastery over it.

The challenges of our global and personal reality today can seem bigger than your ability to deal with or find peace within. When I listen to the energies and connect with the Earth, I hear again and again that what is happening to the whole of humanity and our planet at this time is a reflection of how much we are loved. The duality of this experience was for the purpose of knowing other, of truly knowing Self by an immersion into all that we are not. But we've gotten too caught up in and consumed by the ego's attachments and so, now the higher realms are stepping in. We are undergoing a radical energetic transmutation for the purpose of dismantling our conditioning, our mental programming and the way we have interacted with each other and life so far. Episodes that bring us to our knees are for the purpose of reversing the spin of a linear identity.

It is tricky for our human aspects because we must let go of what is still held as valued and supported by 3D reality. It is so important to begin living a vibrationally supported interior reality, a reality that we know and believe in and yearn for spiritually, but cannot yet see. There is a stunning interdimensional, interdependent process underway whereby the inner structure of our vibrational core is accelerating in harmony with the entire structure of our planet. All the while we go about the mundane in a reality that seems unchanged, unyielding in the very things we all long to be free from. Gaia, the Earth Mother knows what she is doing, we do not need to know or even understand intellectually this Great Shift of The Ages, but we do need to trust it. Trust Life. Get out of and stay out of the mind and allow for the reorientation of a thought-based existence to give way to the heart.

Interior mindfulness is a prerequisite for conscious awareness. The clarity and awareness of the new human waking up to life is now, more than ever, focused on birth. If you can imagine having the interior of one being born into a new life, that first moment of opening your eyes, all your senses instantly engaged by surroundings you've never known or experienced. There would be a sense of wonder and curiosity, openness and excitement to move into and explore the unknown that awaited you. This is what it is to live in the moment, to be free from the mind and residing in the heart's intelligence.

And what I am suggesting and know to be true for our species at this time, is that energetically, we have been gifted a new start. The ego looks around and sees fear and the destruction of everything that it has depended upon and grown to identify its fragile sense of self with. Yet, we are Spiritual expressions of infinite Creation and we have chosen this now for the opportunity to bring new understanding and meaning to the very things that have dimmed the light of our awareness. The current unsettling of our known is for the greater love of centering in the mystery of a very expansive and infinite life, a new earth emerging. It is in the mystery that you will meet with your highest expression and find an open door to Ultimate Consciousness and freedom.

It is hard to be still without the full awareness of what is coming. The ego wants and needs to know. But on 5D Earth, all is created from stillness. Love is radiated from within and sent out as a currency of instant manifestation into the unknown of a world surrendered to a perpetual state of beingness. Stillness is an energy of high magic, the art of mastery that occurs when you are fully, totally, completely and authentically present to your experience; any and all experience. Today I got a message from afar, a listener on the other side of the globe, so simple yet so meaningful to my being. It was to thank me for being so present. I embraced that "gift" as perhaps the greatest compliment I have ever received. To completely surrender to the moment is to be in your love, in your joy, in your creativity, even in the midst of everything that would deny these. Our power in these coming weeks and months and years of quantum change and foundational undoing is to be fully present to it all, yet compassionately detached and energetically neutral.

These past few weeks on the show I have shared numerous dreams, experiences in nature and energetically inspired meditations emphasizing the very new template of a planetary over-soul. This humanity is genetically ready for the new communities of light that will be seeded in harmony, shared gifts and environmentally sustainable cohabitation. But we must continue to fine-tune our vibrational signature in the way we take in and respond to every moment of our shapeshifting reality of existence. All action needs to come from a state of presence, a center of Self that says "in this moment I make new choices." I hold the light high everyday in asking how I can express this compelling new consciousness and energy in such a way that constantly reorients the minds of the many away from fear and into love. The Mother is on the move. We must move with her. We must let go and detach from all those things, which are causing us to deteriorate as a species. What we cling to sends an amplified energetic runner across the shifting infrastructure of our world, vibrating that we are not yet ready to let go and wholly trust the greater Truth of who we are.

We are not that. Whatever that is. As we continue to lift, to vibrate within the inexplicable golden spiral of vertical awareness and light, it is the death of ALL that has been your identity. Each day our DNA is firing new levels of awareness, of re-membrance, of joy, of peace, harmony and love. And as our physical bodies acclimate to new and greater frequencies of light, we will have greater and greater access to the advanced potentials of our innate capacities; the feminine qualities of creativity, imagination, intuition, following our heart and knowing, living in the vibration of love. When you are in the present moment, all the joy and freedom that is will become apparent to you and you will feel the centering that empowers you beyond thought, beyond fear, beyond the mind.

One of my recent meditations gifted me a vision that encapsulates the frequency and light manifesting in our now. As I surrendered to the inner well and dark void of the pineal gland, I saw a crystal white bowl materialize within the nothingness. The bowl gently floated to the center of my awareness and focus. I continued to breathe into the empty space of the moment as the bowl glowed with incandescent light. Momentarily, the bowl began to fill with gold and silver coins, internally. First it was empty and then gold and silver filled from within the bowl as a fountain coming to life with living waters. And as I observed and breathed and allowed the vibrational sustenance to fill my present awareness, an image of me appeared to sit upon the top of that currency of gold and silver, centered in the abundance of a magical creation.

In dream language, the bowl represents new thoughts and ideas, and that the bowl was white with light suggests that the thoughts were pure and sacred, as well. This vibrational imagery from the void of the mystery is reflecting what we already know in our wisdom to be true. Not only are we being abundantly supported in our determination to be new and think anew and create as very new beings awakening to authenticity, but the treasure we seek, the sustenance of all that we need for happiness, fulfillment and freedom from this sensate plane, is within. Call it forth, new humans. Your ancient destiny is birthing itself into this now on your behalf. Your power, your light, your mastery longs to come to you and integrate with you and it will. Just let go and trust the Process you are in. ALL is truly well.

Shadow And Light, The Mystery and Legacy Of Planet Earth

August 29, 2009

Beyond all time and space, within and outside all known and unknown dimensions, a pause between the inhalation and exhalation of prana, there is a void where all realities and planes of existence collapse into themselves; a nothingness of penetrating stillness and silence. It is the womb of all Creation. In that nothingness is a superluminal pulse, a heartbeat of dominant desire and primary purpose, the unknown giving birth to a known of many worlds and expression of beingness.

The above passage is from **The New Human**, in a chapter called **The Freedom Of Love**. I have been thinking a lot about freedom lately. All across the globe, every organism of life is being touch and affected by a new Light and Cosmic teaching here to reintegrate the language of Oneness on this planet. For some, there is but a glimmer, a pin-light of new awareness awakening from a long and dehumanizing sleep. For others, this Light carries a radiance that speaks irrevocably of a time of peace and Universal understanding settling upon the consciousness and energy of an entire world, a world waking up to itself. Within this remembrance, we each have the infinite capacity to realize greater and greater levels of Self-awareness as we allow the restructuring of an external and internal reality to simultaneously occur.

When I am in nature, walking on the Earth and filling my senses with her essence, I can hear and feel the song of her crystalline core resonating within my own crystalline structure. It is an eternal song of the higher love present with us here, present for all – and it knows no bounds. The Shining Ones reflected in yesterday's show how the higher realms of Cosmic Light and the Crystalline Core of Gaia's Heart are engaged in a co-creative, interdimensional timeline, altering the entire consciousness and energy of the planet through synergy and love. Our relationship with the Mother is manna for our spiritual essence and our cooperation with her through this golden gate of ascension, will assist us in reestablishing and maintaining the energies of our inherent light.

Among the gifts being illuminated within this now of our evolution is the growing realization of just how much life truly is a reflection of the creator god within us. I see it in my clients, in friends and family, and within the interaction occurring on the show, a new light is shining on spirituality and personal responsibility within the whole of our world as more move toward an expanded understanding of who they are. No longer content with an unsustainable status quo, we are asking new questions and extending a new reach and embracing uncertainty as an impulse within which a new way of life can be birthed.

The egoic mind is coming undone, right alongside the dismantling infrastructure of an ego directed reality. Alchemy of the mind is perhaps our greatest obstacle to actualization and freedom. We are just so conditioned by our thoughts and it is thought that hooks us into all the apocalyptic potentials of the internal structure of the egoic mind and the external structure of form. It is so essential to understand and allow the current challenges and limitations in our personal and collective lives as the impetus for something totally new arising from the apparent crisis upon us. As we integrate these very new frequencies in greater and greater capacities, the awareness of our world crisis as an internal crisis is the beginning of a new face and view of spirituality awakening on earth. Thus, the seemingly insurmountable circumstances we are witnessing all around us can be redefined and redirected to the power we all have, to go within. As the constructs and structures within the status quo continue to reconfigure, so too must we reconfigure our minds and the way we have viewed and been in relationship with Self, each other and life.

Love is awakening on our planet and joy is returning to our lives because we are finally understanding that those rarified frequencies are independent of the trials and tribulations, the details and resistances of this reality; that we are the emissaries of that love and joy and responsible to its care. The lack of true joy in our world has been due to the fact our physicality has been so dense... our bodies have absorbed these densities through participation in acts of conscious and unconscious behavior. As a species we have been attuning to the status quo at the expense of the interior realm where joy innately resides. Change within and without is full scale as we crescendo toward the end of one era and the beginning of a new one and should not be resisted in any measure. This calls for a reflective review of lifestyles and attachments, downsizing when necessary for the purpose of reorganizing our habits and needs around sustainability. If we all were to reevaluate our wants and desires around the heart and love for LIFE versus the mind and insatiable appetites, imagine the organic redistribution of form to formlessness, of greed to compassion, of lack to plenty and of consumerism to meaningful service that would follow. In this Age of Light, of activating Christ Consciousness across the Crystal Grid of a re-energized and newly inspired humanity, we have been granted a cosmically and vibrationally empowered choice to now live our highest truth.

We must be more active in disengaging the outer control we have been consumed by. The time and space we create to break free from conditioned thought and habit stimulated by television, Internet and entertainment can be turned into inspired action and awakened passions as we work to get to know our energy bodies... consciously, daily bringing more light and frequency into indifferent routines. There are natural, simple and easily applied methods of lifting our light quotient for all who are truly ready to release their fears of illusion and glamour.

From the most remote locations of civilization to the densest populations of social consciousness, there is a moving force of Unification rising from the shadows of a learned history. Each moment is a reflection of our future and each moment is a brand new opportunity to write a new story for our individual lives and for our world. There are many who question the capacity of humankind to rise above its own acquired ignorance and penchant to look the other way. But to do so is to question love. We are shifting the consciousness of the planet one light, one mind, one heart and one being at a time. We can continue to denigrate our fellow beings and question how our world dynamics could have gotten so out of hand, or we can be courageously, fiercely **in this moment** and imagine how things can be different, as we turn our affinity toward community, kinship, shared responsibility and Unity.

The time is upon us to live the Universal Principles of Love, Peace, and Harmony with our brothers and sisters within our own species and with all intelligent life. The freedom of love is the actualization of Oneness. For too long, the many have sought power for powers sake and we have collectively agreed to this assumed and egregious imbalance. It is so very important in this now to vigilantly keep our focus on the higher vibrations of 5D earth, because energetically, it is already here. There are higher levels of consciousness with advanced technologies, highly evolved civilizations throughout the cosmos that have been interacting with earth throughout its history and want peace for this beautiful blue planet. In order to communicate with them we must raise our consciousness to where they are, offering the very best, positive and spiritually motivated intent of who we are rather than meeting them with fear and warfare. All that has ever been and will ever be is coalescing into this momentous now for that purpose. This moment is all we have.

Reality unfolds as a result of how we are being. In choosing peace, we choose conscious evolution within our own species as well as an intelligent cooperation with a spiritual hierarchy willing to work toward an age of Universal Unity. The answer to every question of every seeker throughout the many shades of light and dark of our beloved humanity has always been within and it has always been love.

Interstellar Wisdom

September 5, 2009

There is a new voice rising through a shadowed history on this Earth. As we witness so much that seems to spin into more and more destruction and chaos, deception and disempowerment, the still small voice of a new legion of Light is gaining momentum. Our planet is expanding toward a new day for all of humanity.

The Guidance speaks to me increasingly so in tones and harmonics, colorful and mesmerizing light-waves and fractals of informational patterns. Each day as I go into the vibrational hum of the Great Mother, I am transported into radiant chambers of enchantment and illumination. The stories that I gather there are the stories of this humanity, past, present and future, in interpreting these stories for the many awakening to their own inner light, their own voice and higher purpose, I become a willing participant in the Unification of a disparate species. The information being streamed to us Now, through these harmonics, is practical, providential and carries the intent of Universal peace. As we move out of the mind and into the heart, out of emotion and into compassion, more and more will be attuned to this new language of Light, the music of all Creation being birthed from the womb of Gaia's Crystalline Core.

So much is happening so quickly in this NOW of our evolution. As the core vibration of our planet increases, we continue to shapeshift into our crystal essence from within, even as we perceive a seemingly unchanging world without. This inner birth of our Authentic Nature and Soul essence is the vibrational conduit for a renewal of the mind, of perceptions and beliefs and unconscious thought. It is our opportunity to be still in the impulse of our conditioning and deepen our relationship with Self, with our known reality and all of existence. We are being fed a new sustenance from our star origins and we in turn must get about the conscious and determined work of reaching for and contributing to a new sustenance within the world of form, a new foundation of sacred sustainability.

I am heartened each week by those gathering within the intent of **The New Human** template. Slowly, but consciously and deliberately they come, guided by the impulse of the unseen, by the frequency of Truth that resonates from the Evolutionary Spiral. For so long we have contributed to a coil of ego driven desire, pushing the envelope way beyond need and into creations of hypnotic illusions and grandiose power. To observe and truly embrace our personal responsibility in the choices we each have made to take us further and further away from Self, is to begin the return back home. We have succumbed to the false safety of giving our lives and decisions over to a system and it is in disengaging that system, first energetically and then in mindful and compassionate action, that we join in the conscious restructuring of both an internal and external new world.

I became aware this last week of a corresponding harmonic to the teaching and embodiment of **The New Human** intent. I have long known that the new consciousness and new energy of this energetic is quite expansive, is indeed on a divine timeline coalescing with many prophecies of ancient wisdom and foreseeing. This timeless model of a new humanity is coming to light in the minds and hearts of individuals across the globe who are encoded with the light-seeds of its manifestation. And what I know to be true is that there are Soul unions activating within this inexplicable time-shift of reality, and beautiful aspects of space that have been egregiously kept hidden from us now joining ionic particles within this golden spiral of ascension upon us.

We must all move quickly with the energies now, adjusting our sensate worlds of attachments to allow for the cellular repatternings to find fruition within the known. If we get still and go into our hearts, we know this all makes sense. The Unification of Life is now enjoining like minds and heart's intelligences in this dimension with the high minds and advanced technologies of many worlds, within and without, aligning the energy grids of many civilizations. The brotherhood of a multidimensional Universe, intent on freeing this beautiful blue planet from a dying system, is activating within the god codes of individuals, re-membering their Authentic Nature, within the greater family of Light!

The Universe is full of living beings from different dimensions that are and have always been interested in developing Consciousness for the sustainable and altruistic future of this humanity. The people in power have lied to us throughout our history, about the presence of star beings amongst us, and will continue to do so. There is, indeed a Galactic Federation of radiant beings working together toward peace and harmony for our planet. It has always been our destiny to awaken to a greater understanding and awareness of who we are within the Cosmos. That the mirrors of our greater potential are now stepping into the heightened capacity of our expanding awareness and vibrational remembrance is a natural and inevitable progression for a species within an evolutionary momentum of great change. We have advanced as far as we can in isolation. We must now embrace the wisdom that we have never been alone and willingly engage the spiritual network of interdimensional enlightenment available to us.

I am a simple being at heart. I have had the blessed, over-soul experience of traveling through many walks of life within this human experiment. My humanity embodies the circumference of higher institutions of learning, the indigenous wisdom of tribal elders, religious indoctrination of secular teachings, emotional fragmentation of spiritual initiations and rich immersion into differing cultures and lifestyles, **all** replete with the sensate and egoic allures of a child given the key to never-land. I know I am part of a beloved species that was given freewill to create in a limitless realm of possibility. But now it is time to give back to the formlessness out of which was birthed this wondrous expression of unconditional LOVE! We are the awakening ones and we are not afraid or apologetic of our Inherent Light and right use of power.

For so long we have resided in a space of not being able to see past the choices made from an unconscious mind. If we are to advance with the potentials recorded in the Living Libraries of all Existence, we must each, everyday, step back from everything we have come to know as true and determine to stop servicing a dying system with our Light. We must turn our focus and awareness, our trust and creationary powers toward the spiritual revitalization of this planet. To move without thought is to engage your reality anew each day, moment by moment. Listen to the silence, re-evalute your choices with loving detachment and come out of the isolation that has imprisoned you in false security and mindless participation in the known. What exists and is held in place in our world today is there by the power of our thoughts. Dare to be guided by your heart and its passion and watch the new landscape of love begin to flower within the many layers of consciousness now activating across the globe.

The New Human potential seeded within the vibrational signature of this humanity is, as yet, in its infancy. I have been guided and shown the developmental, edifying, regenerative and expansive attunement around this template and the many layers of actualization therein. As this species continues to grow in awareness and to eliminate negativity and investments of separation from the Earth plane, the battle between Light and Dark will complete its alchemical transmutation into the New Harmonic of 5D World, a world of Oneness, Peace, Joy and LOVE.

Cooperation, Compromise And Community, A New Season Of Being

September 12, 2009

"We tell you a truth of the universe when we say that reality is unknowable with any instrument save your own sense of unity and wholeness. Your perception of wholeness is unfolding because the culture of the multidimensional universe is rooted in unity. As your wholeness navigator reveals itself in the coming shift, you will dismantle and restructure your perceptions of who you are and in this process humanity will emerge like a river of light from what was once an impenetrable fog."

An Excerpt from The Wholeness Navigator, Decoded from Chamber 12 WingMakers

We are having a really big now, the humanity of this current time/space within the evolutionary spiral of human potential. As we enter the Fall of 2009, there is an auspicious energy settling within the quickening of 3D reality, there grows a greater discrepancy between what continues to dismantle in so many layers of disrepair and what is rising as a revolution within the renewed minds and hearts of this species.

I went to the woods shortly after the show to just be with and express my gratitude to the Shining Ones. Though their presence and wise council is with me always, I can see them and hear their voices more deeply in the sacred space of pristine nature. I know that these magnificent beings of Ultimate Consciousness and benevolent wisdom represent the energy of the future for Gaia and all her sentient beings. Our physical bodies continue to be in one world but our consciousness and energy, the crystalline core of our being is on the move to an entirely different existence where we will embrace the divine in each other unconditionally and walk effortlessly in the energy of peace. As I communed with these shimmering beings of translucent light, their crystal expression towering above me, they impressed upon my awareness how important it is that the chosen ones of this day and time on planet Earth be ever mindful that our actions must consistently mirror the cellular changes initiated within. Though our minds may cling to the same old story and the antiquated structures of our sensate world, in each moment we are vibrationally brand new, gifted with the impetus toward a new and sovereign existence. We are the generation of Self-Knowers, awakening to the only course of action that will advance us toward a truer reflection of our inherent light, that of surrendering the known to the greater mystery of life.

Still aglow with the strong transmissions of consciousness and energy that were expressed to **The New Human** audience in yesterday's show, I met with some friends to talk about the experiences that this intent engenders and inspires each week. While we all reflected on the light and joy of awareness being shown through the encounter of ancient sites, the vortexes of numerically charged shifts such as the 9/9/9 portal and even the phenomenon of technologies mirroring the restructuring of our internal hard-drives, a young man approached our table as if purposely and deliberately called. There was clearly no separation between this being and myself, no inhibition or conditioned mind present. He was instinctively drawn to the energy that spiraled around us. He had heard us discussing **The New Human** show, the book and intent and wanted more!

We talked about the new consciousness emerging for this humanity. No longer just dreaming of a time when we will all wear different faces, the new human is the experience of light interacting with light. All the constructs and mental habits that have imprisoned us in conditions of judgment and fear based belief are giving way to an understanding that we must meet each other in Oneness, to survive and thrive as a whole. For so long we have been entrained to a system dependent on a top-down, masculine, patriarchal model of thinking and ego dictatorship where everything is imposed upon us and we comply. We have gone against our own divine nature and moral compass and lost something of great value, something essential about ourselves for the prostituted illusion of safety and materialism. It is our humanity, the common thread of Unity that we all share in this earth experience that will shift the balance once again to align with our authentic nature. And the return path will not be an easy one.

We are all going to have to create new ways to get along, making compromises we can all live with, doing the right thing not for self-centered reasons but for the sake and love of all. We must get our minds on board with the new light and vibration of our interior. All beings must be able to state clearly what it is we are working toward collectively and then back that up with how we are investing our time, awareness and energy in everyday choice. There is no "other". If we practice separation in anyway, be it with our thoughts via the ego feeling threatened, demanding ownership or fearing various aspects of tomorrow at the expense of being present today, we are denying the true lineage of our star origins and the potential of aligning with the higher mind awareness found, therein. It can be a revealing illuminator that we are challenged to get along and compromise with those we love, those in our hearts, much less the greater world of "other" in which we live. All of the various groups and exclusive segments within our society and world must come together and agree, as vibrationally sovereign individuals, to participate in a common collective of the future.

Community, Community, Community! Unity Consciousness expands as the world within, slowly but deliberately and with conscious intent, transforms the world without. With the simple but deliberate practices of building our light body and vibrational capacity, deepening our relationship with the natural world and engaging actions that honor the Earth, we are strengthening our bodies against dis-ease and our minds against fear and the blissfully ignorant spin of our intoxicating media. We must daily disengage the system, mentally, physically, emotionally, in word and deed, beliefs and lifestyle choices. We are changing our world-view and what it means to be human on this earth one moment of creativity and imagination at a time.

Imagine the possibility of three earths existing side by side. One potential is the expression of known existence, world famine, extreme lack, entitlement, injustice, addiction, materialism and a people who have abandoned the earth, denying their unique gifts and expression of joy for the promise of glamour and egoic fulfillment. All the comfort levels of that world are gone. The second potential is of a self-sustaining organism of harmony, balance and altruistic behavior by a species who have chosen an existence of expansion, health, wealth, wisdom, compassion and love. It is the potential of 5D World where all beings are intimate with First Source and thus with Self and one another.

And where we are today, within a scientifically, astrologically, astronomically and anciently calculated time of a wholly new existence for the solar system, is a moment of eternity wherein every human, every individual expression of the Consciousness and Energy that is God Being, is being lifted by a spiral of light descending from the sky in support of a radical reformation of who we want to be! The third potential is being chosen each day, a bridge manifesting out of new minds, new hearts, new lives and existence of those vibrationally embodying the vision of The New Earth. All potentials exist side by side, as they always have for this humanity of free will and empowered choice. It is a Supra Collective emerging within the fearless and fierce intent to no longer reside in a reality of illusion and pseudo-identity. We are at the edge of creating a new paradigm of humanity from a new base of power. Every day we are being vibrationally fine-tuned toward a super-celled organizing potential of spiritual development that recognizes Enlightenment as Authenticity! You being fully you! In your heart, in your joy, living in harmony with each other, with nature, with the many civilizations of divine beings in our universe and thus, with all life.

We are waking up to ourselves, re-membering as we journey through this now, that it is in the expression of Oneness, all of us be-ing unity, practicing unity, engaging unity and acting only upon unity, that we will be able to break free from this duality of diminished existence and live in the creative expression of our Authentic Selves, together, as One.

Spaciousness, Stillness, Sacred Sound

September 19, 2009

All of my life, I have been a bridge. This is a level of awareness and understanding that I had to grow into through immersion into extreme measures of the duality and separation that has long oppressed this species. And though the collective particulars of my journey since birth are not so important to this fantastic moment we find ourselves in, what is relevant is that that bridge energy, of providing access to a point of receivership beyond the current perimeters of mind and emotional quotient, is still at work as I give voice to the new human potential at hand. This awakening of the 2.0 homoluminous of future earth is indeed, calculated across time and space, and being initiated in timely and harmonically induced spirals around the globe by a Cosmic Knowing System, an ancient wisdom and a profound love. As the separation of two very distinct and diametrically opposed worlds continues to magnify within the tenor of the mental plane, all of humanity is at the edge of a defining personal choice that will shape the future collectively.

It was my great joy to share the frequency of the Blue Light with the listening audience this week, and this opportunity was meaningful in many ways. So much wants to come in and communicate with us in this time of chaos and coerced decision making for our species. For so long we have lived in the mind and taken even our spirituality as an intellectual exercise, something to be achieved versus remembered and allowed. Yet, as I share these "everyday" experiences of the Earth's uncompromising love for us, of mysterious worlds and benevolent beings that want to cooperate with us here, many are enveloped in and feel the possibility of their own mystical experiences with the Great Mother, the goddess/feminine principle currently rebirthing on the Earth. Indeed, a profound connection exists between the language of the Earth and our ability to access infinite streams of knowledge and unlimited wisdom. The rise of the feminine principles of intuition, compassion and fierce love are being supported by the Earth Mother, who is a relentless expert at what she does - teaching balance, beauty, cooperation and the eternal rhythm of life sustaining itself, with love.

This wholly special and interdimensionally observed blue planet is full of unimagined potential, we really need only to provide the space of mind, body and heart for the greater mysteries of "real life" to be revealed. The Blue Light frequency of attunement and quantum healing is present for all. You don't need any special knowledge or "expert" guide to experience it, you just need an intent aligned with your heart and the greater service of humanity as a Unified Organism. We cannot begin to grasp just how One we all are. It is, indeed, time we took responsibility for each other around the world, meditating each day on how every act, emotion, thought and belief is magnified to the whole of humanity, how we can shift our presence in the greater scheme of things to one of allowing, participation and Unity Consciousness. Connecting deeply with nature and the vibration of existence will draw those of high minds and pure hearts together on an internal organization of reality versus an external, egoic organization. This will be the beginning of Quantum Communities of right action and divine purpose manifesting through joy and the authentic expression of Self.

All-inclusive healing and liberation means all inclusive compassion and understanding of where, what and who we have been. All have participated in the separation and duality of this existence. To embrace this aberration is to acknowledge that slavery was not just a misuse of power experienced by some, we have all perpetuated the energy of this lucid teacher for our species by allowing our minds to be freely and indubitably enslaved. We must each now step back from who we have been, individually and collectively. This humanity is walking into a time of choice, engaging choice by exchanging individualism, isolation and fear for community, freedom and love. Love for a species. Love for existence and the absolute awareness of our inherent humanism. When we truly take responsibility for Self, owning all of what we have created and become, we raise the vibration of our physical and spiritual bodies combined, flowing the energy of Unity and sovereign mind out into our local environment and the greater world we live in.

I had a curious encounter in the woods today, given the discussion in this week's show around liberating our minds and moving into heart-centered awareness and decision-making. Most of the natural environment and woodlands where I live are meeting places for lovers of nature and animals. Unlike a cityscape where life is more regulated and restricted in expectation and experience, it is not uncommon to hit the trails here and run into would be family and fast friends with their pets in tow. I was sitting by the river with my dog, Samadhi Blue, when a young couple and their dog came around the bend of the trail. They seemed hesitant at first, almost cautious as they approached. I learned this apprehension was because they had recently been reprimanded, by a woman in these same woods, who called the authorities on them saying that their dog was unleashed and posed a threat to the environment. It was clear to me that these two young beings before me were cooperative and compromising people, that their dog was harmless, friendly and very attuned to them in obedience. So, in discussing their unfortunate encounter with the disgruntled hiker, what I heard the Shining Ones so wisely express as a reminder to us all is that people who adhere to rules and regulations over presence and discernment are fearful beings, beings that don't trust themselves and so look for ways to stir the pot of conformity because it makes them feel safe.

It can be hard to find balance in our everyday reality because the 3rd Dimension is conditional by design. Our purpose here is to find balance within an existence that has no structures of well-being and upliftment. We have been diminished in our inherent nature to such an extent that we no longer have or even know our own minds. We have learned to make decisions based on conditioning rather than our hearts and consequently walk through life anticipating dangers, which then materialize by the power of the fear and unmet emotions that we vibrate. As the ripple of an awakening consciousness finds a new residence within the sleeping and inert minds of a social collective, more and more are realizing that the lives they thought were their own are actually the manipulations of a social structure. When you can stand in your own truth, independent of the dictates and expectations and impending threats of economic, financial, environmental and health care structures that are not and have never been in balance or concerned for humanity's well-being, that is when you know you have stepped into a state of higher dimensions. When you follow Spirit first and know whom you are within that understanding, there are no wobbles in standing in your sovereign mind and truth, no doubt in where your allegiances lie when choosing love over fear and doing the right thing always, for the sake of Unity.

The first step to divine sovereignty is to understand that most of the thoughts you think are not yours. Energy follows thought and thought follows energy, always. The first and most important thing we can do to take back the power of our individual lives is to cultivate stillness. Stillness has to come first. To create the spaciousness for stillness in your lives, for nothingness, emptiness, not knowing and surrender, is to pursue peace and tranquility at the expense of fear. Fear travels without bias through the social consciousness field, the collective of group thought and a conditioned mentality. If we are truly present with Self in each moment, moving without thought and in our hearts, intuition and inner knowingness - much of the mindless routine we have given our sovereignty over to would shift to lives more aligned with the wisdom we came to share.

It is my personal nature and providential position to focus my work and energy on the higher frequencies of this current evolutionary impetus. That does not negate my awareness of the precarious circumstances we are faced with as a whole and the challenge, everyday, of being alert and awake to what is going on around us. It is not a given we have a wonderful future ahead of us. The only way it can be wonderful is if we are willing, on an individual and personal level, to truly look at the way things are around us and how much of our humanity and heart, our love and essential nature we are bringing to the everydayness of our lives. An evolution of awareness is underway. We are in the most dramatically transformative place in human history and the future lies in the actions of who we are being in this now. This is a time of heart-centered engagement with existence, with your life, your community and your world. We are all charged to create a positive reality not just for our own well-being and the sustainability of our immediate environment, but for a planetary and cosmic viability. Each must hear that the shift from conflict and negativity to love and growth begins with Self and that Oneness is an invitation and resting place for us all. As we grow the Light and energy of its harmonic in the experience of who we are, fearlessly and uncompromisingly around the globe, that Unity will balance out the disturbances within our individual lives and consequently, our world. When we move from the limited duality of consciousness to the higher dimensions of reality, we exchange individuality and fear for community and freedom. Love is the teacher of us all. And in our pure essence we are all teachers of that very same love.

Spiritual Integrity, Re-membering Love

September 26, 2009

How could we possibly have imagined a time for this wayward yet inherently beautiful species when we would be so enjoined with the wonders of Creation? A time when the lines of division and illusions of separation would give way to the yearnings of a Love that is Absolute? It is as if the song of a resonate harmonic has been given new spaciousness that is slowly but deliberately and truly, filling the hearts and new minds of a humanity waking up to Itself.

I went for a run in the Shining Ones woods the day before the show, to ground down the energies swirling with high intent around the new human potential. There is just so much new information being streamed to all of humanity, new vibrations of unification and the ways we can each unfold the future for the benefit of all. Over mountain passes and through pregnant streams, I surrendered my mind to the rhythm of my feet drumming the trail as my heart lifted into the mystery of the Earth's enveloping wisdom. It is not unusual for me to find myself at the end of an hour-long commune, feeling like I have just arrived - attuned, cleansed, rejuvenated and newly inspired with deeper insight about this current evolutionary spiral for our species. When I came to a stop this day, so filled with gratitude for life, this experience and my own determination to know Self, I looked down to find a white woolly caterpillar effortlessly clinging to my shirt. Somewhere within the journey of my ritual of connecting with Gaia for pure reflection on a time of Collective Transformation, a caterpillar had offered itself into the equation with vibrational information and medicine.

We are, as a Collective, moving through our human aspects to full embodiment and fearless activation of our Spiritual Selves. The humble, woolly caterpillar reaches a point in its lifecycle at which time it knows instinctively that it must change, it knows what it must become. This is the message this rare white caterpillar was expressing to me as I contemplated the ancient template and reawakening of a wholly new human. The Divine and Cosmic process of activating Gaia's Crystalline Grid, her radiance and beauty, is coinciding with the crystalline core, radiance and beauty being activated within each of humanity. Within the folds of the Earth and her instinctive wisdom, the caterpillar knows when it must die to its caterpillar nature and in so doing, emerges as a gorgeous creature of beauty, joy and Light. They become butterflies, the ultimate symbol of transformation and freedom. And that this caterpillar was white reflected within this consciousness and energy, that the pure essence and Christed potential of humanity is transfiguring within the apparent limitation and appearance of what has always been.

The new human is a new consciousness. What does that mean exactly? What does it mean to be conscious? More than anything else, being conscious means to be fully, wholly and utterly in the present moment and only there, body, mind and spirit. And in this present moment, there is only Love. To be conscious is to make decisions for love and joy and harmony and not from conditions or expectations outside of Self. If we could truly grasp that there is no past, no awareness of wrong doing and mistakes made and bridges burned within our trials and tribulations as a human species, then "this moment" would not find us suspicious and doubting, judging and drawing attention to the details of what is trying desperately to transform. To truly see and know the world as energy is to understand that there is always a higher realms perspective that is greater than the limited scope of our human emotions. When we imitate the caterpillar, surrounding ourselves with a cocoon of light by going within, we go beyond form, beyond thought and the mind and dis-ease and the ultimate fear of death. If we determine again and again within these rarified energies of new light and new awareness to still feed into and be fed by the mental plane, then we will continue to re-enact the shadows of our past having never felt the aliveness and joy of Existence.

We are all charged to find the good in our world situations. It is challenging in the least and seemingly impossible to the many to witness so much that remains unchanging and bathed in the shadows of a painful history within structures and institutions of imbalance, to attune to the fact that there is a new energy present. Yet, the consciousness and energy of **The New Human** is built upon a foundation of that new, an understanding that we created the current imbalances of our world by where we have focused thought. In voicing that we want change, we must redirect that very same thought and energy in how we are representing the frequency of love. Each moment and everything is always about energy. If you are decrying and bringing attention to what is still wrong within this positional ascension process, then you are in fact stalking that deception at the expense of your own peace and tranquility. Things are not nor have they ever been as they appear to be. The only way for us to lift as a Collective into our inherent humanism is to make every choice and decision, every action and deed one of directing the energy toward what is right and of love, peace and joy in our world and not toward what the egoic mind still sees as evil. It is such a beautiful and empowered way to live when you understand that we can each reduce terrorism, disharmony and deception in our world and increase Love and Peace by controlling our own emotional and ego-bound environment.

There is only Love. If you truly believed this and trusted that love as the most powerful force in the Universe, how would you be spending this precious moment of existence? Be-ing an ongoing conduit to creative flow with clear-seeing hearts and free minds is what we were born to do. As the Earth Mother continues to refine her own essence, she will no longer tolerate any energetic that is not aligned with 5th World. We are aligning with this level of integrity in tiers and the gift is, we get to decide, must decide what life we want. And then let our actions speak that intent.

To be conscious is to acknowledge that all beings are playing a role of mastery, liberation and ascension within the greater awareness and Inclusive Wisdom of Creation. As we struggle with the difficult economy and bridging of an old world politico, with a new, world sovereignty, it is wise to emulate the energy of the caterpillar. Our safety and emancipation lies in keeping our energy neutral, in the cocoon of stillness, nothingness and non-reactive being-ness. There is nothing that happens outside the vertical spiral of Oneness, of higher realms influence, of omniscient wisdom and of love. I trust that, do you? These changes will happen and how they happen for each is about individual perception and the integrity to rise, let go, and re-member.

I encourage the many and the few to **stop** being the past. When we live in fear of outside events (which is what the energy of control is about) we are living like the caterpillar. We are crawling through our lives, bound by the world of form. We are letting mass consciousness and media consciousness create our lives for us, rendering us unable to fly. The Ultimate Freedom is freedom from the mind. This is quite possibly the oldest truth and teaching to our awareness as humans. Now it is time to **be** that surrender.

When we go within, when we touch into our Inner Divine and the utter stillness found therein, we are going beyond that part of us which is limited, bound and enslaved. We are transforming beyond death. We are saying yes to the divine union of the spiritual and physical aspects, to emerge as a homoluminous being of Light and only Light. From this place of Authentic Self, we can silently visualize the world we would like to see and that vision will have the power of stillness, of center, of unbound faith and unconditional trust. If we are truly still, we can feel ourselves changing, becoming less dense, becoming filled with Spirit. Light becoming Light; fully actualized as the change that will manifest a New Earth. It is the step up from participating in creation to **be-ing** Creation and that is the elemental piece in our truly re-membering back to Oneness and love.

Field Of Dreams

October 3, 2009

I went to be with the Mother, as I always do, shortly after the show today. Life and people, existence, and the many shades of our becoming throughout humanity's history all swirled within the interior of my own awakening wisdom. And as I climbed an ancient mountain, filling my breath with the warm envelope of nature's regard for this species, my liberated mind went into stillness and the deep well of this magnificent story unfolding, the return of the homoluminous. Imagine for a moment, being suspended in the brilliance of stars, free of atmosphere, no interference from the world of form and thought and fear, Imagine how brightly and beautiful those stars would be shining. Talk about clarity! That is the love and freedom and peace I feel in the woods, in nature's embrace and mystery. And it was in those moments of lucid receivership, that the Earth began talking to me of the *Field of Dreams.*

There is a field of knowledge, of wisdom and memory and patterns that unite everything in a quantum web of One Organism, One Life. These morphogenetic fields carry timeless information and serve as non-physical blueprints, created by patterns of physical forms throughout time and space. And what I have learned and been shown and guided by within these pristine woods of my classroom of the last eight years or so, is that by tuning into and opening the heart and mind to morphic resonance, one can collapse the veils of illusion that keep this humanity ignorant of its greater history. This field is vast and encompassing. It contains an intelligence that mirrors its vastness. This field of dreams is one of the many gifts of Creation and carries the opportunity of our knowing ourselves beyond this reality, of dreaming the greater dream of humanity awake, by uniting the seeds and artistry of ancient civilizations with future worlds.

When I reached the top of my mountain climb, I found a nice perch offered by a small cluster of rocks and sat to gaze out over the valley below. Hundreds of trees provided shade as the sun speckled through the changing fall leaves and I just allowed my mind, my heart and consciousness to be informed by Spirit. I contemplated the movie *Field of Dreams* that is, of course, in the ready recall of social consciousness. This movie was about a common man who spent his life following the rules of society, yet internally searching for meaning, the thing that would give expression to his dreams. It was this internal search and the quiet desperation of a life that did not resonate with his heart that allowed him to connect with the voices of the mystery. And as I sat in that vast wonder of nature, in awe of this analogy the Guidance offered me on behalf of the energies within today's show, I reflected on the prominent theme of the movie, *"if you build it, they will come."*

Stillness is the wisdom of the **New Earth**. Joy and Light are the vibrations and power of the **New Human**. These magnificent scalar waves and higher harmonics of our planet's move to a new galaxy are here to inform us through a new intelligence and creative potential. No longer creating from lack and fear and greed of the old masculine mentality, the new human is a new consciousness of understanding that the frequencies of God, of Love, of all Existence, reside fully and only in the present moment. In each moment lies our individual and collective power. This now moment will ever lead us to the dream and transformation that we seek. The mind is so conditioned and the ego so rigid with unconscious drives that it wants to create by will. Yet it is the heart's intelligence, the heart's wisdom and trust and intuitive faculty that will create the physical foundation for the 5D World of our Collective destiny. When we master stillness, we master the power of the resonate field to draw to us all that is essential, opening humanity up to the higher dimensions and co-creative partnerships of love, peace, joy, harmony, freedom and abundance for all.

The field of dreams of this very pregnant and historical moment of time/space for humanity is the potential of a dramatic, collective shift for a spiritually awakened species. As we move out of thought, out of mind and need and into innocence and love, our level of receivership shifts exponentially to an evolution of understanding just how much we are loved. Loved for who and what we have been and for the dreams we carry of who and what we might become. Because the morphic field of unified consciousness connects us to one another across the globe and within all life form, the door is opened as well, to the possibility of concurrent consciousness with the many civilizations of existences within the entirety of humankind. It is in being here now, embracing this time of spiritual opportunity with all of our hearts and being that we position ourselves to step into agreed upon roles of synchronistic activation with ancient peoples and future Selves. The DNA spiral the Earth's ascent and all Creation is pulsing cosmic memory through the radiant chambers of individual codices within those re-membering their divine purpose and evolutionary promise.

It is increasingly evident that we are coming into some potentially grave scenarios of foundational restructuring for our planet. These potentials are no longer a distant possibility. They are unfolding before us with ominous foretelling for those with the courage and sight to behold evident truths. That we chose to experience this time in alignment with the Galactic Center and intensification of the First Source Beam speaks powerfully to a renaissance of beings no longer content with operating at a diminished spiritual capacity. And so, with the collaboration and cooperative intelligence of many worlds and universes, this magical blue planet and all her sentient beings have the vibrational opportunity to move into higher levels of human functioning through an internally organizing operating system of genetic repatterning and cellular rejuvenation. The humans operating in these higher levels will unite together in the behaviors of love to activate the Etheric Heart Center of Oneness.

Life as we've known and understood it to be no longer exists or is even possible for the species of planet Earth. There are so many beings in so many dimensions waiting for us to acknowledge them and join forces toward a new point of harmonization within the Crystalline Grid of Gaia's heart. Daily as I commune with the Shining Ones and the greater Family of Light within her luminous fields, fractal patterns and rainbow colors speak to me of Collective Intelligence, and the true nature of reality. Could it be that we are linked in Consciousness to all Creation and that the bridge of Unity that has for so long eluded us as a species can be found in the Earth's many chambers of crystalline memory?

The mind and heart of the new human are ever in state of open-hearted wisdom, trusting existence, following Spirit, communing intelligently with the Earth and mirroring the innocence of joyful wonder at the secrets of her eternal rhythm. The only way that humanity will evolve into its rightful position in the Omniverse is to dislodge itself from the historic mind and inertia of habit by moving into the transparency of a new consciousness. This is the path of innocence regained as we expand into the specialness of a humanity intentfully recalibrating the Harmonic Field of a Collective dream.

Hidden In Plain Sight, Giving Voice To The Mystery

October 10, 2009

When you experience the mystery, you are given access to information from the mystery. Each seemingly insignificant moment such as hearing the night bird sing or witnessing a portal of invisibility between 5D and 3D reality, is an opportunity to go deeper into the wisdom and greater knowing of many unknown worlds. Indeed, it is ultimately through nature that the human family will come back together and be awakened to a greater awareness of Self. To be in tune with her frequency is to truly understand that we are One interdependent organism where all are equal, all is in balance and there is only One Truth; Love.

The energies around this week's show very much emphasized the energy of movement. We are on the move vibrationally, lifting in awareness as Gaia completes her journey to an entirely new galaxy. This expansion is both physical, as the ascension energies support a lightening in our physical vessels and in understanding, as we shift from an ego directed belief system to a heart-centered consciousness. This moment in time for humanity is about choice within the potential of many different realities and the power that we have as a species, to focus on directing our energies toward a different outcome. It is so important within this evolutionary cadence of awakening minds and awareness to now use our spiritual insight to restore balance to what has for so long been in a state of imbalance. Change is and has always been who we are being in each moment. We must take personal responsibility for what energies continue to be perpetuated and our determination to choose anew, to be new.

As Gaia continues her quickening, she is calling us into deeper communion with her. Part of our Soul agreements and spiritual intent within this time/space window of opportunity was to open up and activate energy portals around the globe to usher in a new era of co-creative existence. A pure intelligence is at work within her metamorphosis and these planetary portals are mirroring the portals re-activating within the human family. We are discovering these ancient places because we are discovering our true natures and these alignments are key to the rebirth of the feminine principle for our planet. When we are in our hearts an entirely different world opens up; new sight, new vision, new understandings of compassion and the awareness that an evolution of consciousness is underway and Gaia is the wisdom keeper. Each person is a portal unto themselves with access to multidimensional worlds, able to navigate through the densities even as they remain free of the deceptions unraveling.

This shift is changing personalities and asks for a deepening of relationship on all levels. As the ego based mind surrenders to new understandings of what it is to truly love, to see clearly the light within all not through the filter of fear but the clarity of no need, our way of interacting with each other, with Self and the world around us will shift accordingly. Old relationships are transforming to deeper understandings, new relationships are coming into view in alignment with our expansion and it is for us to receive them as brand new. It is then that we step into a new understanding of Self as we all embrace the Oneness and divine impetus to understand truly that everything that comes to our door comes bearing the gift of a freer and brighter love.

We are in the most dramatically transformative place in human history, transforming so fast that it is a challenge each day to be alert and awake to what is going on around us. As I observe how this grand portal of potential and illumination is affecting the many and those I hold dear, I am comforted in knowing that there are forces at work now far greater than any one person. As we shift into the spiral of vertical time, it is not uncommon to experience gaps within the recalibration occurring within, moments of lost time and the sense of being in a different "place," literally. We are bridging the old with the new and sometimes the ego identity can and will get disoriented. Just know that as we integrate new layers of these ascension energies, it is not uncommon to feel lost. The ego's world must be allowed to melt away, little deaths of deconstructing the emotional body. And the new reference point for us all in surrendering the ego, in overcoming our own small fears and patterns of distrust, is to understand that we no longer dwell in the energy of deception, we have transcended to the Age of Transparency. It is a time of trust, of reaching higher within and of an entirely new grid of spaciousness and freedom for our planet, freedom to choose anew in our understanding of Self and each other. This is a time of engagement and participation and Unity versus isolation and cocooning and protection. Unity and Love are the dream of Oneness and the Light is shining ahead of us to lead us to a new tomorrow, for our own hearts and for the love of Existence.

Ascension is a return to Self. Ascension is Awareness, at its base of which, is Oneness, co-creative partnership and truthfulness with Self always. It is way past the hour that humanity truly wake up to what they are participating in and learn that as each one person disengages old, as each person recognizes the patterns within self that are the patterns of our history, each piece of reactive conditioning and automated fear that we surrender allows for a corollary access to your Authentic Self. This new way of being, this new era of what it means to be human is about each of us having the courage and awareness of who we are truly to begin to disengage the system, the machine, that has imprisoned our minds and suppressed our capacity to Know and Imagine and Create from Love versus fear.

The Earth is radiating a new transparency that is freeing our minds and clearing our emotional attachments and perceptions so we will see her more clearly. As we see her more clearly and see her vibrations emitting from the world of form, as we hear her harmonics, her song beneath the cacophony and distortion of the matrix world, we will necessarily shift our awareness and decision making to heart-centered consciousness where there is no fear, only more love to step into. This transparency, this time of authentic alignments and staying fluid in your thoughts and life choices is about recognizing that the encounters and alignments and intuitive knowings activating within the heart right now are about re-unions with our familiars of Light and destinies therein. We can trust that.

Real life, existence, has always been about knowing Self *through* perceived other. Our mastery in this plane is the Unification of all that is perceived as duality. As we dare to deepen our connection to the Earth, we deepen our connection to each other and thus to Self. She is breathing a little freer now because we are letting go and trusting the magnificent frequency of Love, above all else. It is a very fierce Soul that wants to have life and deepen the well always of our understanding and awareness of Self through other. It is time to come out of our separation, knowing that we all have equal and necessary gifts to bring to the playing field of the human family. When you open your heart up to the mystery, to change within and for this ultimately transforming world, you express a new and authentic level of visibility to existence. Then all that was once hidden becomes the new Light of a transformed future for planet Earth.

Sacred Journey, Remembering Home

October 17, 2009

I was given a mudra back toward the beginning of this year, directly from Source and the transfiguration of Gaia's Crystalline grid. No longer moving with and following my mind, it is energy that speaks directly to me and informs my actions and thought processes. Out in the woods one day my arms began to move, incorporating a certain numerical rhythm and expressive gesture that both danced effortlessly with the totality of the energies around me yet equally refined those energies and brought them back to my Center. The language of the Light affirmed to me that this mudra would serve to rearrange and balance all incoming and outgoing surface energies as I walked the center path of the days ahead. And in the stillness of this moment, being with and feeling all the energies that are pulsing and humming within and around me in relation to the New Human Consciousness and Energy, the information of this mudra comes to me... reflecting the current contraction within the evolutionary spiral for this humanity. We must come back to center before we can move forward into a new dispensation of what it means to be human.

We are very much in a deepening, a pregnant pause in the Process of this Shift and stillness commands the present moment. Planets are orbiting, Earth is transitioning into her rightful place within the Galactic Core and the surface complacency of humankind is being unsettled by a discrepancy of mind and heart that can no longer sustain the egoic miscreations of an unconscious system. For so long we have lived outside of center, following the mental conditionings of a reality that is essentially nonsensical to our spiritual natures. It is fascinating and Soul infused to observe how this necessary momentum into Transparency and Authenticity as a frequency of new life is illumining the unconscious agreement, between individual and Collective, to exist within a cocoon. The mind can justify just about anything when the Collective is in agreement. Yet the mind is what created the Collective and now we find ourselves in an evolutionary clutch and shift to see if we have truly learned personal responsibility, that there is only this moment and we are either vibrating love and the future, or fear and the past. Love is a fairly simple and unapologetic frequency. It is pure and without ego. To know the freedom and sovereignty of love is to master the discrepancies within our own lives first and in so doing disengage the energy of destruction, sadness, illusion and fear within the crumbling infrastructure of 3D world.

As we become more aware of our Selves as Light, as we see more clearly the light within all things and persons, we necessarily shift into a consciousness and energy, a vibrational awareness that allows for more and more stillness and less and less will-force. Allows that there is a greater Organism we are all a part of that breathes when we breathe, that expands and contracts with each moment of our interpretation of this experience. We are so much more than the mind's need to know and be in control and separate out and live within one endless contraction of self. This vacuum of energy, of Ultimate Consciousness that seeks to know Itself through us is Self Organizing everything, all energy, through the information that it receives from us! This is how this other-powered, fearful, entitled and exclusive reality was formed, by our thoughts and a thorough disassociation from the heart. We are constantly creating our reality and our reality constantly creating us, but we have been doing so through a past or future orientation rather than being fully present to what is and in so doing, freeing the heart from apathy. We've been interacting with, engaging the Field through the mental plane and thus stimulating the egoic construct of creation at the expense of love.

Life is a constant reminder that things change on a dime. We have so much to reflect that even as we follow superficial rules and do our best to maintain the status quo, some semblance of control - that there is a greater sphere of revolution, a cycle much greater than our myopic awareness of why we are here, what truly matters and the deep longing to just stop the repetition long enough to readjust our sails.

"Tell them to feel the energies," the Shining Ones whisper in my ear. The energy all around us is a Presence of great wisdom, foreseeing, intelligence and love. We are in the midst of a great suspension of time; the linear realm is being forced into a vacuum of vertical time, so much density being compressed into a new spaciousness of creationary opportunity. There is stillness and nothingness and wait right now precisely so that we move in the direction that is authentically ours, the direction that belongs to the future. We simply cannot force or will our way to the new. The energies of 5D world are seeping through the thinning veils even as we witness the undoing of so much erroneously deified form. There is a precise, absolute cooperation and coordination happening between you and the energies of all Creation, you and existence, you and Ultimate Consciousness. This is not knowledge for you to learn but awareness for you to feel. The energies want to lift us up, long to gather us into the momentum of a vertical remembrance and spiritual authority. But we have got to be still, let go and surrender to the mystery of our own autonomy, our own sovereign center of being. In understanding Center, we become the New Collective now manifesting future earth.

One of my favorite scenes in the Matrix Trilogy came within the climax of Matrix Revolution. Neo had been given his final decree from the Oracle. He had gained enough awareness of Self, who he was and what his true destiny was to fulfill his ultimate purpose. He and Trinity, his anima, were side by side, a perfectly balanced union of the masculine and feminine principles, flying directly into the unknown of a self-destructing illusion. There was no option but to willingly surrender to the task at hand, even though the known, what could be perceived in the path ahead, was certain annihilation. And what I so love about this scene is that he never looked away - eyes wide open in a fearless focus, doubt was not an option. His knowing and trust were bigger than his fear. He remained perfectly still, a still mind. Even the sacrifice of his anima, his heart, did not deter his devotion to his purpose. In letting go, surrendering to that fate, his power and light and faith transformed all destruction into utter peace and Love was restored.

We came to help raise the frequency of the planet. That awareness alone quiets the incessant chatter of my mind and redirects all my thoughts to my heart. Each day is a measure of surrendering the egoic identity to our greater destiny as Love waking up to itself for the sake of all. We are moving as a Collective, as a planet, as an organism to a much larger cycle of existence, an existence where our sun will transition from the 5th sun to the 6th sun. According to empirical sciences and ancient codices such as the Mayan Calendar, 2012 will mark a change in the sun's quality and I can't help but imagine and feel in my heart that that change is coinciding with, if not a metaphor for the capacity of Light we will be carrying within.

Each day, each of us is within a moment of time ongoing where we are reconfiguring the heart, your heart and my heart and Gaia's heart within the One Heart of all Existence. It is a time of knowing who and what we are and making new choices and decisions based on LOVE and not fear. Each time we do, we vibrate the tone and Master Harmonic of the future through our bodies and out into the grid of Creation. The new human is the new cycle beginning. Close your eyes and feel the light wave of these new energies, let them inform you and fill you and guide you to a new awareness of Self and center of personal peace. As consciousness and energy progresses, our realization of just how beautiful the world really is will increase, we will trust the mystery more fervently and allow for the stillness of our inner being to become the creationary power of an entirely new existence. This is the knowingness and love of the new human.

Unbound Unity, The Lightening Of A World

October 31, 2009

I hear it in each moment, I feel it in my body and heart, I feel it in the hearts of the many who are waking to a new octave of being. There is a tone, a Master Harmonic of Intent and Beingness, of Creation, that has been slowly building beneath the surface of what can be seen and known to the intellect. It is the song of One Love, a constant vibrational momentum that is in a time sensitive crescendo toward a Golden Age of co-created community. There is, indeed, a spiritual hierarchy, many worlds of existence, overseeing this Unity of Intent as the earth song becomes especially sweet with harmony. As each of us dares to embrace a wiser more careful stewardship of Oneness, of the earth-ship as a vehicle of interdependent cooperation and each other as partners of the future, we lift as a Collective toward a new age of Universal Unity.

All of us are being asked to step into a greater expression of who we are, a greater octave within our unique vibrational signatures, for the sake of Unity and World Service. That is the era we are in, one of Transparency, Authenticity and Peace, a new consciousness here to restore balance to this planet and all of existence. The new human is an intent based remembrance of shared responsibility that is being activated within stillness and unconditional receptivity to the unknown. The "you" that you are in the nothingness, in the sacred space of your process carries a wisdom and freedom to move forward in the midst of much uncertainty. Creating from stillness is a high magic that is securing a new foundation within this ancient teaching. When we understand ourselves as energy and begin reordering our personal realities as unique notes within a greater chord, much of our attention and decision-making shifts from personal concern to individual power, power to affect real and lasting change. We must shift our focus to how we are be-ing rather than what we can oppose and are fearful of. We can raise our consciousness enough to create the new radiant zones and sovereign lives we so long for, independent of what is dismantling in the world of form. When we truly put our minds on the things of greater importance, the details of space/time become less and less relevant to our experience. But we must disengage the ego from the illusion of control long enough to understand that the full awareness of the ascension process is in our hearts, in love and remembrance of the language of Light.

We have so much more power than we've had the courage to stand in. What is happening through an incredible lightening of things that have for so long been in shadow is that our inner light is finding greater reflection in this new spaciousness. As Gaia breathes a little easier within her expansion, we too, are feeling the invitation to a more meaningful purpose and greater intimacy with Self and others. Our creativity and passion is being stimulated to deepen our heart's expression of love in our individual lives and in the world; love for Self and love for one another. It is a precious gift within a rarified window of existence, to trust heart consciousness over the mind and thus liberate the world of form to a new freedom. It is for each of us to step out of the groove of well-worn comfort zones long enough to realize that life as we've known it has already ceased to be! Beneath the surface of order and reality as usual is a foundation of sand where everything appears to be ok, until it isn't. There is a certain facade that is still out-picturing and giving the illusion of "life as usual" but energetically, we have already moved beyond.

Each time I observe the busyness of 3D World via a fear enslaved media constantly feeding the energetics of powerlessness, **Walmart** overflowing with those desperately clinging to a rote and imprisoned reality or egoic minds scrambling for some small footing of control, I close my eyes and listen to the sound. The sound becomes a frequency map of golden threads, an entrance to a brand new possibility for the humanity of planet earth. When I observe the reality of form, of materialism and so many living outside of Self, I see a golden city superimposed upon all chaos; a world of beauty and Light. These Master Harmonics carry the vibration of the future. It is the One Heartbeat that remains constant between the in and out breath and when we take time for stillness, we align with this scalar wave, vibrating it out through our bodies and into the Collective Grid of Transference.

The New Human is a **paradigm** and teaching about vibrational mastery. To truly understand ourselves as frequency and light, is to undergo a fundamental revisioning, a new perspective of sorts. By opening ourselves up to the power of a Collective Intelligence that is restructuring itself in the face of a very entrenched reality we are able to disengage what has become a repetitive illusion of recycled fear. No longer can we stand in each instance and make choices based on what we see or have been given by conditions and obligation because then we just recreate from within the same dysfunction or limitation. Now is about extending our reach beyond our grasp, surrendering with gratitude the things that no longer truly fulfill us. We must become increasingly comfortable with the unknown, the nothingness of creationary space. These new energies are expanding the fields of awareness from within which we can navigate our way to a greater freedom. The dream-time is overlapping with our shapeshifting realities, new persons are appearing with exactly the support we are asking for, the second and fourth chakra are being stimulated to impassioned expression of creative service and unapologetic love for one another and life... we no longer reside in what was. We reside in the waking dream of all that can be.

Unity Consciousness is seeping into the fabric of our lives in ways great and small. Each week we gather in greater numbers to embrace the understanding that 2012 is a choice. This new cycle of possibility for our species is the culmination of a process that has been building since the beginning of time. It will represent different things to different people depending on states of consciousness. Wherever your mind and focus are, that energy and experience will be amplified. The level of freedom and joy, of community and interdimensional cooperation implicated for us at this time is so multilayered and intricate and profound. We have worked long and hard to get to this moment in evolutionary potential and it is for us to continue to release our grasp. We are in the midst of a process of activation that is deep seated. We must not only trust this love and align ourselves with this radiant Light, but say yes to the mystery that is unfolding by love's design. This is a lifetime that will catapult us beyond what we currently know to a depth of awareness and understanding that we are just now energetically grasping. Let go of the known, surrender the mind to the heart and allow love to reorder your mind to a heart of fearless mastery. There is only this moment and it is, indeed, a new day. Live it well, live it free, live Love.

Lighting A New Star For Humanity

November 7, 2009

Unity, Oneness, Connectivity, that we are returning to an inclusive world is reflected across the landscape of this now in ways great and small. It is not a question of whether or not we are being guided and supported with immense love toward a new consciousness of peace and harmony, it is a matter of witnessing this extraordinary expansion through new eyes, new minds, new hearts.

We are in a time of culminated awareness within the history of humanity's relationship to everything outside of itself. The lightening of these rarified energies is providing for a shift in the mistaken beliefs that have for so long hidden this relationship from our sight and comprehension as a unified whole. We are the creators, the manifesters, the cause and consequence, shadow and light, pain and ecstasy of ALL existence. Everything is happening in each moment and available to us now from a new field of creationary power. Stardust is disseminating through hyperdimensional mists of ascension energies because **now** is our time, your time, to express and be your authentic nature, the Divine Self. This moment is One within a timeless journey to reclaim the whole picture of how truly wondrous it is to be human. A precious portal of illumination, as thru a glass dim lit to a new Age of Transparency, and each are emerging to a new awareness of Self with the power that resides therein.

Each week, as I observe the gathering on the show of those from distant places and different levels of understanding about this evolutionary phenomenon upon us, I am aware that it is the authenticity and transparency of heart consciousness within this ancient teaching that defies the separation of form. We are on a collective journey to a previously inaccessible possibility. As we embrace consciousness and energy as vehicles of awareness indispensable to reshaping existence, we step into a new radiance of integrity as spiritual beings. This is just a moment of incredible significance for our species. As we are more and more willing to be seen, using our voice to empower the virtues and justices of the heart, we will be less and less fearful of the responsibility that comes with integral living.

The New Human is movement from the lower end of consciousness, states of mental activity, of ego bound perception and fearful reactions, to the higher vibrations of quantum mind. We are multidimensional Light Beings capable of manifesting from pure essence and thought. We can now access all the levels of information available in the higher dimensions because we are at long last lifting up and moving beyond. A new part of the brain is being activated that runs a golden cord of remembrance directly to the heart of our true nature and origins, all for the timely and necessarily heightened abilities of direct insight, telepathy, remote viewing, clairvoyance, telekinesis, lucid intuition and unapologetic remembrance of our Divinity. The Soul is vastly multifaceted when developed, able to channel the wisdom and intellect, voice the passion and artistry of every great physicist and scholar and performer through the whole of this earth experiment. We are musical instruments across an infinite time/space continuum vibrationally attuned to now join in Universal harmony.

To restore balance within the masculine/feminine principle and defy mental resistances of the lower mind is to awaken more and more of the Light Body. The body temple is an exploration vehicle, emotionally indifferent yet compassionately understanding of just how deep the amnesia of duality has become. Our physical bodies are storehouses for cosmic energy with the entire spectrum of bright amperage housed within. To bring the full force of the frequency of love through the body temple with conscious attunement to the Light Body, we empower a generator of energy consciousness to inform the outer world anew. New minds, new bodies, new hearts - all activating toward an unprecedented level of freedom and awakened love for humankind.

Humanity is being so magnificently guided through a perfection of our original DNA Blueprint, the Shining Ones are here which in itself marks this as a significant time for our species! People are starting to feel their world and the wisdom of energy from within, getting back to their innate natures. It will be a gradual process but the Light will prevail in ways too wondrous to embrace beyond each moment. There is only ever this moment and we create the future ongoing within each precious Now... an opportunity to be new and effect change within our individual lives and the collective habitat of our world.

There is just such peace within the fullness of what we are in the midst of collectively. Christ Consciousness is streaming through an entirely new portal of radiance upon this beautiful blue orb of interstellar transference. I see in my mind's eye and hold in my heart the pure countenance of Jesus Christ, Lord Senanda, Jeshua Ben Joseph respectively. This Master of lucidity spoke from the heart of all things and materialized not to be held up as separate, to be idolized and worshipped and used as a divider of those he so humbly adored and walked among. His Presence was a reflection of humanity's ultimate potential as sovereign Light Beings. Christ Light is a light beyond visible light, it is the consciousness and energy of 5D World dissipating into the awareness of an organism ready to actualize Itself. We are compassion, we are understanding and peace, joy and harmony, unity, abundance and unconditional love in our brightest moments. And with the fortuitous ending of one evolutionary cycle and the beginning of another, we are the blessed and entrusted stewards of a new Light manifesting. We are Christ Consciousness returning to Earth through our willingness to take the mantle of a disciple's all-inclusive love into our hearts. The more fully you embody this frequency of Love, say YES to it and fear it not, the more radiant your energy will become. Love is a vibrational state that instantaneously gives new life to everything that breathes. The Sun is but a single candle's glow compared to the radiance of LOVE.

The return of the homoluminous to the earth is the vision that Christ had for the future of this humanity. We are the children of the 5th Sun coming to restore balance within the natural world of an existence that is capable of ongoing sustainability. We are the remembrance of a time when all things of true value and meaning were provided for in nature, when stillness was cherished as a powerful conduit of creationary power and breath as a vehicle for accessing new worlds in a state of constant wait to be born. As I sit in the stillness of the new world being born within me, sharing this expression of heart consciousness with you, I am visited by a downy woodpecker and a flock of wild turkey. As always, the Great Mother is at my side, at your side, gifting her insight and wisdom of these transitioning times. Through the woodpecker she reminds us that we are tapping out a new rhythm of being, an entirely new existence attuned to the heartbeat of mother earth. The woodpecker is earth's drummer and represents the ability to move into other dimensions at will on the way to new discoveries of Self.

The medicine power of the turkey is renewal. With proper care and cultivation of renewable resources, life is constantly restored to balance and harmony for all creatures, all of Creation. We have been blessed with great abundance in the earth and endowed with immeasurable gifts within. It is in sharing freely while acknowledging all of life as sacred that we will come to know peace once again on earth.

There is only this moment. It is your moment and it is unlimited and free. The intensification of the Light in the coming days with this exquisite gift of the 11/11/11 stargate is a rarified opportunity to align with the stargate of your heart and mind's eye. Within this deepening is the potential activation of both Ultimate Consciousness and the Cosmic Creationary Matrix across a new grid of Beingness, a future manifesting NOW, without fear, only Love.

The Journey Toward Unity

November 14, 2009

"The real voyage of discovery consists not in seeking new landscapes but in having new eyes."

Marcel Proust

So much beauty, so much Light, right in the midst of so much that is coming undone: I contemplate often the relationship between the inner world and the outer, the egoic mind and the heart, the world of form superimposed upon the formlessness of untold potential realities. And what I know to be true is that what is within, surrounds us, always, without exception. As our world shifts into another season of being, we are being asked to rectify, not only what is disparate, separate and lacking compassionate care within the creations of form without. We are called to a new clarity of being within, one that carries enough personal light to illumine any thing or person that is perceived as other. For it is wholeness that our nature requires, right alignment, a self properly aligned with Self. Change, imagination, creativity and liberation become the awareness of one who has moved beyond thought and determines to become the complete answer in each moment to what is evolving. Becoming whole is, in fact, a profound secret that can only be realized within the unknown.

Each week we travel into deeper mysteries within the show and within the greater world transforming. What I love and honor so much in how this template is unfolding is that the unseen powers are manifesting as actions that nourish, shape and connect us in more unity. Through an intricate balance between what is being lifted to more Light and what is being allowed to dismantle into states of ultimate disrepair, we find the peace of empowered choice. Life as we've known it is deteriorating because of a lack of understanding of what existence is truly about; shared resources, cooperation, co-creation and love. This **now** is a period of timeless and right action, solutions sought not for the comfort and safety of self but for the good and love of the whole.

Visualize yourself standing before a gateway on a mountaintop. All that has been is behind you, no longer visible to your awareness, yet the future rests in the wait of your own transformation. There is a necessary unknown that becomes the chrysalis of our own becoming as we undertake the journey between two worlds. New clarities may ask for us to forgo existing plans, ambitions and ideals with an understanding that the future is under constant change. When we allow the heart and each moment to decide the next step of necessary forward movement, we enter a new realm of Ultimate Consciousness that is able to see and move beyond.

You cannot describe the mystery to another, nor can you teach it or lead one to it. You can only become the greater mystery of who you are. It is in the mystery that we meet with our highest expression and begin the true purpose of this existence: to discover the meaning and destiny of our lives, not through the mind and thoughts and beliefs of others but through the freedom of our own. Then the future becomes an Oracle of the Self. We must continually go into the unknown within our own potential and the unknown of the greater mysteries of life to build the new grid of a Self Actualizing human consciousness. There is, indeed, an entirely new grid around the planet, a frequency of embodied light radiance being grounded into this dimension by right action and the awakening of the Unified Self. Every prayer is being answered in each moment toward the realization of a new humanity by each individual's ability to extract your own answer and determine for yourself what is right action.

The new human emerging is standing at the threshold of a timeliness of understanding that there is only this moment and our power lies within it. Experiencing the true present is something most find difficult because we spend a great deal of our lives dwelling on past regrets or future fantasies. To catch ourselves doing so is the beginning of Self. Magic, unlimited mind and a fierce lucidity of heart consciousness are always in the present moment. The ability to be what you know and live who you are is an evolution of understanding that any belief we carry or tenet that we follow that does not include the consideration of the whole, speaks to the uncertainty and division you carry within. There is no other. The trees, the rocks, the animals and our dreams are all extensions of the One Force that is seeking a totality of expression; feeling existence, knowing existence, being the whole of existence, everywhere, in each moment. The greatest gift within this time of major growth for our species is the genetically endowed ability to turn off thought and engage the intuitive powers that we have to navigate ourselves through the unknown. Joyousness accompanies this new energy and Light pierces through all uncertainty when we embrace love as a living Intelligence capable of disinfecting the entire illusion of our history! Love is like the parent and those in the mind and thought are still in the infancy of the human potential. Our inherent Light is a trillion times brighter than the sun.

We are in a moment of decisive choice. It is our destiny to change the way we do things, our lifestyles and care of each other, the dispensation of our gifts and talents. At our best, each of us is a channel through which divine wisdom flows. One of the greatest secrets out of which our history has evolved is that the unknowable is the Divine! When we are in nothingness, we are in God and in Love and all the details that we fear and are enslaved to become irrelevant. We have some potentially devastating times ahead of us for those who are in the mind and remain attached to the world of form. Its deconstruction is inevitable. As we cross the event horizon of an uncertain future, we must go deeper into the mystery of self and all of existence and create the new world from within. The humanity of each age is a reflection of the culture in which it evolves. To be responsible and to cultivate trust within human beings is to make known what is right. Leaders within our Sciences and Governments, Environmentalist and Economists alike must move into this Age of Transparency with equal measures of integrity and consciousness. The future of our greater world lies in each individual's ability to change the world within, raising individual consciousness and doing what is right for all.

We are journeying between two worlds, one that can be seen and touched and one that can be felt and embraced all-inclusive. It is the shift from strictness and reason to freedom and the transparency of love. To be self responsible is to shine a bright and fearless light into the unknown of your own creations and step out of what is not authentically you. Then we each become creators of a new reality that is not just a condition or unmet expectation of mind, but a radiant expression of our creativity, our joy, our sovereignty and power as conscious beings of Eternal Light. We can build new societies together based on love, trust, integrity and Self Responsibility. It is an instantaneous decision to be made by each. You are here to enact change, I am here to be change, we are here to cooperate with and listen to a new language of intelligence that is beyond reason, but within love. Together we encompass the full spectrum of all that we have been and all that we can be in the only point of power we ever have, this now: Be it, dream it, see it, embrace it, love it, expand it, evolve.

Chrysalis Of A New World

November 21, 2009

I was out by the river yesterday, cooling off with my dog after a morning run, when a memory came to me that the Guidance encouraged me to share. It is so important to find balance and spaces of peace for our Spirit as our bodies and minds and lives undergo so much rapid change and transformation. I often go to nature to calm the uncertainties of an unknown reality determined to surface to the awareness of our species. On one such day, I journeyed as if in a field of future orientation, beyond time, to a place on this same river. I felt drawn to just lay my weary body down on one of the giant rocks that framed the water's flow. I remember staring a long time into the endless sky above. An occasional red-tail hawk flew over as I listened to the harmonies within the rapids at my side and I felt at once suspended, lifted into another space of being, yet equally at peace with the reality I currently resided in. Hawk provided a reminder, for my awareness and the many, of new vision now coming into view for this humanity and of the interdimensional guardianship present within our expansion.

After a period that felt like forever yet an instant all at once, I got up from my time-space acclimation of beingness and what I momentarily saw will remain with me always. As the sunlight hit the immediate environment like a great illuminator of clarity, every stone, every rock of all shapes and sizes scattered along the river's edge, became a heart. Hundreds of hearts glistened in the sun's rays. They actually appeared animated, effused with the effervescence of radiant lifeforce. It could only be described as magic of the highest order. And I think the reason this memory came to mind within the energies of this current portal of our evolutionary ascent is that it reflects a greater phenomena at hand. Something wholly wondrous is breaking through, seeping into this known and fixed illusion we have understood as life. As the consciousness and energy of this humanity continues to expand, the non-material worlds of interdimensionality are becoming more apparent, worlds no longer hidden.

When in stillness, I see the world of humanity as a closed lotus flower, just beginning to open, and it is crystal. The lotus flower is a symbol of the Buddha-nature, purity and perfection, acquisition through innocence and stillness. There is a phenomenon of crystal energies and DNA molecules merging as the veils that have kept things hidden to this species continue to fade away. We have entered into a new placement in the Universe, in Creation, by raising our consciousness with the Earths. An exquisite symbiosis of emergence is upon this humanity, the air around us and the structure within us changing in each moment. There is a new hologram of reality being projected by these new crystalline qualities and minds and hearts are being affected deeply. Brains are being restructured, nerves upgraded as many beings begin to embody the symptoms of a fully actualized human being. Like a giant ovum in the throes of giving birth, Gaia's combustion as she makes her way to a new galaxy is allowing her to shed the layers of miscreation and deception that have for so long diminished her lucidity. It is a Process more beautiful than we have expression for with our primitive language. But we don't need to describe it to make it real, we just need to allow and become her metamorphosis.

I am increasingly intrigued by the appearance of ancient rock formations within the region of my little spot on the earth. I have for the last year been experiencing stargates and portals in the guise of great monoliths, but they typically would go back into hiding after my brief encounters and experience of their energy structures. Now these sightings are not only increasing, they are remaining. These bleed-throughs, supernatural appearances of giant stone beings inscribed with hieroglyphic symbols are, I feel, just the beginnings of profound new discoveries. I have seen rare plant life growing deep within the woods, as well as the appearances of seemingly new species within the animal kingdom. As this magnificent star tetrahedron continues her evolutionary spiral into 5D World much that was lost is coming into existence, once again; evidential promises of the new earth now manifesting. Dimensionality is exceeding dimensionality because more are waking to their inner radiance and the ancient worlds are being born anew: for us, by us, through us, the new human collapsing ancient and future civilizations into this now. Time is not only folding in upon itself, it is becoming Eternal.

Those who live in secrecy can no longer hide from the expansion of the Universal Heart. The Age of Transparency is descending upon the old world in a cosmic field of stardust, activating the golden serpent of the DNA codex. The portal, the galactic doorway to 5D World is now open to us by our heart, our integral intent and vibrational signatures. The placement, arrangement and geometric lines of these stone beings are potentially creating a new harmonic across the planetary grid as their gates are opened. They are part of the new song of humanity. The return of these ancient cities and artifacts, wisdoms and technologies are allowing our natural abilities to be healed, the appearance of crystal children to accelerate and Unity Consciousness to be the center from which we create new societies and communities of Light. Higher faculties of human understandings are taking flight as we embrace the implicit relationship between the world and individuals coming together in a commonality of intent and shared responsibilities.

The key to experiencing these higher energies with ease and wonder and amazing creative manifestations is to connect with each other in love and respect. This has been quite the journey our species has undertaken. We did so knowing that we had the power and foresight and maturity of spiritual mastery to succeed in transforming a world of duality to a Unity of Light. As our energy and Gaia's Crystalline Grid continue to ascend, divine linkage is happening and we must allow that synergy to guide us to new ways of loving, serving, interacting and living in the world. You are not here to do your work, I am not here to do my work, we are here to do the work of planetary service, together, as One. We have all fought a great battle to recover the true ownership of this crystal blue orb, she belongs to love, you belong to love, we are that Love.

The Unity building within the template of **The New Human** reflects the many facets of a beautiful rainbow prism. We are the sound and light, the crystal essence of a new world emerging. It is with great humility that I share the language of the light and the intelligence of nature each week on the show, as the Shining Ones reveal the secrets of dimensions that dwell in peace and harmony, cooperation and pure intent. They have returned at this time because we are ready to re-member the star-seeds within our DNA. Their radiance and love is a gentle reminder to take nothing for granted – that each of us is the sun in the east that reflects a new mind capable of being fully in each moment, with present thought. It is for each of us to look beyond what we think we know and embrace the mystery as a presence we need to embody. We are migrating to a new level of being and we carry the secrets and radiance of the stars within.

I sat alone in the tranquility of a setting sun, overlooking a still lake. I felt a warmth envelope me with a simple metaphor of our existence here as energetic beings. "You are still waters at the core of your being. You are here to experience the diverse energetics that nature tosses into that stillness. Sometimes the new creates a wave that effects great change in your world and sometimes, just a ripple that fades away. Accept them all, live without expectation, know it is ALL love."

And as the sun disappeared behind the ridgeline, a mysterious light appeared in the center of the lake. It had a shimmer, a radiance that danced in a diaphanous field of new light. Somehow, the setting sun had found a tiny window on one of the homes on the far side of the lake and created a secondary ray of luminosity. Things were not as they appeared but more beautiful than could be imagined. It was the new Light of a new Sun, reminding me in that moment that the world has indeed, changed. The Golden Age is here, we are the awakening ones and the ancients are returning by our willingness to surrender the separation, to **trust** that all is truly well.

A Now Before Its Time

November 28, 2009

I see in my mind's eye, the energy of a giant funnel. There is velocity present of a clockwise movement within a reverse spin, and the vacuum at the base of the funnel is drawing everything back to zero point. The presence of greater and greater polarities on our planet, extreme measures of separation within the yin and yang, the shadow and light, the deceptions and truths of the totality of our humanity - created this spinning chaos of imbalance. And as our planet continues its rapid acceleration into her new and radiant position in the galaxy, this molecular reconfiguration of beingness for all of existence is folding in upon itself. It is the swirl of transfiguration. Gaia is leading us through this evolution of the heart with the potential of Universal Unity available to all. All the planets in the Solar System are changing, just like the earth, and everything that is happening to us is part of this timely change. No longer can the energy of separation, duality, opposites and imbalance be supported. Linear understandings of space-time are giving way to what is the rise of a new human consciousness that moves with spiritual time and the void of infinite nothingness. We are the destined keepers of a time like no other.

The Universe is an exquisite system of perfect balance. There is instantaneous expansion and contraction to deflect the magnetics of an intelligently ordered organism in any given moment. As the expansion and intelligence of the heart of humanity continues to ripple across the crystalline grid of an awakening species, more are embracing the present moment as a teacher of the highest order. Single mindedness, a centered presence of awareness and the willingness to be still are the spiritual disciplines attuning more and more to our power and responsibility as creationary beings. Most fail to grasp the power and peace of being only here, right now. We are conditioned to live in emotional fragmentation over the past or with fear over the uncertainty of the future. Thought has robbed us of the inexplicable freedom, and vast potential of each moment. Yet it is only when you are fully present to each moment, living it, embracing it, accepting it and loving it, that you have the full power of the Soul.

I stood in the kitchen of an opulent home last week with a realtor friend, who was preparing the space for a new tenant. This immaculate, lavishly furnished abode is a secondary home and rarely visited or enjoyed by its owner. My friend and I both observed how perfect and ordered and with such abundance the place was... yet it did not feel inhabited, loved or appreciated. It gave the appearance of the finest material comforts yet there was no soul present, no heart, no peace.

In that moment, I felt my mind and energy zoom through a wormhole of the human polarity. We stood in a reflection of the power of money, what it can do and acquire and maintain in the illusion of social consciousness. And what occurred to me in that moment is that that extreme energetic, of satisfying the egoic mind no matter what the cost and at the expense of insatiable emptiness, is the exact same energetic that created the extreme poverty in our world. They are the magnetic polarities of the same consciousness. It was a simple moment of profound insight into our undeniable responsibility in the world we have shaped around us. We are that powerful. And that loved. We are the god-force manifesting in each moment, the duality of our chosen involution. As we awaken to the Observer of our multidimensionality, we are able to see more clearly the extent of our imbalance. There is a Universal Justice, a supreme continuum of existence that allows for the extreme measures of our choices in regaining our own state of ultimate union within the Self and in relation to all of existence. The Light is seeking wholeness and the return to Oneness through us. The new human is a new consciousness grounded in the wisdom of Unity and drawing new sustenance from the zero-point field.

So much is occurring so fast, with many different levels of awareness and understanding to interpret the unknowable for this species. I had a rare and special encounter yesterday in nature. I feel it speaks to the energies of this newest vibrational increase that came in over the weekend of November 21 and 22, 2009. I had my first experience of a white squirrel. As there are no accidents and the Guidance is ever present with exacting mirrors of the energies carried within, I knew this fascinating creature was providing more insight into our collective progress and forward movement. One doesn't need to do any research to know that squirrels are industrious with high energy and ever focused on their tasks. They store away for future needs, obviously having vision for things to come and being prepared for it. The gathering power of squirrel is a great gift that teaches us balance within the circle of gathering and giving. The significance of the "white" is, of course, rarity and purity of heart and spirit. The new human consciousness is intent on following spirit first and focusing the mind on things of greater importance. This now is about building networks of co-creative exchange and individually preparing the way for sovereign communities of sustainability. We do what we do and act for the purpose of love and love alone, trusting the intelligence of the heart to see clearly what stands in truth.

As we continue to move into uncertain times of extraordinary transitions and transformations for our species, squirrel reminds us of the power of cooperation, coming together with alert mindfulness to the needs and proactive movement of a shifting climate of existence. We are now in the approach spiral of a very new human experience. The world of form appears to be intact and functioning as usual but there is no support under it, 3D dimensional space/time no longer has a foundation.

The world of energy, of frequency and vibration exists within total time. It is fluid and in constant motion. As vibrational beings of increasing light amperage, this eternal world is the unknown making itself known in each moment through the 5D Principles of Ascension; peace, joy, harmony, cooperation, creativity, compassion and non-violent solutions. There are not enough safe guards or preparations that can be made by individuals because the organism exists as One. Unity Consciousness is the new foundation of security. It is time to join resources, talents, inner light and clear-seeing vision as we step fearlessly into the days ahead. Our future is the past embraced with gratitude and loving detachment. It is our choice as divine beings of energy and light to view this time as just an ordinary passage of what has always been. Or we can awaken to the awareness that this interplanetary climate change is affecting our DNA directly and that we are no different than the higher mind intelligences and advanced spiritualization of multidimensional beings throughout the Cosmos. That is what we are awakening to and it is timely, indeed.

Earth changes, from the highest sensory awareness, are an opportunity to migrate to future possibilities, to make use of the past as an experiential teacher capable of breaking the shell around the heart. The energy of the future flows in the direction we radiate our love, our true and creative passions and our joy for the gift of what has not yet been seen or touched by this humanity but has all the potential to be made known to us in this lifetime.

The secret that I have seen manifest from the inverted triangle I described in the opening imagery, is the secret the ancients knew and that we must now remember. We are a species of golden light body merkabas now lifting to our rightful place in the Universe. We are each an exact replica of the star tetrahedron around the earth. Her movement, her transformation, her lightening and evolutionary thrust through the stars, is ours. We are moving in synergy toward a time and place where only Unity and Love will remain. Each and every day, the Shining Ones and many realms of Cosmic Seers are revealing more and more of the seeker's puzzle to a humanity no longer in density and shadow. The worlds are collapsing for the purpose of a new start and new day for this beloved humanity. It is time to exhale...

Void Of Creation, The Return To Zero Point

December 5, 2009

The moon, the stars, every planet, all atoms and molecules, the tiniest seed of a dandelion weed and the complete wonder of the physical body... all connected, all changing irrevocably, all One. You are the Universe, I am consciousness and energy and throughout and within the many different expressions of existence, Creation is unhindered, always, all ways.

As I came up the mountain pass in one of my most cherished nature settings, I was met with the magnificent stance of a Stag. I stopped still in the early morning mists as he met my gaze with both intensity and gentleness. I felt him. I knew he was there even before I saw him. Eight points, positioned as antenna to direct the mind to higher forms of attunement, reminded me in that moment, in this moment, there is, indeed, power and potential of infinite worlds available to us; the balance of a new kind of achievement and victory for this humanity. Within ancient teachings and tribal wisdom, deer is considered our most important link between civilization and wilderness, a gentle, but inciting summons into new realms, new lands and an open door to the greater mysteries of life.

In the higher dimensions above the third and fourth plane of existence, time is holographic. It is not limited to individual understandings and reference points for what comprises life and the meaning therein. Throughout the Universe there is order, perfect balance, harmony - in the movement of the planets, throughout all of nature and in the functioning of the human mind. A mind in its natural state of order is in harmony with the Universe and is such, timeless in what it can access and comprehend and take into the heart's intelligence, as Truth. My intellectual awareness of zero point energy is limited. Yet, in my high mind, where all energy meets everything else, my consciousness expands daily in understanding the manner and significance of this phenomenon.

There is a void where all the energy in the Universe is found, a vacant space with a background of harmonic codes and multiple frequencies working together in precise cooperation and harmony, a truly magical technology of light, electrical currents and infinite free energy. I frequently access and experience this dimension of exacting ratios, tones and frequencies when in the utter stillness of the natural world. It is a dimension and quality of understanding beyond the mind, an advanced awareness that we are that void, the totality of differentials and harmony there in.

In nature, in the woods, there is utter stillness. I can hear my breath, the space between the silences and the sonic hum of the Universe all-inclusive. And what is so meaningful in sharing this experience with the many is that it is reflection of how multiple facets of our existence and awareness across technologies, are folding into shared discoveries. Examples throughout our world and across many mediums that suggests a cohesion of mind, a harmony of heart, a singularity of consciousness; that the design of the whole Universe is toward the inevitable Unification of It, of Self. This void and moment for the human species is an opportunity to expand and flower like never before. It is a moment that has never been and will never happen again.

True life is coming from an energy field. Consciousness is a living, fluid, emotive and transferable energy that is responding to the energy in you. Each week I take the listeners of **The New Human** radio show on adventures of consciousness, examples of collapsing worlds and heightened Presence from the unseen realms. In my own small world within the more documented research of advanced sciences there is proof of the connection between the consciousness of humanity, the consciousness of the Earth and the consciousness of the entire Cosmos. The awareness that every life is linked to all existence enhances the connection between the quality of life and the quality of thought. Individual life and our collective existence is an expression, always, of our mind and perceptions. That is an understanding of great power. When we move out of the field of thought and the conditioning therein, we move into a field of energy that reveals new realms of existence that speak to you from the most unlikely of places, and serve to shift the whole of conscious awareness to a new paradigm of understanding and connectivity with all life.

The old brain is connected to the egoic mind and masculine reasoning, the new brain is connected to the feminine heart and eyes of knowing. I can literally feel and "see" movement, a migration of sorts to a new part of my brain; shifting platelets and electrical synapses rewiring conditioning, to a new freedom. More and more we are having experiences beyond the capacity of the old brain to even interpret, much less put into expression. And we must just allow that to be, accept that it is ok to have a moment before us that defies reasoning, that asks us to be fully present and become the unknown of what is unfolding.

As I stood high in the mists after my providential encounter with the stag, the Shining Ones began to gather in the vast nature that surrounded me. From within the trees and out of the mists, beautiful blue radiances of Light began to emerge as exalted magnificence, Presence and knowing. These high beings of such intimacy with the earth embody omnicompassion, a vast inclusion of all that humanity has been and can be. I started to pivot, taking in all the wonder, the energy and love of this new existence that is manifesting on our behalf. This love... (big breath in) to love one another in this way will change the entire foundation of our existence, this I know. We are to take this love into our being and radiate it out into the possibility before us.

I believe that all high beings and ascended masters from every dimension and angelic realm are essentially One Love expressing different qualities and focus of energy. I understand that the Shining Ones are the link between the earth, our genetics and the interconnected ascension of Gaia and this humanity. They impress upon my heart and knowing each day that our cellular structure is quickening and our consciousness expanding so much that it is our potential to become an extra-stellar civilization! But they equally fill me with caution and foreseen warnings about our responsibility to move with the shift upon us. They recently shared these words with me that I share with you now!

"When you truly begin to cross the event horizon of the new world and your Authentic Self, less and less of your egoic identity will be recognized or find stability. Everything that you have figured out and know to do to keep your life functioning and in sync with the 3rd Dimensional reality will be rendered useless and without merit or credibility. One by one, all doors to your past will be shut because you have chosen to know and be more, to begin investing and participating in Eternity, now. The death of the ego, ideals and power derived from this illusion of mental constructs and material gain is what is often referred to in your world as the dark night of the Soul. No longer content to be a distant participant in an illusory existence, the Soul must now awaken and become the new lighthouse and guide for the dying aspect of self.

Can you deny that there is something more than what you can see and touch and reason with the mind? Can you deny that there is a greater Force of existence calling this humanity to higher ground? Has your heart and knowingness been touched by something deep and moving to the spirit? Why? What is the purpose of such depth if you are to keep figuring things out by the same tired decisions that have gotten your people nowhere of lasting measure.

If you really want to understand and know more about who you are to Creation, you must be willing to continually examine your thoughts. You are a programmed and conditioned people. In order to really allow the possibility of Creation to open up, a new land and worlds beyond your capacity for thought, you must be willing to widen your perception and embrace the mystery as the bridge to interdimensional Unity.

Everyday your mind and heart, your thoughts and actions must reflect a new knowingness, that you need one another, that you are one another and your gifts are an interlocking harmonic, the tone of One Organism. If you are not yet positioned to make the reach yourself, you are increasingly shown ways that you can extend your reach through others who have stepped out ahead. Where you are today as a humanity, was created by thought, steps and actions of individuals. Everything is responding according to your interaction with it, this has always been your power. You have existed as a species long enough to know what has been created that no longer works and what has not yet been created, that must now come to pass. New minds, new bodies, new hearts, creativity, communities of shared exchange, cooperation, compromise, living your own lives of sovereign purpose and an inseparable, inexhaustible, symbiotic communion with your host earth. This will not be an easy transition for your people, but it will be more than worth it and is the only hope for a world of unity and peace."

As I stood there, alternating between in-breaths of gratitude and an exhale of complete humility at the greater worlds I am shown so freely, the light of the morning sun suddenly burst across miles of open mountainside, landscaped with majestic trees. Suddenly, what was in one moment a veil of singular dimension became an illumined canvas of differing shades of shadow and light. The trees became many trees as their shadows were exposed with the rising sun. And the gentle wisdom of the Shining Ones energy echoed through my awareness: "there is a new sun, a new light here for your people, and its radiance will expose every shadow. The Creator is bringing your Solar System back to balance, a new dawn of understanding is coming to your planet and you must change with this new ray activity if you are to survive."

A place of perfect balance, an infinite void of utter space, stillness, peace, Creation, infinite possibilities, a time like no other. More and more we are embracing the individual power we have to create a new kind of world. The earth will continue to shift its vibration as it moves into a new groove in the Universe. Her time is and will continue to be less and less in sync with our understanding of time in 3rd dimensional reality. We must let go and surrender the mind, its attachments to form, to extreme materialization and the anger of unjust creations. The Age of Transparency, a return to the innocence and joy of existence is the wisdom of maturity that comes with accepting that nothing has ever been done to you, all is free will, all is choice. Your future matches the extent of your imagination, the perimeter of your beliefs and the magnitude of your love, an inexplicable love of everything for everything else.

The new human emerging as an empowered creator of a new earth is keenly aware that the you you know and are today, is not the Self that is ready to step in and be the Light of a new world, for your own evolution and all of existence. The new spirituality of 5D World is a return to zero point energy where time is stacked in synchronization with the new energetics of a new human physicality, mind and heart. We must allow for an unprecedented and unchartered change of purpose for all of Creation. This Shift is not just a shift for humankind it is a shift that involves every level of every dimension and every planet in the Solar System. We are part of a galactic shift that is raising the vibration of every planet in the galaxy. That is who you are, that is how much you are loved.

In the background of the space that is the void, once fearful and unknown, is the energy of a new song, a new and beautiful artistry ready to expand our understanding of music as a species to the music of all of Creation. We are now in awareness of the holy grail of our true power and purpose as humankind. All is available to us now through the highest frequency of love and the manifestation of Interdimensional Unity. The future is **now** and it is all happening within.

The Return Path

December 12, 2009

Jiddu Krishnamurti asked the question, "What is Creation?" A great mystic and teacher of the unknown equation, this gentle illuminator suggested that in answering the question, we first ask, "what will we give to it?" (sigh) What energy, what capacity, what enthusiasm and passion, what level of freedom will we give to the totality of Creation. An impeccable reflection of the search for Truth, Krishnamurti in effect answered the question by directing awareness to the one measure by which Creation expresses itself, namely you.

As I write this expression of my own creative capacity, the whole of humanity is in the midst of a stargate triad, yet another time-wave intersection to facilitate the receptivity of cosmic knowledge and greater love upon our planet and species. Daily, around the world there are event phenomena occurring, drawing more and more into the undeniable awareness that the unknown is making itself known, through the energetic of transparency. The emotional climate of earth's people is scattered as so many seeds across a wind-blown horizon, because we are no longer in wait for some distant possibility of transformation to occur. It is happening now, right in front of us, in each moment. This is our moment of decided action in moving away from duality and into the frequency of love, all-inclusive. To understand energy consciousness is to understand that wherever we put our energy and thought in each moment, is to become that which we focus upon. Whatever it is, great or small. It is not our job to check everyone else's action and react for then we are the ego we stand in judgment of. We balance and justify all disharmony in our world and the greater organism not by egoic influence but by turning our energy to the work of Unity! We must put our minds and time and energy on growing more of what is now right, to creative purpose and harmony in all things, leaving the need to correct and defend to denser realities. We are spiritual Joy. We are teachers of Light. We are fractal components of the many faceted prism of love. Our work here is to reclaim the emotional fragments of our immersion into density by retracting all energy from pockets of dissension and distortion, thus embodying the power of energetic neutrality. We must not underestimate the cunning of dark forces to use differing factions of spirituality as yet another distraction to alienate us further from Unity and our evolution as a species.

Our enlightenment is through a thorough command of Self. Our ascension is the remembrance of our authentic nature and how greatly that authenticity yearns to serve as a catalyst for world transformation. The greater consciousness and energy of possibility present for a new human capacity is the ultimate awareness that there is only one event happening, one experience, one world of expression. This emerging paradigm allows for the experience of Self as greater than the holographic component of identity that is experiencing this reality. Life is multidimensional. It is the expression of billions of points of light into different lifetimes and experience holograms.

The new human meditation that came in to express the potency of this current stargate portal, was a visual expression of the interwoven spiral between the physical, Spiritual, Soul, Shamballa, Solar Logos and God Monad. A new bridge is forming within the expansion of consciousness on our planet that is linking the lower and higher self to coincide with a personal spiritual evolution. A new science of the mind is emerging as part of the process of enlightenment for humanity that will reflect the practical application of the inner connection between humankind, the earth, spiritual hierarchies, other planets and greater solar systems. The bridge of our own expansion of consciousness is allowing for many bridges of connections to now occur which all coincide with earth's positioning in a new solar system. Everything within every realm and marker of expanded intelligence within our current development as a species speaks to a coming together, to a joining of forces and cooperation of intent and power. It makes sense that initiation into a new solar system necessarily creates a body of expression at higher levels than the one before. To grasp the implication therein is to grasp that there are no kings at this stage in the game, there is only one event happening and this moment contains only love.

We are engaged in a massive evolutionary spike that is changing our DNA at unprecedented rates to coincide with a beautiful, co-creative cooperation between many realms and the earth plane. New technologies and healing modalities are in development that are part of a future we are still evolving toward Collectively. The new age of humanity is a new, right use of power, a power not of will and force but of allowing and of love. To know is to be satisfied with the awareness and wisdom you embody. Then that awareness and wisdom becomes an energy through you, with greater force and influence than the agendas the mind attaches to. There are so many levels of experiential frequencies present in this now, we are opening up to the full radiance of Existence and our unique and rarified roles in the totality of it all. Every person, every human being is at a moment of completion within one cycle and the beginning of something wholly and wondrously new. And the question of import is have we truly learned the lessons of density? Are we ready to emerge into the disposition of Unity in every measure, to lift the consciousness and energy of humanity into the frequency of Love.

The consciousness of the new human template expands within the show each week in synergy with global events and the suggestion of myriad challenging scenarios. There are an abundance of futurists and spiritual seers endeavoring to direct mass consciousness to a new awareness. More are aware each day that there are many dimensions happening at the same time, that we have a 3D and 5D earth existing parallel to each other along with an empowered choice as never before to choose which existence we want; for ourselves and the world. We must bring ever greater awareness and mindfulness to the power of our thoughts to hold us in certain vibrations. We have the capacity and enhanced vibration in this now to begin projecting our physicality into another dimension, another earth experience and we get there by the power of our mind, or the freedom therein! We must be fierce in focusing our thoughts on love and the greater scenarios of peace and cooperation coming to pass, on forgiveness and right action and interdimensional Unity. New systems and frequency maps are being created right now to support the vibrations of higher thought while those entrenched in the belief structures of the past will continue in 3D, veils intact.

The new human awareness is the emergence of energy consciousness, a scrupulous, unmitigated embodiment of oneself as energy intimately connected to everything else. We are everything and all experience at once and Ultimate Consciousness is the component that moves through all differentiation, as Love. We are in the gift of a gradual process of evolution that has culminated to a decisive moment for this humanity. The return path is the path by which the consciousness of what is and what might be, gradually dawns as a new light of understanding. As I observe the energy still being negotiated between differing camps of spiritual thought and opinion, I see how easily it is to fall into old grooves of separation over what is yet unsettled on our horizon. I do not dispute the unraveling and devastation of one reality of existence, an energetic that has grown too dense to be supported by the earth's new radiance. But, I understand deeply the intricacies of energy consciousness, as well. It is energy and the focus of our thought and action and love that will be not only our individual safe passage through uncertain times, it is the foundation of a new earth now manifesting. Consequently, it is critical that we be of very clear minds, free of emotionality and ego fragmentation. This new space of new creation is equally propagated by pure energy and the consciousness of One, or ego driven agendas and the continued lessons of density.

There are three strands of golden thread that comprise the rainbow bridge of a new science of a new age for this humanity. I could share with you that I became aware of this golden chain as I lay out beneath the stars one night and merged my consciousness with theirs. I frequently will lie on the ground of the earth and ask my future to inform my now on how to best serve this humanity. The answer I continually receive is the one known to the heart consciousness of all Creation, including you. Self Realization is the mastery of three things - honesty of mind (innocence), sincerity of spirit (intent) and detachment from all density and form. To embrace these is to transcend to a new reality where nothing has ever been done to us or taken from us and where no force has any power of lasting consequence over us as we truly understand who we are. We are creating our next Existence in each moment by how we are interacting with it all. The more one evolves, the more one knows. The more one knows, the greater the responsibility of service and the greater the opportunity for service. We must use our awareness of this amazing synergy of co-creation and cooperation to calm others and help them understand a greater love - that all is being brought into the light of a brand new day for the good of all humankind.

The final chapter of **The New Human** is entitled **Bridge Across Tomorrow**. I was aware through energy and my own heart's intelligence that at the time that information came through, two years ago, the bridge was referring to the disclosure and emergence of our necessary relations with our extraterrestrial kinship. And what this illumines to me from where I sit today is that what we once envisioned is now reality; that the hierarchies of humanity are merging with our minds and hearts through a new receivership and consciousness of an expanded reality of Existence. We have lifted now as a whole to the vibration of a higher possibility for harmony and peace. We are being informed by Consciousness Itself and asked only to imagine a reality free from duality, aversion and strife. As we head into another year of quantum reconfiguration for what it has meant to be human thus far, may we all remember and embody that the return path is and has always been, love.

The Immeasurable Now

December 19, 2009

I was driving with a friend across at best, precarious roads, determined to get to some sacred woods for a solstice ceremony. Recent, record breaking snowfalls in the Carolinas made getting even to the market a test of ingenuity and fortitude, yet the importance of this Winter Solstice of 2009, called deeply and reverently to stay true to our intent of honoring the Spirit World this day. We set out across a barren landscape of snow and ice, on a two plus hour journey to the heart of the Joyce Kilmer Forest. Many were to be a part of the ritual planned for this day, but only two were meant to partake in the experiences ahead. And so, my spiritual companion and I set out with much joy, trust and faith in the greater forces of love to always provide for exactly the experience that aligns with your heart and intent in each perfect now moment.

On the way to the ancient site that we have talked about in recent shows, we came upon an owl that had been hit on the highway. We doubled back with a tightness in our chests to retrieve this winged creature from its harsh environment, determined to honor it in the ceremony planned for the day. We tuned into the moment, understanding that all events are purposeful and that the Guidance is ever present with gifts beyond the scope of thought and reason. By the time we reached the entrance of the forest, it was clear to us that that owl had medicine of great import to contribute to this day, to the passage of time two beings of light were transitioning through on their own journey and the transition as well, of another great portal of energetic for a humanity being offered new eyes with which to see life.

The excitement and wonder by the time we reached the entrance of this ancient site had been building exponentially, but nothing could have prepared us for the events ahead. At a certain point, we reached roads that no car had dared journey upon because of the wintry blast that days before had dumped up to 18 inches of snow on various parts of our region. The vehicle we were in was not 4WD and we were driving into increasingly remote territory. But we forged ahead with determined knowing. At one point, driving in low gear very deliberately up the snow blanketed mountain pass, we came around a bend and felt an immediate shift in realities. We saw with our 3D eyes what looked like a wintry white passage of uncertain outcome, but our eyes of knowing saw a pristine wormhole. The energy of this Winter Solstice was taking us into the mystery. A promise was being kept and met in one inexplicable moment of understanding. There was nothing to be afraid of, we simply disabled our mundane eyes and let go into the magic, our focusing abilities were instantly enhanced and we were surrounded by a Presence filled with substance and peace.

We made our way to the face of the ancient site. There was an indescribable reverence present, such stillness and utter beauty. The sun glistened brightly on untouched snow. All around us were sparkling veins and crystals within the bed of wintry white and the nothingness enveloped us with a static charge of clear communication. We created a medicine wheel of tobacco on the snow with the owl as the all-seeing center. We burned sage, danced, sang, drummed and effortlessly channeled the expression and vision of 5D World. This day and the events that have spiraled since are multifaceted and unending, but I wish to share a few key elements with you as a bridge between where you are as you read of the experience and the greater truth that you were there, in ceremony, receiving the gift and wisdom of the owl who sacrificed itself for greater energies now rippling across the planetary grid.

All around us is death. Depending on your vision and level of understanding, death is present within the thinning veils of so much that is becoming Transparent. The earth is our conscious mirror and through the recent winter storms that are serving to disrupt routine and dislodge complacency, Gaia is reflecting a greater Process that this humanity must not only acknowledge, but embrace. A great force and frequency of illumination came in on the 20th of December, it opened yet another portal in anticipation of the empowered presence of the Winter Solstice. The cooperation and interconnected communication between worlds of true life cannot be measured or fully grasped by the human mind. Energy is constantly informing energy in a seamless spiral of divine synergy. The invisible molecule is informing the night sky that is a part of the winter storm that guides the flight of the owl that provides a new insight to the expanding mind of the seeker. All life is interwoven and generously speaking to us through the frequency of love, a love greater than all separation, a love beyond measure. The greater portion of medicine the owl gifted to all in receivership this day was about vision, profound vision, the ability to see with the light of the sun even in darkness, the unknown and mysterious worlds.

On Christmas Day 2009, while many bustled in the normalcy of family traditions that carried differing levels of personal meaning and consciousness, an energy permeated from the skies that offered this humanity a new awareness of our ancestry. I have had some amazing experiences with off-worlders of late, direct communications from the star beings. I spoke of such encounters in the December 19th show and revisiting the lightcodes within the show that day will reveal much about your own other worldly encounters, conscious or not. It is a very great love that is here now, informing our past from a future orientation so that we can free ourselves in this now from a perpetuated insanity. The energy and focus of minds and hearts on December 25th very much reflect the two worlds now separating into very distinct intents. The gift present for the many, the offering from the higher realms and planetary alignments that day was a chance to look at your past and heal the past with all relations. We are constantly interacting with our ancestors through the day to day interactions we have with our immediate relations. We're being challenged at our deepest core level as never before with an opportunity that will not come again. It is time to depersonalize and heal events across space/time, within and without. These new energies coming in will spin those who have not done their homework. The new human is a new consciousness, an awareness informed by a new science of mind and heart. Those attached to 3D and conformity, operating from mental constructs and ultimately fear, will not see the new light and possibilities now manifesting for greater understandings, a renewal of our humanity.

So many yet dwell in their own inner darkness, unaware. Their sovereignty has been usurped by an unconscious entanglement with their history such that the new is in a constant strangle by what has always been. The energy amplified by the owl within the power of the final of three stargates is the ability to see and hear through layers of density and shadow that allow so many to remain in their own unclarity. If you are still and within the intelligence of your heart, you will feel the presence and connection of this divine energy. There is a more intimate and powerful support present for you and the intent you carry deep within. The Light is deeming to express through you now, to be a portal of clarity so that others can see their way out of deception and shadow. In the realm of Light, there is only you and all of Existence is dependent on your remembering that there is no other.

This now is about authenticity. The new human is authenticity, journeying through this now with joy and the understanding of what is truly unfolding for our world. The prism of 3D is shifting to 5D World ongoing in ways great and small, you need only pay attention! December 2009 has been one event phenomenon after another; disclosure is here. New evidences of something previously unknown to this humanity are manifesting at quantum rates and we don't need government to tell us what is. Love and compassion are shapeshifting the laws of reality. The vastness and beauty of the universe is bending what could previously be defined such that discordant, unharmonious puzzle pieces are linking together to reveal a new Unity for all Existence. It is so important to take these personal and global phenomena of experience within and make them our own. There is nothing to be feared and no one to worship because all that was once separate is folding in upon itself. This is our evolution. Our ancestors are everywhere and all present and we now have the vibrational support to SEE and embrace them.

I observed myself carrying that dead owl as if it were a baby. I felt great love for it and felt loved and seen by the owl, as well. Each day, hidden in plain view, are evidences of the Spirit World reminding us that we are not alone and that there are hands reaching through the veils to guide us to a new existence. Sometimes I feel as if I cannot get a deep enough breath to take in all this love, love that is present for you, and me and the whole of a species once lost, now awakening to itself. In the stillness of my knowing I am constantly reminded that it is Gaia's essence to restore; she does not judge or take sides, balance is being restored. The Eternal Process of death and rebirth is the breath that is carrying us to a new earth, for all. The grave atrocities we've visited upon one another in a cycle that no longer serves, that is now complete, is being balanced by a compassion and love that is necessarily uniting heaven to earth, one tribe of many nations in interdimensional harmony. Something that knows more about you and the path ahead than your beliefs and perceptions is deeming to convey that to you in each moment, in likely and unlikely measures. Go within. Know yourself. Know your relationship with Creation and follow only that. The new human is your future self, extending a new awareness to you now and that new awareness is empowered with the insight and intuition of a very fierce love. This is our new freedom.

Touching Center

January 2, 2010

Close your eyes, take a deep breath, and feel. Can you imagine if the whole world truly understood that all the secrets and unknown mysteries of this existence are mirrored within one's own heart?

As we take the first tentative, yet wildly anticipatory steps into a brand new decade of an evolving world, what can we expect? How do we best proceed? Where will the stardust settle and who will we be in the settling?

Everything is so new, beautiful energy has found a permanent residency on the earth through a crescendo of energy portals attuned to the importance of a critical mass threshold on the horizon for our species. This new, that we are seeing and finding beauty in the things that really matter, is an energy available to all, capable of gathering the many into a positive momentum of inevitable change and transformation for this planet. Imagine standing in a shadow, and then the sun comes from behind a tree or cloud. At first, it shines on just a portion of your being, yet you feel its warmth and the joy of that radiance. Then a portal widens and the sun illumines your face and soon your whole being. What was previously dim lit now glows in the fullness of an incandescent new light for a humanity that has tired of its childish and transient ways.

The Light is here, great love is here, the High Ones have arrived on behalf of an evolving world. The Shining Ones and Cosmic Seers and Masters of many dimensions are all here to assure that this new Light radiance continues to expand and ground into a new season of being; a new reality of joy, happiness and abundance for this species. Everything true and of greater importance is coming into view, we can see now. The signs are growing more prevalent to dismantle fear and shine a new light in the direction of more - if we are in heart consciousness and center. 2010 initiates a decade that will go on to ripple for hundreds of years to come. We are ready to be conscious creators with the understanding that this brief passage from now until 2012 will be the foundation of this new decade and the many decades to come for this planet. This new energy is here to fill the new spaciousness within, the space created by Gaia's new light. These stargates and portals have been as great gates that have opened to pour more Light onto earth, and in so doing, pour more Light into you: your physical body, mental plane and heart center.

The unknown is your joy. It holds the potential of everything you aspire to as a creative being. Each moment is continually altered by your energy, an energy that grows and expands each day with new light radiance. This next phase we are entering for our species is one in which expressing and being your spiritual joy will be effortless, if you nurture your creativity and allow space for this potential. We are remembering and in this awakening realizing that we were each given gifts without measure and those gifts are seeded within our passion; passion for life, for existence, for experience, embracing the senses as conduits for a Creator in love with its Creation. You can confidently begin feeling how you want to creatively express this amazing, unconditional, universal love energy present with us now. It is here to empower your purpose, to begin using your voice and focusing your mind on a new world being born through you. How would this world look and be if you were its creator. Ungovernable, inexplicable, exuberant power comes with the realization that you are. Close your eyes, put your hands on your heart chakra and just feel the love of Creation that is now manifesting there as intelligence. Breathe with gratitude, breathe with the joy of one who now knows what has been given, entrusted to you, to give birth to at this time.

I was driving home from the woods yesterday. People marvel that I will go to the woods even in sub zero wind chill conditions. I imagine those who have mastered the earth plane did so by first dismantling the ego, disengaging the mind and demystifying the mystery of our spirituality. I love to defy the mind. An invaluable understanding of the **New Human Consciousness** and energy now present is that we are capable in any moment of transporting our physicality into higher worlds of frequency and light. As vibrational beings endowed with the DNA of higher mind technologics and starseeded capabilities, we can transform any circumstance into an experience that reflects our radiance. Consider that that blue light that spiraled over Norway was a fantastical event phenomenon that mirrored the smaller yet no less significant event phenomenon of everyday life for increasing numbers. To experience a wormhole, an energy transfiguration in our anything but ordinary realities, is to be cognizant of 3D and centered in conscious awareness, yet be enveloped in a field where all the elements such as time, location, temperature, physical limitations and the like, change. Wormholes transport you to a very purposeful experience that enables you to collapse worlds, fold realities and gather new insights. Ideas and opportunities that would have otherwise gone unnoticed just manifest right before your eyes.

I experienced two wormholes in the space/time between the December Solstice and New Years Day. Both were in nature, one I was by myself, and the other with a companion of like resonance. The natural forces are kicking up in intensity and that intensity can either support the reach of a greater trust, or it can further spin the chaos of 3D experience. When I go into nature, I don't take my mind with me, I am in my joy and gratitude unceasing. I am quite certain that the core temperature of my body has increased vibrationally, but I also know that we are increasingly empowered to assimilate frequency and acclimate the physical body to the circumstances at hand. This will soon be a vital understanding as we transition though the eye of uncertain times, environmentally, economically, financially and morally. It is so important to grasp that our mind and intent are decisive factors in the future we will experience. I have had the vision of myself standing in the midst of destruction and desolation, yet I am unscathed, beautiful, in peace. To understand how much we are loved is to recognize the power we have to choose the way we want to experience reality. You can be standing next to a person that chooses to experience in a fearful and ignorant way, yet not experience any of that insanity.

In 2010, anything that you desire strongly will manifest in your life. Discernment and a strong connection to Gaia's wisdom, are essential. It is so important to align your heart chakra with the Earth's core and the Cosmic Heart, unify your central column of light with the vertical axis of transcendent knowingness. There is so much information being disseminated and it will prove to be crazy making at best if you listen without center. It is your Authentic Self and Soul that can claim each moment as one in which you are the one who knows. The most brilliant minds and seers among us still have ego influence, ultimately you are the best source of information available to your expansion if you use discernment, use the breath to ground and learn to follow energy. There are so many unseen events happening that cannot be fully grasped with the mind, but they can be felt vibrationally, with heart consciousness. The unmoving is starting to move, the Universe is folding into a location inside of you. Our evolution is in understanding that the physical vessel is a portal for unconditional Universal Love and in following your heart you becomes the gateless gate to the totality of Existence, the totality of you.

The **New Human** is the mastery of energy. The ancient teachings and future worlds are merging through this timely and new consciousness of understanding. The process of Creation and our power as creationary beings is the simple understanding that we are frequency and light interacting with vibrational reality. 3D is held together by a focus of thought and energy, belief, perception and fear. 5th World, which already exists in a hologram of infinite experience, is a frequency of existence, as well. It too, is a consciousness. And the simple yet profound objective is to practice and live and **be** the frequency, the vibrational choice of the dream you wish to dwell in. You don't need to understand quantum physics and scalar waves and the mechanics of the speed of light to gather wisdom from the stars. You need only choose and orient your reality around love, joy, compassion, peace, abundance, doing what inspires you and gives you the freedom to create. 2010 vibrates to the number three and three is about creativity; your ability to create with a joy not of this dimension, and the courage, power and tenacity to do so in your own lives, but also in relation to the world. You are a creative being, as is the earth mother. She is giving birth to new life, for you, in you, though you. Your creative nature is a key element of the new roles each will be playing in these very new energies. Surrender what you think you know and give yourself permission to not know, yet love more deeply and create from the well of that love.

As the media and cinema of our times always reflects a greater Process and vibrational momentum of this humanity, it only makes sense that the movie Avatar come into being in this Now. The upward spiral of momentum around this species is so fantastical, and it is positive, heart centered creations such as this movie that impress our inner knowing with the fact that we have already dreamed the dream... we have seen it, been it, embraced it, mastered it and transitioned though all the light frequencies of our becoming. This IS the journey of our multidimensionality. We are in the upward spiral now looking down at all that has been, at a cycle now complete. I saw *Avatar* on Christmas Eve 2009 and could not help but feel the truer gift it reflected upon a still materially driven world. It is an adventure story and a love story, much like the story of this humanity. A movie in many ways before its time reflecting a future we can choose now. In our interior we are a love-centered humanity with full awareness of our interdependency with the earth. Through stunning visual and special effects that serve to effectively draw in the Collective, the greatest message and underlying theme that *Avatar* rippled out into that very same Collective is the importance of our connection to the earth to all existence. It touches deeply the Unity we all carry within and the magical, rich, peace and abundance that come from living in harmony with each other, and all life.

The first few weeks of January 2010 will be filled with strong energetics, opportunities to rise up, get out of complacency and free yourselves from whatever is perceived as limiting. It is not uncommon in this intense passage of ultimate emancipation to feel utter bliss in one moment and complete despair and hopelessness in the next. Such is the journey from forgetfulness to new light. We are re-membering to a new race, a new earth culture, a new world, "hallelujah mountains," and all. New energies are arriving from within the earth as she sings her way to a new song for all of Creation. These same energies are birthing in you, as well. Be kind and gentle with yourselves, compassionate for the journey you have undertaken and equally grateful for whom you now get to be.

The New Human is a remembrance, a remembrance before the past of our attachments. We are re-connecting with our true selves, our authenticity and heart. It is happening at a cellular level by a Process that is deeming to gather as many into the new as are willing to forgive the duality and embrace fully the language and light of love. This new transparency is allowing us to see and be seen as never before. Soul memories and blueprints within are NOW aligning with our conscious awareness. We are Unifying, Self Actualizing, meeting with our true selves, "two mirrors, facing each other with nothing in between." *Avatar* stirs many ancient memories and at best, leaves one longing for home. As we step fearlessly and authentically into a new year, within and new decade, within a new spiral of evolutionary humanity, may we all know the joy and peace of a journey so vast we can't help but embrace the gift of it as home.

High Magic Is Here

January 9, 2010

All energy came to a stop, all motion stood still. I was completely present to the reality before me, seeing the animated expressions and smiles of three faces sitting at the table with me. I petted the dog who could not seem to quiet the impulse to jump up into my lap and talk to me with her eyes. But something very magical was occurring, as well. A vacuum was present, a portal? a wormhole? A moment within a deeper moment that didn't need to tell me to pay attention, this experience was my attention. I observed myself at the center of a mystical event that felt at once like nothing else existed outside of that moment, yet all of life had equally folded into my present awareness. It was a moment that was bigger than all that had come before and included the entire future. It occurred to me that I was in the midst of my moment, that this extraordinary experience on an otherwise ordinary day was something that not only had I been preparing for through many, many lifetimes, I had arrived to the experience as destined. I had, in effect, caught up to my Self.

We are all in the midst of high magic. This humanity is the humanity that all the heavens are looking to as a gift that is about to be opened. Wonder is everywhere present, we have stepped through the looking glass and are now looking back at all we have been with new sight, greater awareness and an entirely new level of surrender. Is it a coincidence that the classic children's tale, *Alice In Wonderland*, has been remade into an epic story brought to life at this time? The themes within this tale abound with metaphor for the discerning eye and expanded wisdom of a species ready to see itself clearly.

Lewis Carroll recognized and honored the unprejudiced and innocent way young children approach life. *Alice In Wonderland* is the reflection of an adult world through a child's eyes, the silly rules and random nonsense of societal etiquette we've created for ourselves, along with the development of an unruly ego that to a child, is anything but logical. This story is a story about a child's struggle to survive in the confusing world of adults, to understand the adult world. Alice has to "overcome" the open-mindedness that comes instinctually for children so that she can be an adult, make her way through the incomprehensible, often arbitrary behavior she experiences in **Wonderland**. She quickly learns that apparently adults need rules, and lots of them to live by. Yet, most seem to live by these rules without asking themselves why? In **Wonderland**, Alice is constantly confronted by the motif of identity; the spiral of the rabbit hole disorients her sense of self. As each experience and encounter reflect back to her mirrors of closed minds within a conditioned world, she begins to doubt herself. Alice adventures through an unfamiliar land in search of a true reflection of herself only to find creatures full of unstable identities! She does learn to cope with the **Wonderland** rules and gets better at managing them as life goes on, but by the end, has adapted and loses most of her vivid imagination. She realizes that the creatures in **Wonderland** are 'nothing but a pack of cards' and wakes up into the 'real' world, the world of adults.

2010 is here! And this NOW is really happening! lol I chuckled on this week's show that 2010 sounds like a future event, some futuristic, prophesied time far in the distance. Yet, the Future is NOW and we are living it. It is like we've have caught up to ourselves. We are ready to grow up and become again, the astute awareness and free mind of the children we once were. The future is meeting the past in a Now vibrationally supporting the innate gifts, knowingness and wisdom of our authenticity. Everything truly does feel a bit surreal about this now, it is as if things, life, humanity has kind of come full circle. We've fallen through the rabbit hole, landed in a make-believe world and are in the return spiral of our re-membrance. The awareness is awakening in greater numbers each day that what we do here, we've already done, and we're here to understand and embrace the love of why?

The **new human consciousness** is aware, first and foremost, of ourselves, as energy, light meeting light in an anything but random experience. This reality is not something that happened to us, it is something that we anticipated and chose. It is a game of mastery if you will, in which the players embraced a duality with the intent to know Self more fully. Down, down, down the rabbit hole we joyfully leaped, wanting for adventure, trusting who and what we were to align with certain "markers," switches, experiential awakeners along the way of our journey here to help us step into greater and greater expressions of who we are. What I am observing, increasing so, is that those alignments, encounters and magical moments are quickening. I see it greatly in my own life and am a witness to it in the lives around me, ongoing. Increasing reflections of the future gathering up the past, through us. You will find yourself talking with and meeting people that you are either being an expression of the future for, "you" as the something that they have not yet awakened to, but are ready for. Or, you might find yourself in the midst of an experience that feels a bit ahead of where you now are, that asks you to step into it now, without thought but with greater trust and knowingness. At any given moment we have one of many possibilities before us that either become the new direction of our journey or keep us in the loop of patterns that soon shape a false and unconscious identity. The **new human** is capable of using energy to transform energy, in each moment, from what it was to what it could be. We have collectively transitioned into a new field of awareness that is awakening the many to their power to create not with thought and habit but with passion, joy and love.

These beginning weeks of a brand new year of a brand new decade are providing great momentum to our creative imagination. As children, we were fearless at jumping head long into new experiences, moving day to day through life, not with attachment and agenda, but with freedom of mind and joy of unlimited discovery. It is so important to move through your experience with an awareness of what is conditioning of belief, patterns that perpetuate the unconscious loop of societal expectations. We are entering the mystery and the ego will and must be necessarily disarmed. Patterns within nature and light-codes within the whole of existence are present as a higher information system to lead us into the Consciousness of 5D World.

The more new you surround yourselves with, the more allowing and in surrender you are of this new adventure, the more the unknown will become you and you it. We are downloading information from the stars everyday to help heal our DNA and activate a new awareness that we agreed to steward in at this time. Our power is about truly understanding ourselves and all of life as One Organism and our job here, our work that we must show up for each day, is orienting your current reality around your spiritual reach, the purpose you agreed to manifest at this time. Not sure what that is? Lacking momentum in breaking away from old patterns and groves of familiarity? Prayer, meditation, the power of intention, creativity, spending time in nature, eating a vibrationally aware diet, drinking pure water, relaxing, and allowing time for spiritual joy are powerful tools of transformation.

We are creationary beings in partnership with existence. The Creative Universe works through us. Without us, in our joy, out of conditioning and **being** the love of Existence in our everyday lives, nothing new happens and the loop we've long existed in, continues. If you get stuck, look for a pattern, if you go into fear, you are in a loop within a cycle of this humanity that is complete. Our karma in this lifetime is the purpose that drives us and that purpose is to expand beyond the illusion that we are separate. We are here to gift back all that we have been given so that new worlds and universes can manifest out of the universe we carry within.

Lewis Carrol wrote a sequel to *Alice in Wonderland* called *Through the Looking Glass.* In the first book (sleeping humanity), Alice is bewildered by the crazy adult (ego based) world. There was no joy or imagination. Children were told there were things that they could not do (which every child knows is not true!) and made to follow nonsensical rules that brought sorrow, pain and division to a rather uninspired life. In the sequel, Alice has grown up and having observed and better grasped the rules of the game, she is more confident with herself when interacting with the **Wonderland** creatures. In the first story she is chastised and told what to do. In Through the Looking Glass, she begins to teach the characters in **Wonderland** lessons that she has acquired in watching their silly ways. In so doing, she did not become, she transformed.

Alice had a goal in the second book. An astute observer will see the theme of patterns clearly represented in this fairy tale come to life. Fractals make the connection between our physical bodies, the ancient sites on our planet and the stars in the Cosmos. Everything is connected to everything else through patterns. Once we begin to **see** that Creation happens through patterns, we are empowered to interact with, move through and manifest our lives not through a repetitive cycle but through awareness and power. We can ride the wave within each cycle of existence without becoming that cycle.

The game within the game in *Through The Looking Glass* is chess, and Alice is determined to be Queen. To achieve this, she has to move within the understanding of the rules of the game, yet she does so aware of herself and with intent; it is her choice. She knows she must reach the final square and to do so, she can only interact with the creatures that are on a square directly next to hers. This reflects the necessity of sovereignty. She is not governing her decisions based on the anticipation of what other players or creatures or memories from the past might do. Nor is she focusing on where she wants to go at the expense of the current reality and moment. She is fully present with an analytic, discerning mind and using her intuition to guide each next move.

Alice In Wonderland was perhaps, a story from the future, an illumined ray from the foreseen of a species barreling down the wrong road. Magical with metaphor, I am sure that more than a few of us are feeling a bit like Alice, spiraling into a new land, a new adventure, a very unknown world. In the final passage of her journey, Alice is trying to reach a higher social position, she aspires to a more lofty position in life. She has mastered certain rules of a game she always saw as a game and learned her mastery from the very creatures stuck in the loop of this nonsensical reality. The story ends with Alice, at first, fearful of what will happen when she wakes up, that perhaps she will cease to exist.

"Now, Kitty, let's consider who it was that dreamed it all... you see, Kitty, it must have been either me or the Red King. He was part of my dream, of course, but then I was part of his dream, too! Was it the Red King, Kitty? Oh, Kitty, do help to settle it! I'm sure your paw can wait!" But the provoking kitten only began on the other paw, and pretended it hadn't heard the question. Which do you think it was?

And here we now are, dreaming the dream awake, a humanity not at all afraid, to wake up and remember. In just this last decade we have come through the awareness of Neo, in the *Matrix*, observing himself, as part of a cycle within a cycle of a loop of unconscious choice and powerlessness. In *The Last Mimzy* we were reminded of the world of pattern and light, codes and sacred sciences that exists beyond the adult mind, yet very much in the awareness and innocence of children. With the current phenomenon of Avatar, a ripple is being sent into an awakening consciousness that is stirring the memories of Unity and Oneness in our hearts. Of being seen in our authenticity while acknowledging our interdependency with Gaia. We have indeed, come full circle in this evolutionary spiral of our species. Alice leaped into the mystery with the innocence and trust of a child, a bottomless unknown where time slowed down, then sped up, and then collapsed when she decided to wake up. The unknown of her imagination was but a fragment of the greater prism of who she was and she was fearless in staying true to herself. Don't be afraid to remember and do what you came here to do.

As I sat in the midst of my own beautifully collapsing world yesterday, I knew that it was a moment that I agreed to long ago and that others are dependent upon my remembering. Everything is here in this now. All that has been and all that will be is present **in this now**. It is greater than we can make sense of with the mind but everything that we hold as intelligence in our hearts. We are free now. The Light on the horizon is here and high magic is our homecoming. Love Is.

Bridge Across Tomorrow

January 16, 2010

"This is love: to fly toward a secret sky, to cause a hundred veils to fall each moment. First to let go of life. Finally, to take a step without feet." *-Rumi*

I imagine if it were possible to collapse a rainbow, all the colors and centripetal force of that energy would be the swirl that encompasses a very radiant now. And although I have never been a trapeze artist, I imagine, as well, that I know exactly what it feels like to be suspended so high above the ground, the known reality so far beneath you. The fierce trust and faith you must have in your own ability to remain balanced as you walk a golden thread from one secure base to another. In other words, wow! We're really doing this. We are straddling dimensions, becoming as comfortable as we can with so much that is unfamiliar, unsettling to the ego and taxing to the physical. All the while, feeling the pull, yearning and remembrance of our own Soul as it rejoins the energy of home, 5D World emerging in the upward spiral of our journey here. A reunion with Self is manifesting and we just need to trust the unknown mystery, trust Gaia, trust love to continue to light the way.

Everything is here now, all present, in each moment and depending upon where you focus your thought and attention, your current reality will either be fed from the loop of conditioned consciousness and what has always been or from the higher frequencies that just exude inspiration. There is energy present to connect the dots of your whole existence, truly, past, present and future. As we continue (and we must continue for we've ventured too far out into the mystery to turn back now) as we continue to re-member to ourselves, align our 3D identity more and more with our Soul, we will align more and more authentically with our family of light, coming together in force, not out of need or agenda but out of a genuine love and honor and appreciation of one another. It is time. As transparency continues to ground into a new age of beingness within our world, we are seeing each other and life as it is, uncloaked, unmasked, out of shadow and into new power and elucidating light!

I had an experience this last week at the ancient site. We were turbo blasted once again with a power concentration of a new moon, solar eclipse and mercury turning direct all on one day. I see these alignments and portals as just so much love, cooperation of the highest order from the natural forces and elements of Creation stepping up on our behalf so that we too, can continue to step up, let go, know and be more. I was called to the ancient site in the Shining Ones woods to help my physical body integrate and assimilate this great power surge. There is a pyramid portal on the site, one of three, that sits at the base of the feminine face of the entire community. This portal is two-sided, with a masculine and feminine entryway. The pyramid of three giant slabs of rock is held up by a central white pillar, speckled with silver shimmers and shaped like a Madonna. I have spent time in the portal, just absorbing the energies into my body's composition, yet prior to this visit I have not been able to crawl through the gateway. I have tried several times, but something, was it the energies, my own higher Self? It is like there was an invisible force field that prevented me from going through. But on this day with the support of these higher energies that are only and of, such love, pushing us forward, higher, freer, I was able to crawl through and out the other side.

And what this reflects so clearly about where we are now as opposed to just last week much less the entirety of our history, is that we have access now to places we could not access before. Our bodies are adjusting, our minds attuned to new information and we can, by love, now venture into territory we have never journeyed before. This is the potential now available for each. New doors are opening every day, special and new earth grids are activating at this time to allow us greater access to ancient information and future awarenesses. And these earth grids are about **re-union** - across and within all dimensions. All of existence is a vast web of energy with endless dazzling directions and events and connections of dimensions to explore. And what I am observing, increasingly so, is that all intersections of your life and my life and greater existence seems to be folding into this now - everything available. The future potential is meeting the past awarenesses with unlimited potential in this moment. Greater forces are available now to help us, to assure we "get it" right this time out. This is the lifetime of personal evolution, from the inside out, Creation through us, into new Existence. Any moment that feels dense to you, unmoving or unsure... CREATE! Create, Create, Create. Creativity is the golden ticket, interdimensional access. When you create, you are **in** love, attuned to an entirely different flow of alignment and centering. It is time to be action oriented, putting your time and energy on what brings you joy, taking the mind away from things of lesser importance.

The way we experience this transition is up to us, to you! You don't change the world you're in, you change your frequency, so that you can move into alignment with and see the world of greater potential... and that it is all love. There are infinite parallel realities and frequency shifts happening simultaneously and where you put your focus is the future you will experience. The **new human** is a new frequency of being. It is the work of activating DNA codes within, through intention, sound, light, frequency, water, diet, awareness, cooperation and uncompromising attunement with nature. When you change, everything around you changes. Align yourselves, your reality, your choices and actions and heart with the consciousness of 5D World, joy, peace, harmony, compassion, forgiveness, abundance and creativity. Surround yourselves with others of reach, who aspire to greater love, greater service and positive attitudes about the future. All persons will remain in the reality that is appropriate to their frequency and belief. There is no right or wrong or judgment, just choice, and it is all is love.

The theme of this week's notes express thoughts still very much in the energy of a brand new year of a brand new decade. **Bridge Across Tomorrow** is actually the final chapter of **The New Human**. This final chapter of a new story for this humanity reflects a point of egress for our species, the bridge a reference to interdimensional unity with our extraterrestrial brothers and sisters. Expanding the circumference of our reach beyond the veils of separation is a necessary piece of embracing a greater family of light, as we complete a transition to a new and greater technology of being. I feel the bridge energy so potent in my everyday reality and observation at this time. It is very much like the ascension version of a life review, a near death experience just before being given another chance, new life, with the awareness of one who has gone through.

We've lifted above the insanity enough to know we can opt out of it. We see where we have been, the consequences of 3D consciousness and the futility of that game. And here we are, with new awareness and greater love, now seeping into the spaces of fear. We are learning to trust ourselves now, to live from the inside out and embrace love as the new center of a Humanity ready to Self-Actualize. Our hearts are opening each day, through events great and small, as balance is restored to the Earth. Stay in your forward movement, out of the mind and old habits and conditioning... eyes straight ahead. We are the more on the other side of the bridge that calls us. We've waited lifetimes for this moment and have immeasurable support in many realms to land safely on the other side, new life in a very new world.

Love Serve and Remember

January 30, 2010

I am remembering my senior year of High School. I am sure there was a level of excitement at the thought of being free, all grown up with a brand new world before me. Yet, I imagine there was a certain level of apprehension, as well. What would the unknown of the world be like? Who would I become as I emerged from a safe, dependent reality to my own unique purpose in the world?

In the infinite world of light and mystery, Spirit communicates to us through energy, tones, symbols, imagination and our intuitive nature. Yet, we tend to pay attention to and notice least what we know most. There is not one moment, in this rapidly changing now that our Authentic Self and a vast interdimensional support system is not present to walk with us into a new understanding and experience of Existence. Greater sight, greater love, greater joy, this moment within lifetimes of gathering and initiation, is about standing in your center of Self, strong in the awareness of what is True. We are in the pivot, old to new, limitation to limitlessness, futility to necessary purpose, unrealized potential to inspired creations of the Eternal kind. Our knowingness is love and we must trust the positive outcome, for our individual lives and for our beloved earth. A new potential is manifesting through our heart centers and an essential trust in the Shining Ones of our potential.

After 11 months of a weekly format on BTR, this final show of January, 2010, marked yet another transition for the Intent of this timeless teaching. The consciousness and energy within this **new human paradigm** is a starseed, carrying and distributing something that will assist and help others grow. It is not a dogmatic or exclusive teaching. Its golden net has been cast wide to include all who are ready to know without the need to know, to surrender uncertainty and feel the joy of re-union. To truly embrace the consciousness of this mastery is to know and understand that our ascension is but our own radiance, remembered. There is nothing more for us to learn or grasp, we need only be willing to be real... and that requires the full acceptance of the Law of One.

My job here, your job here, the *journey of our christed consciousness* is to vibrate out all that we are eternally and to surrender the rest to the mystery. Then, everything that we need when we need it comes by virtue of our true essence and love rather than will, force and manipulation. The expansion of the **new human** consciousness into the minds and hearts of an evolving world is happening by the very technologies it teaches. Our power is not in what we do or the cleverness of the egoic mind, it is in who we are in the shining light of our love, the pulsating rays of our joy. That is our power and purpose within the greater roles of our contribution to this time for humanity.

The new human is a 5D being, intimately connected to 5D World. We are transmigrating back to who we are and a world we not only know but remember well. The process and alchemy of this remembrance is a reverse engineering of the egoic mind, a mind entrained by duality to attach to a construct of conditioned known. Building upon what is has served a useful purpose on this plane of demonstration in that, we have discovered the undeniable capacities of human intelligence. Yet, if we are to fully embody the Golden Age of Enlightenment for this species, we must understand that it is Intuitive Intelligence and Spiritual Sight that are the most important developments of this time. Seeing through the illusion of the mind to the wisdom of the heart is the path of a higher mind technology supported by very new structures being built within the light body temple. While our 3rd dimensional identity experiences the insecurities and fears of a teenager graduating to a life of independence, our sovereignty as spiritual beings lies in our willingness to surrender the dictates and expectations of a very bound and tired world. These very rarified new energies here with us now are about a power that is timeless, resilient, effortless, and engages all "other" through the awareness of One.

The new earth of the new human revolves around sustainability and creation, two objectives that will evolve naturally out of truly committing to priorities aligned with the new feminine. Intuitive Intelligence is the return of the Great Goddess and our ultimate alignment, human to 5D Earth. I am aware how instinctively men are drawn to the pure essence and energy of this template. Women are nurtured and empowered here through inner knowingness, they see their true reflection in the vibrational light of this energy. Yet, it is in observing how balance is being restored within the masculine energetic that truly speaks to the omnipresent Unity vibrating within this Consciousness. There are so many of our light brothers of humanity that long to stand in a new power, to come from love and receptivity versus force and rigidity. And this will come in truly understanding energy. We need only recognize the eternal cycles of the earth mother to recognize that her ability to create, restore, regenerate, renew, nurture and sustain are instinctual in nature and grounded in love. A new harmony is sounding, balance is being restored on so many levels, as we learn to observe energy from the anchor of an open heart, a consciousness of light.

We are a fantastically blessed race of beings entrusted with a choice that will affect the entire Cosmos. That awareness alone fills my heart and sets the trajectory of my own reach every day. Our individual lives teeter right along with the balance of our planet. Each day more are waking up to a wondrous, remarkable vision of a far away star. The star is curiously similar to the one we now inhabit, yet there are evolved beings, living in cooperation and peace, creating with love, all is joy. Each day, that distant star shines a little brighter on the horizon for this humanity. The new human carries a one pointed focus of higher mind and intent, not for self-gain but for collective freedom. We must determine to stay in the present moment, moving forward with an innocent mind and open-lighted heart. The two worlds now present are much closer than imagined, two earths existing side by side for our empowered choice. Living with your whole Self present, loving with your whole Self, is to vibrate with the frequencies of 5D World; creativity, abundance, peace, joy, love, light, mercy, compassion, wisdom, understanding, sharing, caring, strength, beauty, harmony, allowing. Ask yourself in each moment how much of your reality is filled with these vibrations and you will know, in comparison, where your center of being resides.

As **The New Human** expands this coming week to **The World Puja Network**, I encourage you to find and embrace the symbolism of this apparent movement in concept with the greater movement in consciousness for all of humanity. Our whole heart and strong wanting rests within the internal drive to share who we are, to serve through our gifts and shine the light of our joy out onto the world in greater and greater measure. This movement within the greater awareness and teaching of the new human represents the new beginnings you each stand on the threshold of. Follow what you know, listen to the language of your creative nature and passion and trust the energies present with us now to guide you. Ultimate Consciousness is an energy expressing through you now, a new understanding of reality, an authentic and enduring love.

5th World Emerging, Return of the Crystal Beings

February 4, 2010

I have felt very much in a vacuum of late, the noise of 3rd dimensional reality seems to be lessening and information of a higher order is quickening within my being and the world around me. I see the 3D world clearly, perhaps with greater lucidity than ever, yet it seems very much removed, distant from where my mind and brain are currently processing. Event phenomena are magnifying yet emotionality has resigned itself to a newly empowered Observer. And within this vacuum of amplified awareness and compassionate detachment to all that is moving, shapeshifting and transitioning for the whole of this humanity, there is a persistent stream of higher consciousness over-riding the known of this reality with greater wisdom and love.

Epic changes are afoot, residing in the immediate sphere of our understanding and we must position ourselves to witness, observe and see the positive path, narrow as it may be at this time, because the positive path is expanding by our loving participation with it. We must each deliberately determine to ride the higher light frequencies above the seeming chaos of a dying, unsustainable consciousness and world. Each moment is decisive and exact in the opportunity it offers to gather information and make new choices within spiritual awareness, versus linear time. The **new human** is an emerging prototype, a timely renaissance of being embodying and illuminating a quantum leap in human consciousness and within that consciousness and sight, is the intent to be and respond as love and only love. Many are being tested to the strength and center of their current level of consciousness, split second moments to shift conditioned patterns of reaction to stimuli. The **Age of Transparency** invites Truth into every nook and cranny of our beingness. There is nothing that is not as a crystal brightly lit with many facets of mindful response; a still, courageous adaptation to fearful illusions as we create a new reality from center point being.

The weather has become an increasing phenomenon across our nation and world. Mother Nature is mirroring the profound unrest and reset of a species entering an entirely new genetics of being. It is a wondrous, humbling observation to step back from nature's unrest as an opportunity to see where and how strongly we reside in a center of trust. The events of nature are out of our control, much like the inner phenomenon of a changing cellular structure. Our light bodies are way ahead of the egoic mind in allowing for the necessary restructuring of the physical vehicle on our journey to 5D World. Gaia's discord and unpredictable patterns are very much aligned with the changes occurring within. We are intimately connected with the earth. Her renewal, rejuvenation, regeneration, re-balancing and reset of residence within a greater vibration and consciousness is our transfiguration, as well. We have a hands-on, teaching classroom of evolution present in each moment, no matter where we reside on this earth ship. And within that classroom there is a sea of consciousness from which to retrieve the data of our ongoing response. Fear, restlessness, becoming unnerved by what the mind is observing, or calm, peaceful trust in the earth's consciousness and intent? How we perceive her events is key in the ultimate consciousness we will be residing in and the earth we will transition to.

I have been given a visual guidance in the recent years of volatility and uncertainty for this humanity. Teetering very much on the edge of an existence that could spiral into self destruction or evolutionary victory, our power to transcend beyond limitation and defeat to a world of greater light and possibility has everything to do with thought, the allegiance of our belief and where we ultimately turn in times of danger and fear. The vision I have seen in my mind's eye is of my 3rd dimensional self, appearing happy, safe, whole, unscathed. Yet, immediately surrounding me, juxtaposed within the same visual reality, is complete destruction, a war zone of devastation and demise. And what this communication from the greater consciousness, expressing so clearly through insightful awareness, is that our ultimate freedom and protection within this unprecedented evolutionary cycle, lies within our focus, the ability to go within and be still, anchoring our being to the vertical spiral as the lifeline within a dismantling reality and transitioning world. What we have known, the reality we have grown accustomed to is not real. We created it, imagined it, with fearful and limited minds.

The new energy present with us now will not sustain that illusion. We are residing in an entirely new structure of vibrational reality aligned with the consciousness of 5th World. We must now rely upon our inner awareness, the mastery and training of our spiritual identity to help us stay clear about how the pathways of the infinite Self are opening for us in each and every moment. There are fundamental changes in our genetic codes happening on a cellular level; our experience of reality is being rewritten within. Our power within the transition from one earth to another lies in divine perspective, a living awareness that allows the personality to be integrated into our divinity, the christed self, the homoluminous of our light identity, the new human of a very new world of being.

In the midst of so much unknown and uncertainty, life as we know it coming undone right before our eyes within nature's fury, shifting financial structures, lifestyle grooves and the whole construct of work within 3rd dimensional reality. And yet, a very rarified state of being is manifesting for this species. The multidimensional nature of the human soul is coming to life within a very new frontier in consciousness. We are now poised delicately yet powerfully between probable realities and which reality you choose is greatly dependent upon the essence of Self you give your energy and intent more fully to at this time. There is present with you in each moment a brand new being, the crystal essence of your luminous Self. This self is the natural Self, innocent, child-like, authentic in expression and experience of the world around it, seeing wonder and magic versus fear and decay. The true self of our mastery is physically alive with joy and sees beyond what is interpretation, to a greater Truth, that where we are is perfect. Who we are is perfect. Each moment is a totality of expression of an existence that extends far beyond the perimeters of mind and emotion. So much beauty and new life is here now. Awakening implies new awarenesses on the things that hold your mind to fear, lack, limitation, joylessness and the mundane as the extent of your freedom.

You are a crystal, being re-birthed through a Self that is multidimensional. You are everywhere at once and in love with the experience before you. Consider that the presence of more crystal beings and those referred to as indigos in our evolving world is by virtue of the new spaciousness that you inhabit in your inner reality; a reality very much capable of transforming your physical health, your relationship with abundance, your ability to see beyond the known, align with your passion and step into the role you agreed to play on a very new plane of existence for this humanity. There is a magical reality present, a strengthening of your energetic field to bring those things you require to evolve into physical manifestation. There is a triumph of spiritual, psychological, emotional and physical identity within you that is informing your everyday awareness about the true nature of reality. There is no other. There is only one of us here. We must open our hearts to the beauty of the true Self, the pure essence we carry within a crystal core of knowingness and mastery. It is a captivating pulse, a melody of creative purpose that lifts you into the sacredness of every aspect of your life. Stand in the center of your own transformation even as the world around you transforms beyond the mind's understanding. Many more changes and new will come. Wherever you are, your consciousness will determine your experience, ongoing. We must let go of any energies and attachments that no longer serve. All is transforming now by the energies of love. Trust it all as love, see it all as love, elevate your sight to the frequency of love and 5D World will manifest effortlessly at your feet, returning all to love.

Radiant Mind

February 18, 2010

The fullness of this now is unsurpassed, but make no mistake about it, whatever sure footing and foundation you have grown accustomed to in 3D, whatever your ego remains attached to or fearful of will be unsettled and upturned. So many variables of life as we've known it remain in limbo, yet there are beautiful things happening moment to moment to the mind that is free. As we're pushed out of old grooves in our lives, it is not to judge or question what we have done or why there often appears to be more that is uncertain than known. We are in the movement of our transition from linear to spiritual time. Our new spaces and grooves of residency are already prepared and waiting for us, but we cannot take our old structures with us. Our primary objective as spiritual beings is sovereignty, to fully inhabit and belong to the Self. Only then can we truly love and see the new landscape of a world that is sustainable, a co-created earth of cooperation, harmony and shared gifts. Know that whatever you are dependent upon in 3D via attachment, is vibrating not freedom and trust, but slavery and fear.

I have had the good fortune in my life to travel many different roads on my journey back to Oneness, the opportunity to experience many different walks of life, culture and race. Within the circle of my Native American Lodge family, I learned about the long red road. My understanding of the red road of initiation is that of being conscious, fully present to the lessons of physical life and the experience of being human. We are meant to share this fantastical experience of 3D life, our authentic nature is oriented toward unity, but you will discover deeper meaning of this existence if you first become sovereign and are able to be fully and only in each moment as it comes to you. What does it mean to be in the moment and how is that connected to both our freedom and a new radiance of being?

I talk a lot in the show and book about moving without thought because the new human is governed by an innocent and lucid mind. It is so important to stand in the center of your being in each moment and make a decision based only on that moment. To do so is to shift your awareness and perception to spiritual time versus linear thought. Spiritual time is stacked and expansive; all is available in each moment along an infinite space/time continuum. When you are in thought, you are automatically connected to the past and your decisions are but recycled versions of where you have already been and what you've already known. The gift of this moment in all of eternity is that the energetic space around you is brand new, ongoing! You have an opportunity to lift above linear conditioning and habit, ego and imprisonment to a new paradigm of thought, one that is emerging from a newly empowered vibrational identity. When you think about any situation, you are in linear time. When you act upon each moment with the higher technologies your mind is capable of, you make split second decisions within each instance based on your intuition and heart consciousness. This automatically reorients your entire being and intent to the vertical column of light, where there is innate joy and infinite power available to you.

For the first six weeks or so of 2010, the energies have been at full throttle intensity, much like being behind a ski boat, pulled along, but without the skis! We have got to let go and get out of our grooves. And maybe your grooves are of service and you are long on the path of being a light worker. Still, your groove must shift, open up to more and expand beyond the perimeters of what the mind thinks to what the heart knows. We are all stepping into very new spaces. Things that worked before will not work with this new consciousness and energy present with us now and we cannot take the egoic mind with us. Each day, the space around you, the field of light enveloping you is increasing and it is for each of us to move with that light. Let it take you, allow it to reorient your sense of self to a new understanding of who you are as a Universal Being of Light.

Another beautiful and exacting shift came in this last week, around Valentine's Day that is serving to flow us more effortlessly with the higher frequencies, but only if we relax into it. Every day is brand new, I encourage you to make that a mantra in the days and weeks and months to come. We have to face each experience head on in a neutrality of emotion, expanding beyond what the mind perceives to the trust that it is all love, thus becoming One with the shift that is all present with us now. The ski boat zooming across the sea of consciousness will not slow down anytime soon, but you can learn to glide more effortlessly into your new grooves by trusting *everything* you perceive and experience in your reality as part of a greater process unfolding.

Every day my reality is so vastly different than the day before. I **see** this and I know what is going on. The hologram is more apparent and we are all being given many scenarios of choice to decide where and who we really want to be, what world we really want for ourselves. Beyond what is before us that the mind focuses on, there is a greater momentum pushing us, preparing our minds and bodies for the upgrades to 5D World. As the magnetics of our earth shift, a very new part of the brain is being activated right along with the mutation of our DNA. Waves of Light are penetrating the magnetics of our brain and a new consciousness is emerging that is attuned to what is true and lasting versus temporal and fixed. I can see this spaciousness of mind as a room brightly lit. There is no memory or conditioning of lack or fear, limitation or unworthiness. The red road of our experiential and emotional history no longer binds us to the past, unless we choose that. Because, the energy around us now is free, we are free to act within it in ways that better reflect our humanity as One People within One World. If you are paying attention and staying really present to your experience and the love within it, your physical world will increasingly reveal the reality of the non-physical because the worlds are merging more and more each day. As Gaia and all of humanity with her continue to lift within the Golden Spiral of a New Age, more will see evidence all around us of the shift from linear time to spiritual joy, an entirely new Creation of being.

Each day, we must embrace everything from an entirely new perspective. We've been traveling the road of thought, making decisions out of ego and fear, living outside of our heart center and reacting to our experiences based on conditioning and habit. Think about that. Yet, a new awareness is here, our hearts are experiencing the new vibration within. And that is allowing for a global shift to a new road, a journey of heart consciousness and actions governed by love, and only love. Time is folding in upon itself, pay attention. The world of form is collapsing into the world of formlessness and light, pay attention. There is a new foundation beneath you that will become more and more visible as you let go of the groove you have grown accustomed to.

Love is a frequency that allows you to first, truly show up to your experience, be present to it, trust it as your highest good and embrace it as your freedom. Don't think... live from the heart. No looking back or dwelling in what if. The Age of Transparency is here. Truth and honesty will continue to be the order of a very new day as more and more that was hidden continues to be revealed. A new Unity will prevail as we continue to come together in alignments of authentic love and higher purpose. Don't be afraid to be who you really are and step into the new roles of power and light before you. Love is a creationary force, a vibration that moves through you and reorients your entire reality around it when you say yes to it. The heart's wisdom is instantaneous and always in the present moment. Continue to go within and rely on the True Self. The you that you are in this very moment, holds the key to everything... for the future of your own existence and divine purpose, as well as the future of a very new world.

Standing Before It, Walking Into It, Becoming the Dream

March 4, 2010

I was sitting high atop a mountain, surrounded by new; new friends, new family, new environment, new world... and most important of all, a new sense of peace within. The details of the 3rd dimensional world seemed a distant event on a far away horizon. The metaphor of this seemingly localized moment in time was not lost on me. We are constantly enveloped by the consciousness and energy we are vibrating. The setting of this teachable moment was high above the density of an old reality. From that vantage point, not only was the environment new and abundant, it was surrounded by wide, open spaces and a freshness that allowed for new breath, new vision, new possibilities, renewed promise.

It occurs to me that one of the main reasons this humanity has not succeeded in the intent to evolve beyond the trivialities of form is that we try too hard. Always out ahead of our true center, we have learned to be in a perpetual state of striving for who knows what so that we can feel content within the circumstances of our lives. We have adapted a false identity with which we have learned to push and will creation into being with an egoic focus that is never satisfied. Creation Is. It has been and will always be present for humanity, a species of inherent divinity and light. Our presence within it is and has always been for the purpose of bringing our capacity to love and create with joy, to a living canvas of beauty and light. Yet, we have given our joy and creative instincts over to routine and the mundane. We allow the mind to drive us beyond the heart's best interest and knowing. Then we try to fix the details of what we are observing rather than look at the deeper emotionality and energy of what is actually being expressed through the intelligence of natural instinct.

What comes to me as I observe the everydayness of a reality desperately clinging to what is known, even if the known is not answering the more meaningful questions that linger within is that these new frequencies of higher light will cause greater dis-ease and unsettledness in the lives of those who are not centered in their spiritual identity. I imagine the relationship to food will become more distorted and addictions will increase within social consciousness in attempts to alleviate a mentally driven orientation as the world of ego continues to dismantle. Many continue to address physical symptoms with medical solutions while the emotional body screams for a new consideration in the composite picture of who we are, have been and long to be in wholeness. The Light is walking right in the midst of all distortion and illusion, in the guise of persons with a new message, carrying a new energy, offering an alternate reality, yet the known is a very comfortable and well-worn groove. We must get serious about bringing our spirituality, the light of who we are, out into the everydayness of our lives. This is a time of integration, allowing the inner mind and higher light of consciousness to change our level of understanding, our sensibilities, wisdom and spiritual integrity bit by bit as we view the world around us with expanded sight and greater love.

The box of Self is expanding, everyday. There is a new spaciousness around you that is bigger than it used to be. You are no longer confined to the identity you've known. Your choices and ability to think new thoughts have greatly increased. But, you must begin to interact with that spaciousness and you do so with imagination, intuition and creativity. The more you act on the spiritual foundation of your being, the more your mind and energy will be fed with more of the same. YOU are a technology. All the abilities and awareness you seek or can imagine are within you, that information is in your vibrational body. It is just a language we are not accustomed to in 3rd dimensional reality.

These new energies are the teacher. The new light permeating the density of social consciousness is the gateway to a greater probability aligned with your spiritual identity and purpose. But we must engage them, we must interact with them, we must act outside the box of our habits and conditioning and turn our focus more and more to the gift and treasure we carry within. Free yourselves from thought, go within and let the heart's intelligence empower you to new vistas of possibility. When you meditate or pray, when you find moments of stillness within the insanity of an unconsciously spinning world without, call to your future self, acknowledge the higher mind technologies of your inner revolution as a source of information that is ever available to you. We cannot continue to love the light from afar and pray our way to infinite life. We are the actualization of the new human transforming the earth with heart-centered action and love.

The 3rd dimensional reality that is visible to the naked eye is a finite amount of energy that merely recirculates and takes on different shapes and experiences. We have fallen into the sleep of creating from our emotions and fears, ingrained beliefs and unconscious programming passed down to us through generations, ever looping us back into our ancestry in unconscious patterns. The egoic mind is limited in its ability to break free from that because it dwells in the known, it thrives on predictability, routine, habit and the illusion of control that that engenders. This humanity has become lazy in its innate ability to dream and imagine, create and manifest in unlimited measure. We are the ones who have confined our sensibilities to that prison and we are the ones that must step out of that groove. This experience on earth is crazy exciting with a permeating joy that is enlivened by our imagination and creativity. The human spirit thrives on engaging power from within and channeling it out into the world with joy and limitlessness, love and impassioned freedom.

In the 5th dimension of existence, energy becomes infinite. We are no longer creating from our emotional bodies but from our vibrational body. The new human is a 5D being walking through experience as vibrational awareness, attunement with the energy of the reality engaged rather than the limited constructs outpicturing. We are constantly viewing our experience through our level of consciousness, interpreting our reality not necessarily with the fullness of what is but by the level of our awareness and understanding of the true nature of reality, which is love.

It is fascinating really to observe this wondrous game of evolution from a place of compassionate detachment, acknowledging each piece and every person as a Universal Being of Light embodying the patterns of their own unique story. Every being is moving at the pace that is suitable to each, which is why two people can be in the same 3rd dimensional environment and yet have totally different experiences. One is vibrating in 3D consciousness, the other in 4th or above. Neither is right or wrong, we are just all on the move and most have settled for a very limited perspective of a much greater story.

Part of the awareness of your vibrational body entails opening up to new and higher mind technologies. The technology of mind that served us in the 3rd dimension – order, control, reason, logic, using the known to create more of what we don't really want or need, they will no longer serve us as we pivot to a new probability of existence. It is your creative nature, your passion, things that light you up and feed you, that will guide you to a new life and divine purpose. Every day I observe. If asked, I will shine new light into experiences that I see people running a loop of unconscious programming. If not, I know my work within this new energy is to gravitate more toward the unknown and to do so with a happiness of one who knows they are already free. We are creating from the void now and that void is an unlimited canvas of quantum dreams waiting to be engaged. Consciousness is the secret Force of future humanity. It exists within all of nature and all the heavens, from the body electric to the human aura. All connected by Ultimate Consciousness that is ever present to expand each moment beyond the observable, beyond perceived limitations and resistances. The new human experiences this consciousness in all things, hears it, sees it and feels it as an interdimensional harmony that expresses itself as a love song, really. The love song of creation, you waking up to you!

Right now, in each moment, with the earth changes and economic debacle and psychic unrest, there is a new consciousness pushing through. Pushing you out of structures and beliefs that no longer serve you. We are being prepared energetically within Gaia's reset and Cosmic waves and social undoing for very new spaces. Our bodies and minds and lives are upgrading, transitioning to 5D World. Things that worked before will not work within this new consciousness, be it mental habits, how we interact with life, or the beliefs we so dearly cling to. Everything that we are and all of life is moving within the intention to create a planet that is more aligned with Light, a higher level of living and being. And people are ready for that, gratefully so. There is not one among us that is not getting an inner prompt to *do something different.*

As linear time continues to fold into vertical light, we are being sourced by a completely new and greater information system. All around us life is speaking a new clarity because the instinctual foundation of existence is returning, being given new life. It is critical to unplug yourselves from the matrix world and reorient your decision-making and values to the inner world of knowingness. I can assure you that the ego will latch on to whatever opportunity, experience or person that gives it the illusion of being in control. But the ego's foundation is a world of sand and will not be sustainable for much longer.

We are the transformation of this planet. The new human of future humanity follows the instinctual nature that is one with the instinct of all life and all Creation. The instinctual nature is stillness, quietude, creative, aligned with nature and motivated by love. Every day, we must face our experiences head on and if they are not aligned with immeasurable joy, freedom and new light we must have the strength and awareness of Self to STOP, go within, and see where we losing power, seeping energy, not in authentic alignment with ourselves. The frequency of 2010 has everything to do with the power of Creation. The Universal forces do not judge or punish, they respond to the focus of your thought, which is energy. Energy is responding to how you feel about what you say and think. You must be increasingly aware of the frequency of your thought, your words, attitudes and feeling, because that energy is a song you are sending out into all of Creation and Creation will ever send that same song back to you. What kind of world do you want? Are you being that with your actions? We must continue to shine the light of our knowingness and love every day, feet forward with faces to the sun, and that action will continue to permeate all.

The new environment, high above the everyday reality that I found myself sitting in yesterday, is the new possibility present for **you** in each moment that you are journeying through. Your actions and the lens through which you view your immediate reality are the pivot to a very new view of existence for this world and the new humans inhabiting it. Two beings standing side by side, one sees the past with many known possibilities within a perpetual loop of recycled old. The other, nothing but beauty and light, wide open spaces and love. You are the future you are stepping into in each moment. Let go. Surrender the known. Be your vibrational body of awareness and say yes everyday to the things that take your breath away. Follow Spirit first and you will soon be surrounded by the reality, relationships, purpose and abundance of your dreams!

The Decision to Endure

April 29, 2010

What can you hold center in the midst of, how much spin and unknown and chaos can you integrate as the new center of power now manifesting within? I have days I feel clueless as to what I am doing. But greater still are the days that I am filled up with the absolute knowingness that I am standing in the center of my purpose and meeting my Higher Self on the event horizon of a very different world of existence. We are in a ubiquitous passage of understanding, a divine intent manifesting out of a collective purpose. To accelerate the evolution of life and consciousness within an interdependent Cosmos the Universe and this humanity must now find a new balance between what can no longer support us and what longs to be our new foundation.

For the sensitive and awake among us, we feel we cannot bear one more moment of exemplified separation within this reality of experience. As the Age of Transparency continues to magnify the imbalances that have long held us in varying states of paralysis and apathy, both the ignorant and wise of an evolving world are witnessing the culmination and consequence of a humanity disconnected from its conscience, its heart and the divine nature our being. When I first felt the oil spill in the Gulf of Mexico in my body, my emotions went numb with dread and unbearable sorrow for the ecosystem and kingdoms of life affected by it. I was transported immediately to the birds, that juxtaposition of the bird kingdom representing freedom and then *feeling* them all covered with this toxic sludge. It was a penetrating shudder within my sensate being and my heart *knowing* their innocence would not understand what was happening to them.

Then I breathed in deeply and centered myself in a greater energetic of understanding, a greater trust, knowing that we have to **let go**. Not in apathy and non-care but increasingly let go in what will be the consequence of so much unconscious action for so long. *Everything* is connected to this shift. The duality will be amplified in every facet of life around us, touching all levels and layers of existence and love will prevail. However much the illusion of separation and pain, loss, suffering and greed determines to veil it, the beauty, the love and light of sacred codes within Universal design are weaving a new web, connecting galaxies and universes, all densities and realities, into a more authentic and unified expression of Oneness. We must ever put our thoughts and mind, emotions and powerful feminine re-membrance on **what we can do** to bring balance and wholeness back to our own lives.

Each day, within the pejorative spiral of so much that is coming undone, the prism is turning, the crystal hologram is rotating and we are being gifted with the opportunity to see with new eyes, to BE the repatterning of this humanity within every facet of our lives. The energy we engage, extend and embody each day is the energy of what is becoming the new future. The emotional body and ego will take you into absolutes and overwhelm. Your growing light and the re-membrance of your true nature and divine purpose therein, will return you again and again to stillness, to nothingness, so that you can know the moment and trust it as perfect. Even as the spiral tightens, and tighten it will.

What do you see when you witness this humanity? Where are your behaviors and thoughts focused in the ongoing moments of decision we are entrusted with? Even as our beloved Gaia, a conscious, living organism continues to experience the waves of photonic light in her own heart center and light body, so too must we, fine filaments of her authentic nature, simultaneously prepare to receive the heightened waves of an evolutionary, shifting consciousness at all levels. We must, everyday, in each moment, understand increasingly so that the distribution of energy in our lives is equal to the distribution of energy on the planet. Period. We must bring exacting mindfulness to how we are running our energy within conditioned circumstances, for **we are** the repatterning of this existence.

Even as the world of form and the domain of the ego come undone, we, you and me, are repatterning the grid with our passionate devotion and higher mind commitment to this evolutionary process. Gaia is in the upward spiral of the very same accelerated energy emissions that are currently anchoring our DNA to a new level of mastery in this physical realm. We must ever step back (the Observer is a greatly amplified energetic at this time) step back from our humanity long enough to witness a new resonance and capacity within. We have the tools to begin the process of Light Body Activation at this time and more than anything else, it is the decision to know versus be consumed by, to follow spiritual instinct over egoic habits and grooves and to trust love more than the extreme polarizations we will continue to witness as we ever climb the spiral of Light in our return to Source; the all that is of who we are.

One of the most beautiful experiences of this new Light, the power of this higher emanating love here with us now that I have been gifted a ring side experience of, is the masterful, sovereign expression of a newly awakened and inevitable feminine hierarchy on this planet. The true power of the planet is being returned to us through the melding of the God and Goddess, the masculine and the feminine, the yin and yang... the gentle breath of a newly embraced understanding of the role of females on this planet. Since the beginning stages of this Paradigm Shift, the planetary grounding of the new human template in 2007, I have been increasingly aware of and intrigued by the response of the male population. In many ways, the nurturing consciousness gifted within this ancient codex and future teaching has been embraced, recognized and seized more fervently by men. Or perhaps it is in their magnetic response to the energy within this template that men have been more overtly swept up by and called to a new possibility within themselves. Within the authentic mirror of this consciousness and energy, men have the opportunity to feel and witness some of the greater gifts of the feminine that our history has egregiously usurped.

There is no doubt that women have come into a new level of power over the course of our history. Yet, much of that power has come via anger and resentment over a patriarchal society and ancestral lineage. We must first own that, as females. Men have had to bear their fair share of "conditioned expectations" and forced roles on their innate spiritual natures. The old system of submission and control can no longer survive but neither can we not allow for and create room for our male population, the new masculine conduit of expression that wants very much to join with the feminine power gathering together to create a more heart centered and lasting change for this world. The divine feminine is manifesting and whether it is a natural or forced response within your history and opinion of the masculine energetic, women carry the gentle task of compassion and miracle of divine forgiveness.

We are all undergoing an evolution of love on planet earth within which we must allow new relationships and partnerships to form organically, no agenda, no tapes and dense projections as we all create the space for a healing of cellular memory! We must step outside of our conditioned experiences and celebrate the new male that is now here with us, willing to learn a new way of existing and creating and owning their power in the world. Women are by nature, problem solvers, always seeking to resolve conflicts instead of creating them. Together, in conscious participation with each other, we empower the melding of the God and Goddess that will be key to sustainable peace in the world. We are the creators, participants and blessed recipients of an amazing real-time change in energy within the everyday understanding and newly recognized positions as agents of change in how we interact with, engage, embrace and truly see one another in the Light of a new era of being. A wholly cooperative energy evolves out of duality when you recognize the balance of your being in other. The body of We, is the **return path**, to One.

So many things to share today, so many things to talk about to illumine the bridge within as we make our way to spiritual self-awareness - bringing new energy to an old, unsustainable humanity. As we continue to witness more unrest in our weather (that will only increase) in our relationship with money (to which we have given so much of our power) in our psyches (as we are increasingly manipulated into survival mentality), know that we are equally faced with the opportunity to shift the entire planet to Light. Yes, this is what I know, this is what I believe and trust and so, this is the experience I will have. Because **I am** a powerful, creationary being, as are you. I exist as energy and Light, as do you. We are at the peak of intensity in the breakdown of old to new. It is happening inside of you, around you, within and upon our earth and affecting the entire Cosmos in immeasurable ways. It is for each of us to accept our part in the unfolding of our reality, to strive to make it better not through duress and discontent, but out of compassion and a deified remembrance of what it means to love. In our inner most being, in the heart of our truest expression, we are here to adore, because we are adored. We are light vehicles, pure expressions of energy composed of various frequencies, vibration, color and harmony here to give voice to that which we adore. Do you remember?

Gaia is preparing for this shift each day and we must continue to trust her and not cling... the Earth will take care of her own. As the polarities continue to magnify and the many find themselves within scenarios that most of us have not had to experience up close and personal, we must be responsible enough to see and have courage enough to own the way we have misappropriated energy in our own lives. And then determine to **stop** playing with duality. When you are being your Light in every area of your life, in every facet and decision and wielding of power that you have control over, you will see a greater and more enduring power emerge in our world. We must embrace each moment and all that we witness with the power and light of Christ Consciousness, of the Goddess and the Solar Logos within, even as the spiral tightens and we become a truer center for the new dawn of this humanity.

Recognizing Center, Owning Your Light

August 12, 2010

The Guidance is all present now, in the midst of every experience and powerfully redirecting errant thoughts to radiant reflections... of existence, each other, the Self and the true nature of reality. A new consciousness is streaming so profoundly and with such exacting measure that it is **increasingly effortless** to reside above the chaos, uncertainty and ambivalence that is an old and dying vibrational reality.

As I entered the Shining Ones woods early this morning, I was deep in thought, suspended in the inbetween space of dismantling duality and ascending awareness. Yet, my mind was instinctively drawn to a bright reflection in the earth as the sun shone brightly on the path ahead of me. I knelt down to discover a beautiful, transparent quartz crystal, a tetrahedron shape, about two inches in width and depth and quite dense in weight. As I picked up this glistening star merkabah and held it to the light, what was immediately impressed upon me is that my time in the woods today would be immersed in the energy of "radiant mind," the new mind of a new humanity being reflected in this crystal manifestation of the Tree of Life.

The New Human Consciousness and Energy is an ancient to future teaching, attuned in each moment to the Collective passage of a transformational humanity. The greatest secret that hides in the determination to seek sustenance and information outside of self is that all power and presence, illumination and life exist within the individual who is present to each moment, with the consciousness of love. The metaphysical doorway to endless worlds of possibility and Light is no more or less than a mind that is free from its history. Indeed, each person is their own connection between matter and energy and the compass for the new life journey we are all participating in from varying reflections of reality is the untapped power of the mind. Know your own mind, know a new freedom and the power to see new realities of existence.

With the prism talisman of radiant mind clutched tightly in my fist, I was guided to go and process the current energies on the right hand, masculine trail of these pristine woods where the energetics and Light Codes magnify the consciousness stream of the masculine influence. So much of the inquiry from and observation on this current phase passage of energy on the planet is reflecting a heightened sensitivity to all things mental, dense, fearful and unsettled. Even the veteran lightworkers among us are hitting pockets of doubt and oppressing fatigue, both of which cloud the mind. A dominant theme within the energy of oppression and discord is that of imbalance within the divine masculine and a new feminine radiance within the individual and collective matrix of being.

It was not surprising then that within minutes of entering the forest vortex, I had a completely foreign and equally revealing encounter with "old masculine." It bears pointing out that I rarely encounter a human in these woods, much less one whose energy is wholly antithetical to the serenity of the environment. But this is energy consciousness in action; an attunement to reality that rests just above the pervading consciousness level and sees always the bigger picture and gift of every experience as energy informing the spaciousness of an inherently free mind. A man I have never seen before and am sure I will never see again, with two large male dogs he clearly had little control over, outpicturing the errant, chaotic energy of the old masculine. The dogs reared wildly and with uncontrolled power as the man yelled and gripped their leashes. All the while my female dog, Samadhi Blue and I passed gently by on the trail, she off leash and myself, calm in center. "What was that about," I asked the higher realms and consciousness of Light surrounding me? And as I headed to the top of the masculine trail, the stream of higher mind reflection impressed on me a few considerations of import for those who are poised to embody the distinct feminine power of a wholly new existence of reality.

It has been an **intense** energetic the entire month of July 2010. Basically, we are in a profound phase deepening, it is getting our attention through the physical body, our emotions and patience levels, sensitivities in all environments that we can no longer "hide" within. All things to the surface, all things in greater light, all things to return us to a greater love than what we have allowed as a species. Sometimes it can feel as if the energies are literally knocking you around within your reality. This is actually the transparency knocking up against density, the old energy and aggressive masculine juxtaposed to the new and empowered feminine. These oppositional forces (as reflected by the encounter in the woods) cannot co-exist. One must and is giving way to the other in evolutionary cadence and each individual is empowered to know a new integrity of center, to be authentic with the Self in each moment. You must get still and know your core and stop sending your energy out in lack, lack being expressed in the part of you that still seeks outside of Self, wants outside of Self, sees other outside of Self. There is utter fullness in this moment. Any reflection of limitation, reactive emotion or need in your reality is an indication of imbalance, within.

Time and reality as we know it are shifting via the vibration, frequency, energy and consciousness of the planet. This will affect each individual differently depending on your current vibration and level of consciousness. I will sometimes be running trails in the woods and get to place on the trail I could **swear** I just ran 10 minutes before. Or I will finish my run, knowing the trails so well, and feel like I didn't go on certain parts that I would have had to pass to get back to the starting place. These are "time loops", which can occur when you are in an especially high frequency or attuned via your guides, energy portals that hover during the day, etc. So "eerie" and an example of a high strangeness now dawning within the Light of a new part of the brain, energy phenomena made manifest to a consciously participating mind.

The work of the new human and the consciousness and energy I stream on the show each week is activating DNA and opening your field up to light frequency and energy waves, which is very necessary because the planet will continue its ascent and our bodies need to be able to integrate the new vibrations to continue in a forward movement into new atmosphere with her. I can unequivocally note, as well, that your mind IS being altered, unraveled, "loosened" up in perception so that more can come in. Along with the DNA, our brains are being rewired so that we can "live" full time in the residency of our Light, creativity, joy, passion, abundance and freedom from form. Anything that does not resonate with these new human templates and to the degree you are aware and bringing expanded consciousness into your known of reality) the mind will be vexed (a favorite new word) and old stories will be amplified as no longer fitting in the groove they've long resided in.

Feeling "woozy, weary, sick, not well" are all symptoms of imbalance between the energy you are residing in within a current experience and the greater energies, trying to get your attention.

The two main drags on your natural energy field, which is being supported immensely by the new spaciousness of these higher frequencies, are number one, **extreme density butting up against extreme high frequency**. (an example of this would be a day last week for instance. I began the day with a client in the Shining Ones Woods… two hours in those pristine frequencies basically streaming information from 5th World. When I left there, I had to immediately jump in the car and drive to the next city in heavy traffic and on a deadline. It was too jarring of a shift from one activity of extreme to another and I felt the spin of it within and without. This will be increasingly hard on the body. And secondly, just flat out need for more stillness. Usually the two will overlap and coincide in some way, so listening to and addressing one will help alleviate the other.

The biggest support and relief come via **balance**, i.e., the distribution of time and energy in your reality between old and new, old groove versus new spaciousness. These frequencies and your divine nature **need more space**. From mental chatter and shoulds and the angst of indecision and routine and known, to an active participation with the Divine Feminine of our inherent nature. We are **never**, not responsible for the energy around us. We are moving quickly from a consciousness and abundance based on lack and misdirected power to a responsible stewardship of a Divine Power. The most instinctual practices around creating space are: **Conscious use of breath:**- breathe it **all** in, each moment, deeply. And when you think you have taken a deep enough breath sip a little more. **Frequently moving the body:** either to music or out in NATURE via walking, yoga, etc. Feel the energies, let them express through you organically. **Diet:** really pay attention to what you are ingesting! Think, how can I assist my dense body with higher vibrational sustenance? **Pure water:** Drink lots of fresh water, spring or distilled never tap and Ionized or Oxygenated is GREAT! Finally, if you feel weary, for goodness sakes, **Be Still, Go Within** and **know** that you **know**, because **everything is different** and you are receiving new supports from many new directions now. Create the space to **allow** that in and challenge the mind to be ok with "not knowing or seeing the Process!"

So much work is occurring on so many levels for us all. Dreamtime is especially deep. We are journeying far out and reuniting with realms and higher light family that we are poised to join in partnership with to assist 3rd density alchemy. Those in power are fully aware of extraterrestrial life and the activities underway to prepare you and the Earth for an interactive exchange of commerce, technology, resources, creativity and partnerships of empowered Unity. I encourage you to consider that any fear you have around the topic of Galactic Brotherhood is ultimately a fear of your own power. Because we are what is higher, we are the Earth's supreme efficacy of power, we are that to which we have knelt and prayed and we are the new light currently blanketing a once displaced star, newly positioned in the Galaxy.

Know that the Light is never disappointed with you for it is an impartial energy that only knows love. Disappointment, frustration, sadness, fatigue, these are all constructs of the ego to keep us ensnared in the same perpetual, mundane loop. Everything that is fixed and known must give way to a wholly new, vast, unknown mystery of Divine Power. The greatest pivot at this time in the prism of crystalline humanity is knowing the difference between mental processing and energy. Take care that the egoic mind is a consciousness that you are now vibrating beyond. Every show, unique, transformational and exacting, of the **New Human** broadcasts for the past eighteen months, is a divinely calculated repatterning, restructuring and Light Encoded transmission to Activate DNA, stimulate the Pineal Body, free the mind and prepare the Light Body for a new sustenance that is as far reaching as the Cosmic Intelligence it resides within. The energy of these shows and the new human meditations that come through each week will help stabilize, ground, and "protect" your energy field greatly.

Stay out of mind about what is or is not real and just allow. The 3D zone is pushing, forcing, figuring and making things happen, 5D is utter allowing, "It is ok now, you are ready to re-member." The Light needs you to remember. It is time. Know that your creativity is your Authentic Self and your most efficient and natural avenue of participating fully in life once again, allowing love for yourself, through yourself, as the vehicle of which your creativity can be a legacy to the earth. What do you want your energy exchange with the world to be??? Answer this question with the heart, your love and effulgent connection to Source and you will know the center of a newly empowered human.

Free Your Mind

November 11, 2010

"Someday perhaps the inner Light will shine forth from us and then we will need no other light." -*Johann Wolfgang von Goethe*

Strange weirdness, all around... each day new light frequencies penetrate very worn grooves and archaic thought-forms of a species in the throes of an historical pivot. The psychological climate of this humanity is increasingly chaotic while people try to go about life as usual with numbed expressions. Perception is being subtly altered each day in the physical world of form. Many who are re-membering are moving toward becoming masters of the known reality, extracting the Self from the linear constructs and structures that have served to dominate and manipulate us for so long. Yet, fear persists!!!!

This last week I have been inundated with **SOS** communications regarding bazaar, at best, etchings in the sky and questionable travel plans from the powers that be. All the while, the dominant interdimensional communication that persists for me is, PULL THE NOSE OF THE PLANE UP!!! For many are still focused on the ground and impending crash.

Try, try, try as we might the egoic mind is hard pressed to not fall into the patterns of its own destruction. Who are we really? Who do you really know yourself to be? Are the patterns of your thought and decision-making reflecting that to the highest expression of your consciousness? Make no mistake about it, thought form and belief systems are being challenged far beyond the mind's ability to find stability. There is a new gravity present, a new center within which to find balance. We are poised to access and bring new information into the foreground of human knowledge, the godly wisdom of Creation, but you must be willing to disengage the old to find the peace therein.

The Earth's ascent, the acceleration of her electromagnetic field is being mirrored inside each of us and as such, there are ongoing and intense waves of energy pulsing through the physical body even as they serve to disintegrate the grid of the planet. It is the single most profound, inexplicable design of nature and cosmos for the purpose of reorganizing DNA into a complex weaving of the multidimensional sacred geometries of the Light body. Can you fathom? And if you cannot fathom, can you at least be still long enough for the music to penetrate the busyness and attachments of the egoic mind?

Gaia is fine-tuning her physical and etheric body each day, in preparation for her passage into new and higher dimensions of residency. As such, all living beings on the planet are in process of undergoing extreme energy shifts in their auric field resulting in incredible emotional, physical, psychological imbalances and magnified survival/fear issues. It is so important to be still and breathe into the moments of your shapeshifting reality. Full-scale recon-struction of identity is underway. This is the process we chose and are ultimately empowered within. Yet, we doubt. Yet, we fall easily and ignorantly into the grooves and bandwagons of so much drama that if we were still, we could identify as the oldest ploy of the veiled reality to keep you in the spin of your own insanity. Trust and separation cannot co-exist. Who do you know yourself to be? Who are you ready to be? Do you truly know the intelligent wisdom of stillness, non-attachment and no mind? When you put your heart and mind on trust, a new level of freedom sets in. Turn the page. **Pull the nose up on the plane.**

Within all conscious beings lies the potential for expansion and higher awareness but equally so, the potential for recreating an illusion of destruction and mayhem. We have the power and choice to transmute the physical realm into a new experience of life as an interpenetrating of mind and events, a blending of the myriad elements of consciousness and layers of personality. Are we getting this? Read these passages again and again and feel the energy therein. There are new codes of evolutionary Light coming through the language of the Light everyday, the world over. There is not one moment of any action rippling across the planetary grid that is not received and attended to by the cosmometry of the Light. It is so important to understand, fully grasp the power of the mind to both keep us ensnared in the same grooves of the lower realms of consciousness or set us free, once and for all? **Pull the nose up on the plane!** And do it swiftly! There is and has always been more than one probable reality, always, all ways.

There is a higher form and order of design, a vertical light and intelligence magnetizing to imprint your cellular being with hyperdimensional blueprints, a sacred geometry of this species' evolution into a new humanity. Gaia is doing her part. She moves with instinctual wisdom, free from thought. There is no safer place or more important purpose than our attunement to her, not with emotion and fear, but with trust and knowingness. Gaia knows what to do. If you are in heart consciousness you will not have time for petty, elementary phase passages of egoic disbelief! Let go of judgement and separation because it will keep you from seeing, it cloaks your energy field from these lightwaves. Now more so than at any time on this planet, everything IS: the potential of your greatest fear, and the possibility of your Mastery. There is always more than one event happening and the level of consciousness you give your awareness and energy to **will** be your experience.

And so we find ourselves out ahead of the last decade and the millennium concerns where so many stockpiled food and braced themselves for the destruction of their physical homes and livelihoods. Are we wise to the understanding that fearing such events creates far more turmoil and destruction on personal and interplanetary levels than does our allowing of events to unfold within the natural process of cause and effect. The higher choices of this increasingly evolved game of our own evolution is in choosing well the state of mind, consciousness that you call home. For it is there, you will reside. That which is unfolding before you remains yours until you alter your vibration and pivot out of the separation that exists in your own being, the house of your fear. Conscious or in shadowed perception, there are those that want **so desperately** for something to happen to justify their anger and base needs for destruction and warring, relegating them right smack in the middle of the separation that has always been. The consequence of which will be that those determined to focus on and direct from linear rule will likely remain trapped in the 3rd dimension, experiencing the death process. And it is a choice and all is love and all are **in** the expression of their own mastery.

The most important "purpose" you have right now is not allowing fear to cast its dark shadow on your soul. **Who are you really?** When is "IT" going to be the most important thing: IT being the Light, our true identity and power within that identity? Are we behaving like ascended beings, in each moment, with all our **thoughts** and **wonderings** and **being**? Because, as it has always been and will continue to be, the gift of potential and power and wisdom through us is that WE ARE THE CREATORS of this reality. We are, in lucidity, visionary creators that carry the genetics and intelligences of every other dimension, Ascended Master to star being, in the light frequencies of our DNA Matrix. When the calculated and manipulative practices of the media spin information for the precise reaction of your own fearful agenda, do you revert to the patterns of the past and throw the egoic self into the chaos or breathe the Light of Creation into your heart center and KNOW the peace of your own godly wisdom? **Everything is different! Are you?**

We are surrounded by a new spaciousness of nothingness, a beautiful vacuum and void of raw, unformed potential. This unknown mystery is the womb of Creation and the earth is moving through the galaxy as an ascending celestial body so that we can remain earth centered in the higher dimensions. There is no option but to mutate with her. Our physical aspects will continue to follow the mind and so the question is, can we raise our vibration to the extent that we experience the ascension in full conscious awareness? What does that mean?? What does that look like for the individual and Collective? The Authentic Self **knows** and there is no fear! The Authentic Self views the game from the Observer, without attachment or the egoic mind's propensity to immerse itself again and again in the shadow of perpetual deception, unrest and imbalance. Beware not to delude yourself with the bravado of the uninitiated mind that leads again and again into psychological chaos and entrapment! The Soul has already set its course. Your personality aspects are here to navigate a dream within a dream, wherein your every thought, every action, every word is leading you either deeper into the dream, a perpetual recycling of old energy or up the ascending spiral of an evolving humanity.

What does it mean to love unconditionally?? This is not a question or condition of the mind, it is a frequency of remembrance. To love unconditionally is to make a conscious choice each day to move beyond ego gratification and the past concerns of the personality matrix. **When will IT become the most important thing?** That we finally and for always give the WHOLE SELF to It! Think deeply on the things of the heart? Listen to any and all information that comes to you through the heart and use discernment about the sources of information. Get off the lower realms games that will confront you again and again and AGAIN with the dissonant remnants of what has come through the third dimensional density. We just don't have that kind of time any more. There will be greater and greater "plays" of the shadow as the light continues to weave the golden thread of freedom. IT is in the heart, out of mind, the whole self in, where nothing but the purpose and devotion of your Soul is more important and your actions back that up!

Each day, I hear the hum of the Earth, of the Cosmos, when I walk and offer my heart to Creation. This experience has increased with decided measure over the last several months. A harmonic of haunting purpose and weighted intention, I can hear the music of the spheres change in color and tone, harmony and frequency as it penetrates each realm and dimension in the Solar Logos of higher realms existence. This is knowledge that we are re-membering in which we are capable of restructuring and designing a new and higher crystallization of being. It is possible to perceive the music of the spheres and recognize cosmic waves as they pass through the body, activating the signature tones of the Soul with wam vibration. The planetary bodies of our star system speak to one another – share energy fields and exchange the love that permeates the Cosmos, a new song of exquisite harmony and haunting melody that comprises all life, all form, all planetary beings, all consciousness. I "remember" that our conscious identities are but lower expressions of higher realms templates and that, in effect, my unique Soul coding is known and recognized throughout the Omniverse. Then I come back to the gravity of a consciousness that has not quite surrendered to its own next level of expression, where the mental and emotional body so readily send precious energy outside of center and ego's tout their gifts as superior to another while fear pulls again and again on the psyche of those not quite done with the drama of the separation!!!

Yet, there is **no separation.** You are the density of the consciousness outpicturing a past of slavery and entitlemen and you are the wisdom of the ascended realms you aspire to. It is all you. Do you remember that we were never meant to stop? We have the choice to put our energy and the focus of our thoughts into recreating the illusion or to disengage the linear, lower consciousness games thus acquiring in equal measure, greater awareness of the new.

Tell them to PULL THE NOSE UP ON THE PLANE and CHOOSE WELL, the place you call home. When you are in your heart center you serve as a lighthouse for those lost in ways you cannot imagine There will soon be twists in the plots and unimagined scenarios unfolding before us. The perpetual looping back into old and lower levels of consciousness is a well-worn groove for this flawed yet resilient species of humanity. In willing to move through, as an observer, and beyond that which is on the course of self-destruction, not attaching to it, you gain wisdom. With each moment that we remain still and in our center, the Self of our destined Mastery and true identity, we gain wisdom. Every question you send into the nothingness rings out to a guardian host of receivership in the cosmos. Do you allow the stillness to HEAR the answer? Stillness is the space between your known and grooves of past pattern.

I encourage you to work with your light body each day. This will bring new levels of self-awareness and points of reference and you will be better able to recognize the cosmic waves that are passing through you. And **much** is passing through, each day! The invitation is always processing. LIGHTEN UP your awareness and care of the physical body. The destruction of the biosphere that has been this humanity's care of the earth is reflected in the care of the physical form. This unconscious relationship with the physical body and destruction of the biosphere is the way of unenlightened civilizations, not just on earth but on other planets, as well. When it comes to navigating the mind as the frontier of unimagined yet very real worlds, we are but children.

"Someday perhaps the inner light will shine forth from us, and then we will need no other light."

As visionary creators there is only love and it penetrates the known and the nothingness of all unformed potential, all lesser and greater worlds. All else is a projection of the mind. Focus all your efforts, all your discipline, all your energy and intention and devotion on things of the heart and you will find your way to freedom. Devotion is the essence of your joy. Joy is the essence of your devotion. Within the awakening and understanding of a higher potential of Consciousness and Energy, the frequency of Love as an evolutionary driver toward a more unified and heart centered existence, you will begin moving with the **New Human Paradigm** shift and recognize it as an ascending matrix of evolutionary energy and information. Disengage what is dense, get off the illusion, it cannot be managed or controlled. **Engage the pivot!** Ultimate Consciousness is a radiant spiral of God Force, Creationary Light, Intelligent energy that is fluid, ever changing, ever evolving, ever free. Attune yourself to the pulse of the present moment that is as constant as its power to reorient you always to a state of balance, a center of peace, a re-membrance of the Authentic Self.

There is a center of Love that has Intelligence, it is deep and vast and it is a re-membrance in you. In your devotion to your love of Self, your path as the most important thing in your world, you are loving your experience, loving your relations and fear of stepping into the unknown, loving it all as a Process that is happening **through you.** Give your whole Self to and IT will become One, with you.

Recapturing the Connection to our True Selves

December 19, 2010

I had a sweet dream last night, a dream with many layers of meaning and possibility, as most dreams are. Dreamtime is so amplified right now, interdimensional "transmission stations" of a sort, where every potential influence is present to our mutating fields of light. I am not at all sure if it was a dream within a dream within a dream, or an actual probability that I briefly revisited. But the relevance to this current phase passage is rich with meaning for the many, so I am inspired to share it with you.

In the dream, I was transported to my childhood and the memory of a favorite doll. I was about seven, eight, nine years of age and was up on the second floor of our barn, playing with this doll I had innocently named Carolina. Now, the play of light, past to future intersections and vibrational overlays of the many aspects of self that are always present to us, are numerous within this experience, so I invite you to feel the energies of expression and drop into the greater wisdom and meaning found within.

The structure of a barn reflects scenes, backdrops, memories from childhood and the doll was my most beloved toy and best friend. The memory I had forgotten that came rushing back to me like a future I had finally remembered, is that I named this cherished companion of the heart after a place I had never been or had connection to at the time, but that would become a crucial and significant part of my becoming. I would eventually migrate to the Carolinas thirty or so years later, thus an intersection, past to future, collapsing into a very recognizable now. This time travel experience to my perceived past beautifully illumined that in effect, many aspects of Self are always interacting with us, that we meet with more and more fullness of ourselves when we are truly ready to recognize that you have always been who you are today and who you are today is a fragment of an entire omniverse of existence!

Transparency is here. More light streams onto the planet everyday and it is elevating the potential of all levels of being, of the Self, of all you have been and are now awakening to! We are seeing the wisdom of the choices that we've made, the connections and purpose beyond reason to the lower realms of consciousness. Greater light means more seeing. Yet that seeing is not always welcome or comfortable to the egoic mind. We talked about the intense shift that came in around Thanksgiving on the December 2nd New Human broadcast. There was so much joy and freedom and authenticity, but that was within a certain vibration of being. For some, a lot of emotional stuff surfaced that was really hard on the egoic identity. This shift lasted about a week and then around the 7th of December we had yet another major energy shift. There is yet a newer, lighter, higher consciousness and energy streaming onto the planet right now. It is amplifying the bioelectric fields of your bodies in ways inestimable. Imagine electrical voltage prodding your physical bodies - as in WAKE UP, RE-MEMBER.

Where does your mind go when your body expresses a new "symptom," feels strange or odd? It is so important not to go into fear because our manifestation abilities are significantly amplified and will continue to be so. When my body gets a twinge or tingle or sharp attention getter, I instinctively ask what it is about and consider the new "behavior" as I would a child who was outpicturing in a new way. My mind secondly goes to the Light, knowing we are in partnership and that anything I am experiencing in the physical realm has a higher realms expression that is always for my highest good. In remembering who we are, all that we have believed and sorrowed over and held in false perception swirls in the liquid light of Self, right alongside your magnificence. Are you ready to evolve beyond who you have been, to let it go and trust your Spirit to help you create a new reality of being? A Consciousness Grid exists around the earth that allows us to travel to new levels of consciousness, that is the gift. The question is, are you ready to allow and become the gift, to lift to the more that is here now? Transmutation is.

The Light is so prevalent and such a force that we must let go of the lower frequency emotions, that is where chaos spins. In many ways, it is as if every perceived failure and unmet expectation is being sifted through the egoic mind and if you cling to your lower self identity, viewing the old self through the lower consciousness streams, you're going to feel pretty crappy at best, or be reeling the uninitiated mind outwards in blame and condemnation at the reality and people outside of you. Go deeper. Shed the layers. Be naked and vulnerable to those things you do not as yet understand or have control over. What is apparent, every bit of it is coming forth for your discernment and the possibility of release. It is only as real and limiting as your belief in it. We must get very clear on who we are now and live from that center. The path ahead is both simple and profound and will be an exacting mirror for the light and consciousness you carry within, no exceptions.

Everything is. Everything exists. A huge galactic event is happening right now, and you are right smack in the middle of it. By choice! What has been programmed and conditioned into the bands of energy around your body throughout your many experiences is now getting pushed to the surface of your being, is in the spotlight of your own quickening light. Many beings from many dimensions are involved in this event. There are interdimensional spirals moving in and around you and then out through the galaxies and deep into the Great Mother. Gaia is an immense, powerful consciousness, so much bigger than her physical form, as are you. The whole of the evolutionary process is about shifting the consciousness connected to matter; an earth body dense with toxins and abuse and a humanity separate from the whole, instilled with old programs from the outside in. All must be transformed from within. That is where your responsibility lies, getting real with your self about the lower frequencies of emotions you carry.

You are here to go to another level of consciousness, beyond anything you can imagine. Yet, **all that you can imagine** exists. If you are not yet complete with who you have been and the experiences of your becoming you will continue to be burdened with the drama and limitations and separations of the descending spiral. Only you can get out of the place that perceives your being trapped, you are each Divine Creators. The light here now is to expose all shadow and deception once and for all. This alone will do wonders in healing the world of form, freeing the physical body from harboring the past within the frequencies of guilt, fear, sadness, sorrow, unworthiness and victim-hood. THE LIGHT IS HERE. Be the pivot. That is your power from within.

Imagine yourself as liquid light, flowing through your reality, swirling in and amongst the density, fully present to the experience yet, not of the experience. Your whole being and energy field softens as you allow from a new center of residency. You can let the experience inform your reality or you can inform the experience with your light. The earth really needs our support right now as she moves into her new radiance and we must trust her process as she ascends. Gaia is not in sorrow and she does not want our sorrow, beloveds. She is simply gravitating to a higher expression of being, because it is time. It is the evolutionary movement for the good of all. We, all-inclusive, are processing many levels at once. Deep wounds surfacing, emotions all askew, earth changes present ongoing in increasing consequence. Because everything is present, when you determine to stay stuck and see the separation and stand outside of it, you open yourself up to the influence of beings and energies within lower intentional fields of influence. Know that the higher ones of Christed Consciousness exist in the same field of energy as you; they have just dropped the lower consciousness influences and moved beyond thought-form and separation.

As we come into the winter of the year, we are vibrationally supported to embrace the death of the old and the birth of a new season of being. This whole last week leading into the Full Moon Winter Solstice has had certain magic within it. Independent of the madness and busyness and frantic pace of the holiday season, the energies have momentarily quieted in vibration to an almost stillness. We've had wave upon wave of intense shift coming to initiate us into higher dimensional awareness, yet this last week, a vacuum devoid of time. It is quite high and mystical, very liquid and etheric in nature, yet equally palpable all the same. I sense a cocoon of opportunity within which we are being given the grace to leave what needs leaving, behind. The Wam Vibration has deepened and you can almost hear the clutch and shift of the space-time continuum, in stillness. There is a powerful Presence, a higher octave of expression that knows the magnitude and fullness that 2011 holds for this Shift and the higher realms influences are once again, holding space for a new level of co-creation, on our behalf.

Right now, we are being gifted a "moment out of time," a breath in between thought to connect on a profound level with the god within. Knowing Self is no longer a luxury. The movement and Shift of the Ages will continue in full force come the New Year. It is of paramount importance that you keep going within, breathe in the new human templates of love, joy, harmony, peace, abundance, oneness and creativity – the radiant light and true happiness of the Authentic Self and breathe out all the troubles of the day, any worries, all that turns your mind to fear. Set an intention at the beginning of your day, before your meditations, all obligations and experiences, and take a moment to clear your energy, as well. It is the utter joy of the higher realms and ascended ones to assist you, so call upon them, knowing that as a being of light, only light can come to you and only light can be in you. Everything begins in consciousness. Choose now, from the One Light within and everywhere, to go to the higher fields of consciousness and live your intention from there.

Trust each day that there is a level of consciousness within you that understands precisely what is happening in each moment. That consciousness has been informing and guiding you from the innocence of your childhood through the landscape of your dreams and within the all the choices and decisions of your journey toward the light. We must allow the events of great intensity to play out, unimpeded, knowing that everything and all life is always within the perfection of love. A New Consciousness is here for this humanity, this energy and consciousness and love is impregnating and permeating this dimension and there is no turning back. I encourage you to give the gift of your True Self, your authentic essence of being to the world this holiday season. Make the decision to surrender to the Process of Full Being Transformation, the alchemy of a new human being sparked from within. When you own this moment with your power, whatever it is, you are making choices with your heart, a deepening love and trust for the mystery of what lies ahead.

A New Earth Harmonic
The Shining Ones Speak

August 8, 2011

The ascension energies coming to our beautiful blue planet at this time are awe-inspiring and profound. Every day, I feel the something wonderful that is happening for all of humanity if we only have the clear sight and open hearts to receive. This NOW is about a new dispensation of beingness, where we all dare to step out into a light that defies all that has been in shadow. Moving out of duality and into Oneness means living a life true to your heart, true to the purpose you came to fulfill, true to a Love that far exceeds the perimeters of the mind. The Vibrational World is a Presence that has an Eternal Rhythm and Intelligence. Only when we are willing to let it all go, whatever it is - concern for our safety, fear of lack, questions about family and loved ones, attachments to things, allegiances to false structures and misconceptions of the bodies innate design - it is in the willingness to surrender the consciousness and belief structure of an old reality that a new reality of existence comes in and supports us as new Life. Trust is a direct realization that comes when we are truly ready to know and be a new people, co-creating a new world, as One.

Everything that speaks from the subtle worlds at this time vibrates Unity, reconciliation, a return of all opposites, to One Organism of Light. If you have been following **the New Human Paradigm** in its weekly transmissions, we have seen truly how everything from the dates of Disclosure to the increasingly intelligent design of Crop Circles, the return of Jaycee Dugard and the energetic significance of the Caycee Anthony drama – Solar Flare activity, droughts and floods, new deceptions ongoing connected to our politicians and a Financial Crisis that **will not get better** within the consciousness that created it!!!! All these things and themes and facets within the 3rd Dimensional realm have been looked at and restructured within the higher mind template of **The New Human Paradigm**. All seeming reflections of separation, returned to balance through a Consciousness and Energy that is both future oriented and ancient in design. This new paradigm is a genetic re-membrance, and the Shining Ones are the Extraterrestrial Race committed to activating the individual and Collective Codex of both a new humanity and new Earth!

The Shining Ones gather in the Ancient Sites around the earth at this time. They have intimate connection with the Earth's mutating energetics and commune on the planet's surface where the vibrations are refined, pure and of the highest sustained frequencies. I have been working with an area of nature here in the Carolinas for a dozen years now where I am able to commune freely and often with the Shining Ones. Though these beings have been with me in awareness and heart consciousness my entire life and are as near as the breath, to all ready to re-member them, it is in pristine nature, ancient and sacred vortices around the earth, that they can be visibly seen and interacted with. They carry the genetic codes of every race and star system that has ever existed because they are Central Race Beings. I know that when I connect with and hold counsel with the Shining Ones, I am holding counsel with every other intelligence, Culture, civilization and realm that has or will ever exist. Every opposite corrects itself and returns to its true origin within the frequency of these Advanced Light Race beings. All that has been sleeping awakens and all that has been forgotten comes necessarily into a New Light, with the attunement to and invitation of the deep heart, to their vibrational Light.

I was hanging out in the Blue Light of one of the sacred vortices in the Shining Ones Woods last week and had an experience that was meant to be shared, must be shared. I admit I had to step back a bit and just allow it to marinate, vibrate and attune to my own vibrational structure. I easily embodied it and understood from the level of my high mind, yet there was a certain degree of grounding down of its essence and implication that needed to happen for me to express it into words. I was quite high up, at the top of the highest mountain range within hundreds of miles of National Forest land. I had Samadhi Blue with me and was taking a moment to just be deeply immersed in the harmonics present - the tones of the earth and sacred geometry surrounding me like a mother's womb.

Suddenly, my awareness became astutely poised on a looming sound I could not readily identify. Blue nudged in closer to me, sidled right up against me and a bit fidgety with uncertainty. She too, could hear the sound. As the intensity and decibel grew, there was nothing more I could do than surrender to the moment, be in the experience with all my being and TRUST the existence I have come to know as only Love. There was no fear, though there easily could have been! I was aware that "this is a moment that could be interpreted fearfully." Yet, I do not entertain that consciousness anymore. It is just not on my radar or in my energy field because in entertaining the possibility of a fear based reality, I negate the Presence of Love.

The sound grew in intensity, the ground actually vibrated as both a high piercing tone and a deeper roar combined to create a formidable sonic field that now practically enveloped the reality around me. The sound was so deafening, that it pushed everything else, all awareness outside of the moment, away. I was still. There was nothing for me to do but be in the experience. I was not the least bit uncomfortable. I was in what I consider to be one of the safest places on the earth. But the outcome was immensely uncertain, because all the variables were new. I looked up as the sound lined up with the space I was in, to see if I could see something - what? I was not sure. In a moment's space of time, there was a vacuum and everything went still. Instantly, I could see, witnessed, experienced a vapor cloud, translucent, fluid field of energy between myself, and the sound now directly overhead. I thought, "is this a sonic boom"... it wasn't a sonic boom, but then – was it? Utter silence! Imagine being in a vacuum? The forest around me, prolific with exquisite nature glowed, was lit up! Every tree and every leaf had a halo of Light, the same energy field that was pressing into the experience at hand. I then heard the most beautiful melody, a song from the mystery, clear and succinct like cathedral bells. And then voices, like a choir with beautiful harmony! Within fifteen minutes of first hearing the sound phenomenon, all went silent and I was back in the experience of the woods with Blue still at my side! Peace.

Now, if I have learned anything about life here on earth, there are very few things we know for sure. Yet, within the vibrational world, existence communicates with you from a level beyond the mind's understanding, to the knowingness and peace of the heart. This, truly, is the greatest Shift humanity is undergoing at this time, that of moving from the Consciousness of Ego to Heart Consciousness, once again. I know the ancient land of the Shining Ones Woods so intimately. I know the language of the Light and hear the voice of the Mystery with greater trust than the uncertainties of the world of form. So, I tuned in and felt the energy of this unlikely occurrence, knowing it was purposeful, understanding its significance within the current shift humanity is undergoing. I know these woods to be "protected", their resonance creating a frequency band that holds it vibrationally suspended above the denser planes and intentions, not to mention that the entire woodland is blanketing a foundation of crystals.

What few may know is that there are underground bases in the mountains of the Western Carolinas, this area is both used and observed by the Government, as well as a vibrational reservoir for extraterrestrial activity! On the one hand, I have often witnessed black op/military aircraft canvassing these mountains and certain central locations seem to be of immense interest to the powers that be. The President himself has visited here many times since his inauguration, all the while our city is booming, roads and airport being upgraded as if in preparation for unknown events and possible safe zones. Conversely, I have witnessed and commune with several ancient sites, all of which have ancient markings, symbols and codes in geometrically arranged stone structures. Further still, I have seen/been shown the energy field of ships around these ancient sites.

Now, I am not a suspicious person, I personally have little time for conspiracy theories and follow the practice of being present to what is right in front of me versus the many probable potentials that hover in the energetic pulse of a desperate, dismantling world. I simply wish to suss out the backdrop of my experience in the woods on this early August morning, 2011! "Something" invisible to the naked eye passed over Asheville, something that broke the sound barrier and cloaked itself in mystery. But the greater impact that was made, gifted in this synchronistic moment of alignment, is that there was a visible confluence of two very different energy fields. I witnessed a transparent, electromagnetic wave, a liquid plane of harmonic oscillation between where I stood in the woods, blue light and nature all around me and the activity and intention above it. I felt as if I was looking through an interdimensional looking glass, posing as an energy field that delineated two very different realities! All the while, there was peace. All the while, I felt grounded to an assured stillness that invited me to witness a phenomenon of the new energy present, a glimpse into how we will move forward into a new level of existence while the old reality and game plays itself out!

The 3rd Dimensional Earth is no longer present. She has completed her cosmetic and structural changes. This is not a fanciful ideal or information disseminated from the linear plane. 5th World is an experience and consciousness I personally experience every day. Yet the "echo" of the consciousness we once were as a Collective, lingers in shadowed operations and essentially ill-fated attempts to hold a species captive to its past. What this moment of High Magic communicated to me visually, through sound and wave form and the vibrational mirror of my own heart, is that the new structures now in place on our earth, the fields of Light energy and harmonic resonance are capable of deflecting and even over-riding dissonance and negative forces of those still bound in denser planes. Even within this utterly defiant moment of deception and secrecy of a few acting on behalf of the many, there was an Intelligence present that vibrated with a profound stillness, exemplified peace and I heard within the convergence, new harmonics, tones and colors of a new and very different earth. The Light made visible what so many already know in their hearts and that is, what we as yet see with the naked eye are but illusions entrained to the egoic mind. A new Presence and New Earth is commanding a new center of authority and the whole Universe is expanding in response to this awakening.

What was impressed upon me that day is that the earth knows what is coming and she is moving out ahead of whatever else must come to pass. I encourage you to really drink that awareness in, breathe into the deep heart of your own re-membrance. Truly, many prophecies are running, dates loom in possibility, as the minds and hearts of an evolving species peer into the unknown future of our world. We can look to these prophecies and dates in anticipation of what might happen, yet we must equally use care in recognizing our tendency as a species to be in the mind, which takes us out of the present moment and the power we have to change. The greater choice in interacting with and learning to embody these new waves of light is for each to truly look within, get in touch with your own hearts and begin to **live a life** that demonstrates a more conscious existence! You can change your world, I know people who have and reside, gratefully among them. It is so much easier to not change, yet then your world continues to belong to the consciousness of ego, mired in separation versus the wisdom and desires of your heart.

We must begin to recognize that the vibrations of Duality are dense and heavy, leaving us exhausted and without inspiration. Habits, attachments and practices of the world of form are designed to drain us, distort the thinking process and hold us in fear. We can live without the attachments and ego comforts we have grown so accustomed to. So many struggle and are clueless what to do as the reality they have known comes undone all around them. And yet, for those who are awake, we must begin to consciously and steadfastly be the open door for others to see, be shown, reminded of their spirit and that there is another level of power available to them! It is so important to share what you know and are feeling from the higher dimensions. The New Whole is comprised of us, each day, demonstrating the re-membrance of this LOVE and behaving as if we are already free. Because we are! Our freedom is our JOY! Our freedom is our ability to Create. Our freedom is the power of choice we have, in who we give our monies to and focus our minds on and invest our time in. Wonderful things will transpire according to how we handle or interpret what occurs daily. This Shift is happening NOW! The future is not something outside of us, some distant event. The future is who we are being in this moment! That is our greatest power!

The process of becoming a unique and sovereign individual is one of the greatest contributions that we can make to the world in which we live. Connect to what makes you feel good, to your Authentic Self which is motivated everyday by the gratitude of the deep heart, to special friends and those who see you as Light, to your creative nature, to the Earth and the Joy we share with the Mother...we must necessarily bring who we are, our Authentic heart, to the planet at this time. Life will no longer be a chore as we move with the new possibilities all around us. The New Earth vibrates in timelessness. As you release your dependency of schedules and timelines and perpetually unmet expectations of your personality construct, you will know the exuberance and wonder of having all the time you need to develop your creative nature and love unconditionally from a heart that is truly free. Life as you know it today bears little resemblance to one that has been reunited with the vibrational world. A new living language will soon be known to those devoted to the earth's ascension. Loss is not possible within the new consciousness and understanding of your own spiritual light! Fear will return once again to love and the new human nature will be released from dependency on outmoded structures of social and global enterprise.

Something amazing is waiting to be found within your re-membrance of Love. This new Light seeks a voice in you and expression through you. There is not a right or wrong way to evolve, but there is a choice of how the new earth comes to pass for you. Your belief in sacrifice and unworthiness is second only to fear of the unknown. Stay out of your minds beloveds, there is nothing you do not know. You are genetically linked to the greatest intelligences and wisdom of the Universe and there can be no comparison of the magnitude with which you are loved. Though much is dependent on the sentient beings of the little blue planet and your history runs deep in your data banks... a new crystalline structure is activating within your cellular bodies that will continue to nurture you toward conditions that reflect your Light versus those that seem determined to defeat you. Remember in each moment that the new earth is a co-creative environment that vibrates with your Divine nature. Dare to live that divine nature and you will receive all the Guidance and support necessary to transition to a new life. Know there is a general rising up of the Collective which serves to balance every initiative you make toward designing new structures around **being** versus **doing**. You must create space each day to commune with the Mystery, to disengage mind and open your heart to what you love.

This New Light, the Consciousness and Energy of the New Earth now vibrating throughout a new galaxy for this humanity, it seeks expression, through you! That is the most important thing you need know and feel into. Step outside the perimeter of self you have known, each day, with the Intention to know the greater love of who you are. Listen for the generous ways in which the Light responds, the miracle of you responding to you from the highest expression of your own Light. The resonant frequency of the earth is lifting, as is your own unique vibrational signatures. Tune into and allow time for your heart space. Nothing can keep you from your actualization – you must trust that. There is a new harmonic on earth at this time and it is singing you home.

God Technology, Christ Light and the Birth of a New Human Race

December 25, 2011

As we come to the end of a year of multifaceted change and breathtaking momentum, the Shining Ones wish to share some reflection on this current passage in our ascension process and the inestimable quality of the year just ahead.

The **New Human Paradigm** is the destined and prophesied graduation to the highest potential of human consciousness this humanity has ever known. This movement and crystallization of the lower ends of consciousness into Christ Light, a consciousness of God Technology, is a vibrational culmination of a species and planet dedicated to reunification, Oneness and Transcendental Unity. For you see, we are re-membering within a Process we ultimately know Mastery, already embody the technology and cellular information to succeed and recognize ourselves once again, as Light.

The greatest impetus of 2011 was liberation, getting ourselves free and clear of the imbalances of the mental and emotional body and reactive mind. To move without thought is the essential attunement to the moment of NOW, the shift from a linear influence of choice and behavior to a vertical dispensation of knowingness and wisdom.

This is the wisdom piece of a new harmonic of existence for our planet and the beings that inhabit her. We are creating the new earth environment as we go. It is not about planning and logic and sound reasoning, no more "getting your ducks in a row" before adding a new duck. It is about following Spirit first. It is the core re-membrance that on a very profound level you are completely in love with the Light and that within that love is a devotion to the purpose you came to fulfill in these times.

The phenomena of this advancing Light (and there are many) as it activates a new part of the brain for an evolving collective, is that each decision made in the Light, informs the next. No more, no less, but trusting instinct and a still mind to act as the new receptor of a new a very different information stream. The movement is present moment. If you get an inspiration, an instinct, don't think it and qualify or break it into what ifs and shoulds. Trust that feminine light information stream and take action. It is in the action piece, that each next piece is revealed, Creator and Creation dancing together in an agreed upon partnership to manifest a new level of the game.

As we move into higher dimensional light and learn to integrate new levels of frequency and vibration, the egoic, conscious thinking mind is no longer reliable or even capable of seeing what is ahead. The future is an unknown until we step into it, unless we bring the past and thoughtform with us. The manifestation of a new earth is the integration and assimilation of this new wave of consciousness into minds, bodies and hearts of allowing and surrender, a species waking up to its innate capacity to love, co-create and find meaning not in things or a false use of power, but in joining together toward a shared purpose and goal; the commencement of a New Evolutionary Cycle.

The image that I have shared often, especially so, the latter part of 2011 is that of intersecting horizontal and vertical lines. More than anything, this image conveys movement, two different energy flows, diversity, yin and yang, masculine and feminine, mind and heart. As we continue our ascent toward this new dispensation of beingness there is an extreme compression of energy, a new gravity is forming, the potential of which is anchoring us to a very new center.

This new center and gravitational pull is the return to zero point, the duality of a denser reality is collapsing into Unity Consciousness. No more separation, One Consciousness, One Light, One Intelligent Organism and World, One Love. Can you imagine? Because imagine we must, at least until we acquire the vision that accompanies our movement to a higher dimension, state of being, consciousness and reality.

There will continue to be as many interpretations of and experiences of this shift as there are levels of consciousness on our Planet, yet what is important here, is that you do have a choice, always, of the experience you desire to have. This **New Human Paradigm** is a decree of Intention aligned with the higher ends of consciousness and as such, is always going to depict and shine light on the highest probabilities before us in any moment. It is important that we not underestimate the habit of the conscious thinking, egoic mind to gravitate toward denser probabilities. That aspect, a small prism of the Multidimensional Self is characterized by fear, probabilities and influences of the conditioned mind. The disciplines of this new human consciousness are designed to disengage the habitual self, the habit of the conscious thinking mind to see the lower potentials, thus creating vibrational space to see higher probabilities within the old constructs. Each of us entered the earth experience with spiritual eyes, the ability always, to see and know what is true.

There are increasing fields of vibrational joy and very pure streams of Guidance disseminating on our behalf as we near the end of this evolutionary cycle. The mystery and potential of this year vibrates a profound invitation to go deeper into Self and the intention to know Source more intimately. Pain and suffering are optional, always. We must bring care in taking on the experiences of others as a gauge for how we are doing, for each individual is experiencing reality and these shifts through their own vibrational compass and harmonic resonance. Again, 2012 is a probability, nothing more and nothing less. There are increasingly so, two very distinct realities before us, one that is conditioned and known, another that lies in wait for our attunement to and re-membrance. More than at any other time in our history on this planet, each of us has the inner capacity to re-member ourselves to a greater template of light-codes and energetic sustenance. Abundance is here, new possibilities are here, yet they're flowing through new and very different channels attuned to an evolving world.

Your higher mind, consciousness of god light, Authentic Self and Spirit do not even know the vibrations of the dark forces, the agendas of those who manipulate and control from shadow. This is a simple yet profound Truth. When we consider and more importantly take to heart the tactics and threats of lower vibrating probabilities, we are aligning our consciousness and energy with that reality and therefore are subject to those influences. And yet, the aspect of Self that vibrates beyond the reach and resonant field of these persons, agendas, experiences and physical dis-ease are far greater in scope and power than anything that might defeat it. It is the beautiful analogy of the capacity of one candle to extinguish the dark. A single Light, in its power and understanding of Self, deftly and effortlessly transmutes any and all darkness.

The game of our Spiritual evolution is advancing even as the Light penetrates the last vestiges of separation, any and all things that would defy the Light. Those who have danced with the transmutation of the lower vibrating realms for decades and even lifetimes have done so on behalf of Self, of family lineages and the cellularly imprinted vision of a transformed future Earth. We are weary and the desire is strong for the Shift to find resolution, sooner than later. And it will.

Yet, as we move with and into the pure, rarified air of a New Feminine frequency and the consequent union of the divine masculine in balanced reciprocity, again, we must be willing to surrender the conscious thinking mind, old masculine, expectation, agenda, attachment and manipulation of outcome. In other words, stop playing, participating in the games of the lower consciousness reality. In fact, anything less than total surrender is the manipulation of outcome and a direct vibrational impact on whatever future we might have.

And what does this movement out of mind and into heart consciousness look like? The egoic mind has a need to know, the egoic mind wants to direct and teaches from a place of separation, i.e., there is a you and there is a me. The new consciousness is a new energy, in that all movement is vertical. We gather from the still mind and act from this wisdom, as well. Imagine Light pouring into your field, body and mind from a vertical energy flow, liquid light that behaves as water pouring into the top of your head and filling your whole being. As it does so, it alters the mechanics of your mind, body and heart. And because you are present to it rather than in the habitual self or a groove of conditioned consciousness, the reactive mind, you are informed anew, in each moment. A new partnership commences.

Stay with this image of liquid light filling your physical vessel, to eventually seep out at your feet and into your reality. These new light waves are creating the potential of new harmonics within, a new codex of being that will inform your reality, your experience and relationships, all inclusive. We are shifting from human doings who are conditioned to will our reality into place, to human beings who trust and allow our inner light, instinct and capacity for love to inform and redefine the existence around us. As you relearn your capacity to be still, to observe and move through your reality mindfully and from heart consciousness, you will be in a constant state of awe at how synchronized everything becomes. This movement from a construct of separation to one of **Unity Consciousness** is the embodied understanding that we alone create our reality and have the power to reinvent ourselves to a new level of the game.

The new human symbol accompanying this note is a vibrational progression of the vertical and horizontal energy convergence I shared above. In it you will find the elements of God Technology, Christ Light, Heart Consciousness, New Earth and New Sun. A combined expression of sacred geometry and vibrational light, this symbol conveys the evolutionary means to our ascension as a new human race. I encourage you to just breathe that awareness in... place your hand over your heart, smile, let go of the need to understand with the mind and just feel. Allow. This moment within all time and space is a remembrance. Meditate on the harmonics within this symbol. Merge your consciousness with its frequency and light-codes. This will serve as a powerful attunement in the days ahead as we courageously step into a new future of human potential.

When I speak of technology such as god technology and higher mind technology, it is important to open your conscious thinking mind beyond primitive understandings and 3D definitions of technology, as in technical means, applied sciences and industry. An expanded understanding of technology as capacities of light, consciousness and energy, is the movement beyond linear definitions and constructs to vertical information and spiritual attunement.

If you meditate on God Technology, it is Infinite Capacity. To embody and reside in the frequency of God Technology is our innate, divine ability to communicate telepathically, to move objects with our minds, walk through walls, bi-locate, teleport, slow down the aging process and live hundreds of years in perfect health. It is the reservoir of Infinite Mind, the capacity to time travel and materialize whatever we need in an instance. This is the directional remembrance we are moving in and towards as new humans. We carry the codes for a new earth in our DNA and have the power, means and support now, in this moment in time, to activate them.

Christ energy is already in the DNA. Beyond the dogmas and religious distortion of Christ Consciousness, when we run this remembrance through our heart's feeling nature, we recognize the Master Jesus as a representative of the future – a reflection of the highest potential of our humanity. In the Light of Christ Consciousness, there is no separation, no you, no me, no other, just One beautiful all inclusive and unconditional, Love.

This is a critical time for the human species. No longer can we afford to play at spirituality, we must truly begin our merging of consciousness to a higher octave of existence, expand our mind to the possibility of creating other actions and choices with different results. At the core of these new mind technologies for the human race is **Unity Consciousness**, the new human ability to think as One, move with the consciousness of One, act on behalf of Self, as if there is only One. Breathe into that energetic. It changes the whole movement of existence from a top down, linear mentality of separation, to a circular, spiritual relationship with time, each other and Cosmos. Within the Self of an in-dwelling Spirit lie DNA light strands that are waiting to be activated by your attunement to them. It is that simple and that profound. This is no longer a time of gathering and learning. This is a time of stilling the mind and remembering your devotion to Gaia and the great Mystery of worlds beyond this known.

The year ahead for humanity will be turbulent at best, environmentally, politically, financially, in resources and social uprising. For those operating within the old constructs and conditioning, still attached to the old paradigm and duality of form, there will be less and less security, less to find comfort in or derive meaning from. For those on the path of Light and following Spirit, IT must become your only devotion. This is the new spirituality of this final ascent into the gateway of 12/21/12. Either everything is spiritual or nothing is. This alone must be our motivation and intent.

2012 will be a huge disappointment for many, but the gift of many lifetimes for those in a perpetual state of surrender and attunement to the new human templates of a new earth. Just as with the 11/11/11 gateway, we will experience a reality ongoing aligned with our consciousness and energy. There is the reality around you at any given moment and then there is a truer existence that is returning to a state of harmony and balance. Take care with expectations. Your whole being is best served by your efforts to redefine Self and the reality you live in now, not hanging expectations on some promise or prophesied event on the near or distant horizon. The future is woken up by the choices we make in the present. This is the power we bear as Light.

In my own dance of remembrance with the Light, especially so these first weeks of 2012, I have felt myself immersed in a sea of gardenias. Day and night, inside and out, in meditation or in moments of human doingness, I have been enveloped in the aroma and magnitude of thousands of gardenias. For the longest time, I was content to just be with this phenomenon, take it in, recognizing that this sweet element of smell was indeed connected to higher realms presence. But I was guided to explore it a bit more for the sake of sharing the significance and meaning connected to the greater passage we are in just now. Flowers, just as with animals, carry vibrational medicine, essence for our expanding consciousness and energy. Gardenias reflect refinement, pure vibration and the frequency of JOY! For you as an evolving consciousness and this reality as an evolving world, this is the gift there is to have in these times.

Everywhere, all around, in each moment, are worlds within worlds within worlds, vibrational expressions of an existence born out of love. Everything is here in this moment, a NOW orchestrated by you, of you, on your behalf; all dimensions, all possibilities, the Totality of Love, of God, of you as a Universal Being of Light.

Stay in your heart space and feel only Joy, connect with the earth as your most important work for this is her ascension. She will guide us safely to a new dimensional space, the frequency of home. The nature piece cannot be emphasized enough, everything in nature is amplified in tones and colors and harmonics, as is the presence of the Shining Ones. Take time to be with her, with Self, with the nothingness and the advancing Light of these Central Race Beings.

There is a new consciousness radiating as a spiraling light within and around the earth, within and around you. Breathe it in and take it into your heart space. Allow it to flow into your lives as a new energy of remembrance, reunion, Divine Feminine, Cosmic Destiny. All Creation travels together. As we move with new minds, new hearts and new bodies into a new possibility of existence, may we join together in the frequency of Love, for the sake of Love, empowered as One Intention, One World, One Being... One Love.

A New Earth Shambhala
Entering a New Era

The last few months of 2012 have proven to be an unprecedented quickening for humanity and planet. With triple dates and Solar Eclipses, as well as the long anticipated and much prophesied 12/21/12 birth of a New Earth, it will take some time for all that has come to pass to settle in and take new form in our world. But a New Earth, indeed, is emerging. The tragedy in Newtown, CT and the tropical storm not coincidently named Draco thrust us into Zero Point at this time of turning with hearts and fears laid bare. These events, as with many such tragedies and nonsensical phenomenon along humanity's evolutionary trajectory, were influenced by unseen forces with a greater purpose and wisdom than can be comprehended within the old paradigm of mental reasoning and control.

A critical shift in our movement to a New Consciousness and awareness of our Selves, is the understanding that absolutely nothing occurs that is not part of a greater story, a greater plan that Love is ultimately at the center of. There are no victims, no loss, sacrifice or limitation within the higher realms of consciousness and energy. Neither do we have to suffer and endure tragedy to evolve back into our light essence. These are learned conditions and ingrained beliefs within the human psyche. When we witness something that is perceived as horrific, tragic or even evil, we are observing from a very limited consciousness of understanding, a consciousness controlled by fear and survival instincts. The beautiful souls that agreed to be part of the Newtown event did so for the greater purpose of getting as many of humanity as possible into states of Heart Consciousness just prior to the New Earth alignment on the 21st of December 2012.

It is so important at this time in our Collective evolution that we begin observing and interpreting all of existence through a consciousness where there is only Light, and trust that without exception. The 3rd Dimensional reality is but a pinpoint in an incredibly beautiful, infinitely expanding spiral of Light and Consciousness. As the spiral widens and consciousness expands, victims become co-creators with the Light, willing participants in worlds that transcend emotional attachments and illusions of suffering. In truth, suffering and illusion go hand in hand, co-conspirators of a consciousness bound by fear. At the higher ends of the consciousness spectrum, there is only Love. Nothing is separate from that Love and all shadow is consumed by the transparency of unveiled realities, of which there are many.

There has been an incredible crescendo building since the onset of the 21st Century on our planet in 2001, the final thrust of a twenty-five year convergence of Light and awakening for humanity. I've had the honor and good fortune of spending five of those years, thus far, on radio with a weekly transmission of the New Human, New Earth energies. And now, with the transition from 2012 into 2013, we aren't just moving from one year into another, we are leaving an old cycle and entering an entirely new era of existence for planet Earth and humanity: a Golden Age of Light.

An unparalleled confluence of Light illumined the little blue planet on December 21st, 2012 with a glorious Galactic Alignment, lifting humanity and all life into a new octave of being: that of Unity Consciousness. This was a grand, culminating event for our planet and species, equally so an ending and a beginning. There was a lot of turbulence and unstable weather activity on the Winter Solstice of 2012, reflecting the consciousness of those anticipating destruction and finite interpretations of end cycles. But for those attuned to the heart and consciousness of this Cosmic Light, waking up to the new dawn on December 22nd felt like Christmas morning. There was this palpable sense of innocence, wonder and trust in the awareness that magic had occurred, that something wonderful had happened with an abundance of gifts yet to be opened. I personally woke filled to over-flowing with the following wisdom directly from the Shining Ones:

Beautiful Life

Every moment of existence is brand new - and never has that been more true and powerful than this beginning cycle of humanity beyond 2012. Static, unchanging reality only exists in the mind. You are as free as you allow your Self to be, as you believe you are! JOYOUS reality hovers just outside your doubt and questions!

Once you dedicate your life to **living**~ *to that gift and power, and trust who you are in all of Eternity...*

each day becomes an open door to **everything** *your heart desires.*

The great secret of this life is that you are and have always been free -that your joy and creative purpose is God's expression in the world. Open up your heart and allow life to fill you - be courageous in your denial of mediocrity and GO OUT AND HAVE LIFE! YOUR LIFE!! Live it well. Live it free. Live it in Love! Leap to the new Sun of an evolved and united reality - lifted in the Consciousness of One Love.

And so it is that we enter 2013. Can you feel it? Suspend your mind and just feel the new and invitation that is here to step into. Joy is a frequency second only to Love and surely there is a joy not of this known reality present as the Cosmic cycles come full circle and Earth shines as a new star in the heavens. There is an atmosphere of excitement about nothing and everything all at once as the new reality begins to take form.

When **The New Human** was first published in 2008, I felt a distinct and strong presence around the final chapter, *Bridge Across Tomorrow.* The title seemed to vibrate the intention of not only the Shining Ones, but of beings from every star nation; a shimmering presence of Interdimensional Unity forelighting the potential of a very different future for our world and the greater Solar System. This bridge, both symbolic and vibrational, refers to the essential cooperation and partnership of our Earth with other planetary systems and intelligences in our Galaxy.

At the same time *The New Human* consciousness and energy anchored within the Earth Grid in book form in 2008, there was a powerful, albeit little known ceremony occurring on the island of Moorea. This final ceremony of the birth of a *brand new human consciousness grid* on Earth was led by Drunvalo Melchizedek and included the indigenous elders of this ancient and captivating land. The island is triangular in shape, consisting of the ruins of a half-eroded volcano, rugged mountains, lush streams and fertile soil. Drunvelo, a respected teacher and author of the New Age movement described this remote island northwest of Tahiti as one of the most beautiful scenes he'd ever experienced.

You can read in depth about this ceremony in his latest book, The Mayan Ouroboros, but I felt it important to weave in this sidebar of information because it helps to illuminate the driving momentum and evolutionary intention of 2013.

It is time to come together and join forces in our planetary endeavors. *The new cycle begins with the gathering of tribes.* I do not know Drunvelo Melchizedek personally, but there is not a doubt in my mind that we are connected by a greater intention. That ceremony in Moorea and the publishing of **The New Human** on opposite sides of the world was, in effect, one event, expressed through different individuals. And it is important here to lift this awareness higher than the conscious thinking mind, higher than ego. Because this *new paradigm* is not about individual personas – this sharing is not ultimately about Drunvelo Melchizedek and DeAnne Hampton. It is about this something greater that is ready now to become a new expression in our world.

All over our planet for the last quarter century, many dedicated, pioneer light workers have been putting Spirit first and living on the fringes of society for the sake of Divine Purpose and Planetary Service. Somehow, in some way, all these individuals have been tuning different notes of a new song for humanity. There is only One Truth. So, even as these individuals, strategically located around our globe, appeared to be doing their own thing, each was serving to anchor certain coordinates so to speak, new harmonics in what would eventually be the New Earth Grid of a New Human Consciousness. The next phase as we enter the Golden Age of Aquarius, (which is, at its heart, about freedom and humanitarianism and expansion of higher mind technologies), the beginning steps within the Unity Consciousness Grid of a New Earth, is the gathering of the new tribes of humanity. With our sovereignty intact and the seeds of our individual missions planted, we must now merge these foundational pieces into a new human system of cooperation, community, creative vision, equilibrium, right use of power and sustainability for the sake of the whole. We have done all we can do in separation, now we must move as One into Heart Consciousness. I encourage each of you reading these words and considering the implications of this next shift, to meditate on this emergence of new human tribes, the joining together of forces for the Light sans ego and ownership. Imagine the beginnings of New Earth meccas of Light with each bringing what is theirs to bring, a joyful meeting of the minds for those ready to build a New World. Imagine. As this new Light, new consciousness and energy begins to anchor more fully into the new Earth Grid and find expression in our world, it is for each of us to create the space and devotion to discover what is ready now to emerge, individually and then collectively. This is the way forward.

Many refer to this Golden Age as a new renaissance for our people and planet. Deeper still, within the Cosmic Heart of our Earth Mother and all Creation, I feel the pulse of a New Earth Shambhala. As the Mantle of Consciousness shifts on the planet from India to Peru~ the legendary secrets of Shambhala are vibrationally shifting, as well, to a time this ancient and pure land may once again exist for the species of humanity. Throughout our history, the myth and ideals of Shambhala have influenced everything from spiritual traditions to popular culture. And in every instance, the prophecies emphasize a time in our evolution when the decline into war and greed on Earth would necessitate a worldwide shift in the consciousness and energy of our species, precipitating a Golden Age. Shambhala, as with the ancient to future teachings of the **New Human Paradigm**, is a remembrance; it is a vibrational attunement that exists as surely as we have greater, as yet untapped capacities as a human species, a human family of Light. Though Shambhala, as a consciousness, vibrates higher than the 3rd dimension, it is possible for us to experience and recreate it in physical form. It is a pure land in the human realm that each individual has the potential and choice of lifting to vibrationally.

When I attune to the shift in the mantle of consciousness in our world from the legendary mysteries of the Himalayas to the spiritual distinctions and myths of the Andes, I see Light moving across the Earth plane in the way a searchlight penetrates darkness, seeking the lost and weary traveler. Energetically, this shift from the highest to the longest mountains on the planet suggests a more widespread and inclusive reach of the Light on Earth as the balance tips once again from the lower ends of consciousness to the higher potentials of mind, heart and physical capacities for the human species.

The energies and influences of Shambhala, along with a beautiful history and presence of Ascended Masters, have long influenced our world. It has always been the spiritual vision and wisdom that we would reach the maturity of embodying it, thus allowing Peace to return to planet Earth.

Our inner light is a reflection of the light in our world. As we grow that inner capacity to live free from limitations and conditioning, as we are able to integrate, assimilate and maintain this rarified Light of the Divine Feminine as a body of One, a Collective co-creating as One, we grow Shambhala as a new utopia that will reveal powerful truths about how we may transform our world – together – as a human family of Light.

With so much vibrational support and Light emanating onto and within our Earth, there are many who are spiritually aware and sincerely care for our future, yet still feel uncertain in their direction, the chatter in their head garners more attention than the still small voice within and they long for a more tangible, real partnership with their guides and higher realms. And the resounding response from the Shining Ones around this gap is that we must step up our level of commitment. Humanity, as a whole, has not begun to understand, much less experience, what it is to live with commitment; to live as committed beings in committed lives on behalf of a committed intention to our planet and one another. In the 3D zone of reality, commitment is a form of attachment. Think about it, the things we commit ourselves to and understand as commitment in the 3rd dimensional plane, we do so because of what is promised, what the rewards or payoff will be; hence there is expectation. That level of commitment is conditional and automatically affects who we are *in* that circumstance. There are provisions in the contract, so to speak.

Spiritual commitment, on the other hand, is an internal compass – an *eternal* compass, as well. The new humanity is a future oriented species – and the nature of that compass is Love. We came to have life, experience wonder and nurture ourselves with the many gifts of an evolved existence: a living, beautiful planet, rich soil to plant in, abundant waters to provide infinite resources, vast spaces of exquisite nature to fulfill our natural love of beauty and a human family within which to find community and join together with in new creations. This **New Paradigm** for humanity is, in many ways, a giant leap for our species; it is the intention to live consciously, to bring conscious awareness to every moment and detail of our lives. All negativity must be put aside. That we carry burdens, suffer inequities, are unworthy or forsaken, these are all misconceptions perpetuated by our willingness to give our power away, entrust the gift of our lives to an unconscious system. Everything perceived as negative or deficit is ego and that is what must be transcended to know our Selves as Light.

The **New Human Paradigm** is a fluid intelligence, a consciousness pivot from that which is *no longer working* to a new frequency of Light that is here to co-create with us, problem solve and restructure our current way of life toward sustainable, inclusive solutions for our world. It takes courage and integrity to look at what is no longer working in our individual lives. Yet, in order for the greater Light Bodies/Merkabas of Mother Earth and the collective human family to activate and transcend the denser vibrations of an old paradigm, each individual must consciously step into greater transparency within their personal lives while doing the work to increase the pulse of their own Light Body Merkabas. You are a spiritual being, your Light is the Light of this and many worlds. Whatever experience you are currently manifesting is a reflection of the belief of self you most identify with in any given moment. Celebrate the individual work you have done thus far, but understand you are never done with evolutionary endeavors. As you continue to choose and be Love above all else, living your Light and spirituality in every facet of your life, you help recreate reality and build a new world in a very real and positive way.

Ultimately, ascension is an act of Self Love. It is the movement from *thoughts* about a new Earth and possibilities for more meaningful existence, to the consciousness of our hearts. That is the true wisdom piece. True happiness and the freedom of that vibration is found in the simple gratitude of waking up to the Light of who you are and living in the Truth of that Light, everyday. We must cultivate the trust that we are part of something greater, that we are not the only beings inhabiting this vast universe and then begin living as the unlimited, eternal beings of Light that we are. When this becomes the most important thing in our lives here, everything changes.

The Shining Ones are here, now, the relationship I have with them is yours. In the highest expressions of the Source of all Life, God, the Shining Ones, you, me, every star nation and each Ascended Master are essentially One. There is no other. This book and greater visibility of the Shining Ones comes to you now because we are ready, as a species, for greater relations with our Cosmic Family. Will you step up to that evolutionary commitment? New minds, new bodies, new hearts, in harmony with Mother Earth and the living Universe has triggered the Cosmic DNA of an evolving species of Light. And so we venture forth with renewed strength, devotion and resolve. A new awakening and brand new spiritual energy is upon us now, the future beckons. We are the many, returning to Oneness.

About The Author

DeAnne Hampton is the author of _The New Human, Understanding Our Humanity, Embracing Our Divinity_. She is a Keynote Speaker, Teacher of the Vibrational World and a New Earth Consciousness and Initiator of _The New Human Paradigm_. She is the representative and voice of the Advanced Light Race known as the Shining Ones, who herald from the Galactic Center. DeAnne is the founder of _Interior Joy_, _www.interiorjoy.com_, empowering individuals to live authentic and sovereign lives of purpose and joy. Based on the Principles of a 5th Dimensional World, manifesting now on planet Earth, _Interior Joy_ embraces the capacity and power of individuals the world over to walk in the light of their highest potential. DeAnne graduated from the University of South Florida with a Teaching Degree and a Masters in Psychology. She also has a minor in music and is a Certified Sound Healer in DNA Activation. She lives in Asheville, NC with her family, where she enjoys mountain biking, hiking and trail running with her beloved golden retriever, Samadhi Blue.

~

oh great mother, beloved oneness, light that I AM~ fill me today with your peace, that I may quicken my remembrance and devotion here. I am ready to step into my True State of Being, allowing, transforming, becoming once again~ the Power Of Creation, through the vessel of my body, the Light of my heart and the vehicle of my service at this time.

No greater love could I know than the gift of this now - and I accept. My head is held high and I am unafraid. No longer will I give myself to distractions or fear... I AM the impeccable integrity of my Higher Enlightened Self! I now surrender to the timeless ancient wisdom of my Ascended Consciousness~ and breathe in the Unity I share with all existence.

Reflections of Gratitude

I just finished listening to your latest show tonight and wanted to say again how grateful I am for having come across you and your show. Not only do you offer exceptional clarity of the higher constructs, but the powerful grounding energy that flows with your stream of words is SO palpable... a functional, centered merging of Heaven and Earth. My body craves this grounding, so to be able to sense this energy strongly through my body as I listen to your show is miraculous and a relief. The benefit for me is exponential. I do completely believe that the Higher DeAnne and the Shining Ones are one in the same. We are all aspects of the Greater Whole, but your aspect is clearly more developed/integrated/present than most - a spiritual Olympic athlete rather than an armchair warrior. You've done -- and continue to do - the work and it shows. Be well...

Much love, Lee Ann Laraway

San Jose

Dear DeAnne,

I hardly know what to write. Every one of your Shows are exquisite but for some reason your Show yesterday touched me very, very deeply. The frequencies that you used to activate the Anya gave me glimpses of a Crystal New Earth so beautiful beyond the finite form of words. But.... the Visual Metaphor that you so, so generously shared with us all of you toning in the Shinning Ones Woods to restore harmony and balance to the part of the woods that had been clear cut made me cry tears that came from the depth of my being. The image of the Native Americans that came into your view, I feel so connected to them, to their nobility to their truth and wisdom, I couldn't stop crying.

Also for me to feel how right it was, how very very right it was, that you should be honored, deeply, deeply honored for the nobility and truth of your intentions. That your efforts did echo through time to bring them forth. Nothing to be done and nothing to be said just them there vibrating their state of Grace and Presence in acknowledgement of you. I was scarcely able to breathe in reverence of that image. Thank you. Truly - I am unable to quantify the impact your creations continue to have on my own deep remembrance.

In eternal love and pristine light,

Geraldine

Hi DeAnne,

What an extraordinary 5th Dimensional Show you channeled today! I was taken to a place of new creation, new love, and new journeys on a healed planet. When you sang at the end I got goose shivers for a long time. Thank you so much for being a Way-Shower for the rest of us.

Thank you Angel Girl,

With love and light - Jamie in Great Britain

Blessings DeAnne -

I'm so pleased that I finally became ready to hear the amazing information you offer us. I wish I were able to "hear" you several years ago. But, now it seems that the times are critical and I am not allowed to sit on the sidelines goofing off anymore. I have been recruited and I have to get busy remembering that I am truly a Being of Light. Please know that you and your inspirational broadcasts are integral to the opening of my wings and remembrance of flight.

Thank you, thank you, thank you Deanne,

Patty D.

Parker, CO

DeAnne - you are a teacher of high degree.

Christine T. NY

Dear DeAnne,

I am one of your loyal listeners and feel so connected. It has gotten to the point that I fully awake in the middle of night on the day of your broadcast and listen to your message in the stillness. Thank you for your work! I feel such changes in the tapestry of my life's unfoldment. I show up differently. This new work energizes me, feels like my higher calling and is making a difference for others. Each week my work has me driving through the foothills of Mt Hood. I have noticed the "Shining Ones" and known this is what you have been telling me about!

With great love and appreciation,

Mary Lu Taylor

Tigard, Oregon

Loved the power of this show - your words were like truth arrows aimed to open the heart and higher mind! I definitely am feeling the repatterning and de-programming at very deep levels the last 2 weeks! WOW! Thanks for your deep sharing and enlightening us up!! You are a master with your guidance!!

Kate

Boise, Idaho

Dear DeAnne,

I thank you dearly.

I could not have received a better answer to help me remember what I know - and am slowly in the process of anchoring.

Your shows are a treasure, as are you.

In deep gratitude and love,

Marianne

La Conner, Washington

Just finished your article in **Sedona Journal** - very powerful, awesome clarity and communication. Congrats and kudos to you and your higher realms team.

JoAnn C.

St. Petersberg

Oh DeAnne,

.........each week is more profound....the layers of this spiral you are taking us through are so supportive and appreciated. ♥ I often experience moments feeling that I was sensing from a broader awareness. I stopped dead in my tracks with the information around chakras today and started to cry when you spoke of the seventh chakra opening to full capacity. Wow.... Each week when I tune in to The New Human I receive affirmation that I am right where I'm supposed to be and know that it is precisely my quiet little life that allows me the space to do what I came here to do. ☺

MUCH LOVE, jean

Annapolis, Maryland

You are a very special being of light and love.

I cannot thank you enough for all the beautiful vibrations you transmit every moment of every day to all the shiny ones, to all humans, to all animals, to all plant life, in all dimensions, across all multiverses, at all time (past, present, and future). Your vibration of love radiates through all time and space.

From my heart to yours,

Namaste,

Christopher in La Quinta, CA

With each show I experience a state of no separation - all boundaries dissolve and LIFE goes to equilibrium or the manifestation of Life that is. It is as if the system without our illusion corrects ALL imbalance... thank you for showing the WAY!!! Each show is a portal to this New Paradigm of humanity.

Love and Gratitude,

Mike B. NC

DeAnne,

Your attunement to this new light, to the New Earth and ability to articulate these new templates for humanity is equally profound and enlightening. I love cruising the Universe in your spaceship and feel yours is a Cosmic wisdom. Thank you for showing up for humanity at this time and your willingness to be seen in such an authentic light.

You are one of the truly beautiful people in the world and I love you!

Sam G.

Malmo, Sweden

Wisdom from the New Human Paradigm

~

Inside each of us is the capacity to experience wonder, to walk into each moment brand new and fully present. An innocent mind is a free mind, one that sees with the eyes of a child and receives through the wisdom of the heart. We must walk into this NOW with open arms, trusting the Light within and without as the co-creative force of the New Earth. Each moment is an invitation, from the Creator... empowering you to share your Light with a reality ready to be transformed by your Love.

~

To give oneself fully to the presence of Mother/Father God, the true beauty of Existence and the wisdom of One Creation is to dedicate each day to the mystery of the Earth's love for this humanity - and the mystery of the indwelling god. May hearts be strong with this love, knowing that as we give birth to the Christ within, we see God in every face and each moment. We then become the Consciousness of God, where there is no separation, only Love.

~

As new humans, when we look into something - we see beyond it, when we feel the essence of a thing, we are transported. Our transcendence and true liberation is in the full recognition~ that we are the earth, we are the heavens and the world is our creation.

Existence is born through us, by the power of our vision and our Love. Intend it, see it, live it, be it... this is the gift there is to have in this NOW!

~

~

Perfection, Transformation, Actual-ization, Mastery... these are not things to aspire to but remembrances to embody and live. Walking the path with Light and compassion for all living things, living unconditional love in each moment...these are expressions of gratitude for those remembering themselves to that very same love. Each Ascended Master and holy deity is but a higher aspect of Self~ and once we can let go and give ALL over to the Spiritual forces, we begin the reintegration of heaven and earth, human and divine that has always been our destiny!

~

We must begin with the idea that we are the Self we inwardly long to be. This is the beginning, there is no other. It is the profoundly simple matter of dropping all the conditions of the mind, body and attachments to form - devoting oneself once again to re-membering and being that Self, which is Eternal. **The New Human Paradigm** is the embodied recalibration of a new human design, moving beyond teaching and gathering to an empowered service of Planetary Enlightenment.

If each journey begins with a single step - this NOW for an evolving humanity is a moment whereby we can choose to step in a new, conscious and empowered direction of existence. The new human prayer of a new earth is to the future I AM - that we may embody and begin to live our highest light, NOW. A future based not on hopes nor destiny nor miracle, but each of us agreeing to change the inner and outer structures of our conditioning. This prayer of remem-brance is that every facet of our world be understood as a relative I AM - One with all that has been, so that we may now take the Light forward into all that can be; for you, for me, for our planet and the peoples of the earth:

"Dear Beloved One that I AM! Help me to remember that I AM the Light that is coming over the horizon...that every color of Creation is an expression of the frequency of my inner most being. I AM the shadow and light, the ebb and flow, the nothingness and pulse of all Existence. As I dare to know myself beyond the dream I AM now dreaming... a greater expression of existence rushes in to greet me, and I AM whole once again - I AM whole, I AM."

~

You joined the human race with purpose and an Intention connected to Eternity. Though it is "very real" to you here, it is not true reality. You are re-membering another level of Existence and each of you has awaited this time. You are moving into new frequencies as your solar system moves into a new area of space. Within this region of "outer space," which is simultaneously "inner space," you must keep careful watch upon ALL your thoughts and emotions because your powers of instant manifestation are quickly returning.

The Shining Ones

Be The Reach!

As you continue this shift to a new plateau of living in your world, you must be willing to accept that everything in your reality is spiritual and begin to interact with each other and all of life through the heart and not the ego. Once you truly understand and embrace this in all of your experience, your frequency automatically shifts to one of receptivity to the influence and wisdom of the Mystery. For you see, the highest choices you can make are those that emanate from the heart, because you are then positioned to make the optimal vibrational contributions to the Energetic Collective of multidimensional you and the Energetic Collective of your world.

With every breath, I listen
with every breath, I feel
with every breath, I remember...
that everywhere, all around are worlds within worlds...
vibrational expressions of an existence born out of love. There is
nothing for me to achieve greater than the love and gratitude,
intention and presence I bring to each moment. With every
breath I know... the future, and my power within it!

Dear Beloved One that I AM!
Help me to remember that I AM the Light that is coming over the
horizon...that every color of Creation is an expression of the
frequency of my inner most being.

I AM the shadow and light, the ebb and flow, the nothingness
and pulse of all Existence~ as I dare to know myself beyond the
dream I AM now dreaming... a greater expression of existence
rushes in to greet me, and I AM whole once again - I AM whole, I
AM.